JOHN DE ST. JORRE was born in ⌐⌐⌐⌐⌐⌐
and Singapore. After five years in ⌐⌐⌐⌐⌐
foreign correspondent covering ⌐⌐⌐⌐⌐
1973 Arab–Israeli War, and the Iranian Revolution. His dozen books
include *The Good Ship Venus*, a history of the Olympia Press. He
and his family live in Newport, Rhode Island.

# Darling
# Baby Mine

### A son's extraordinary search
### for his mother

## John de St. Jorre

QUARTET BOOKS

First published in 2016 by Quartet Books Limited
A member of the Namara Group
27 Goodge Street, London, W1T 2LD

This paperback edition published in 2017
by Quartet Books Limited

A catalogue record for this book is available from the British Library

ISBN 978 0 70437 440 9

Typeset by Tetragon, London
Printed and bound in Great Britain by TJ International Ltd, Padstow, Cornwall

*For Grace and Olive, in memoriam, and my
family, close and dear, distant yet cherished—
the hidden story.*

'*The past is never dead. It's not even past.*'

WILLIAM FAULKNER
*Requiem for a Nun*

# PROLOGUE

In the autumn of 2009, I went to Kensal Green Cemetery in north London where my mother and her parents were buried. It was a cool, cloudy day with a damp wind ruffling the leaves under the ancient oaks, beeches, and elms. Inspired by the Père Lachaise Cemetery in Paris, Kensal Green was designed on a grand scale across seventy-two acres of farmland. It opened its ornate wrought-iron gates to admit its first funeral cortège in 1833. The city slowly advanced and encircled it, the most prominent newcomer being Wormwood Scrubs Prison, which lies on its southern boundary. I had a map, the details of the grave—Section 33, Row 2, and Grave Number 46191—and a member of the cemetery's staff with me.

The official brochure described the cemetery as 'one of London's oldest and most distinguished public burial grounds,' characterised by 'the important people buried there, its overall richness, and the number of outstanding memorials.' As I followed the guide along a gravel path, a different picture took shape. Headstones, with weathered inscriptions, leaned over at perilous angles, or lay broken among the weeds. Some had disappeared altogether leaving anonymous mounds, covered in grass, lichen, and bracken, that pitched and rolled amid the tombstones. Most graves seemed to be neglected although I saw two new headstones of polished black granite inscribed with gold lettering. Nearby was an anonymous mound adorned with a geranium plant, a rosemary bush, and a child's bright pink plastic windmill, its tiny sails spinning in the breeze.

It was as if an elemental force had swept through the burial ground bent on destroying the Victorians' sense of order and decorum. Only the family mausoleums, vaults and tombs, built of granite or marble, had survived the assault. While the poor might lie close to the wealthy, as they never did in life, the roots of the trees and bushes, underground marauders constantly on the move, sought to deny them their eternal rest.

The guide took me to a particularly wild section, dotted with small wiry shrubs, and pointed to a narrow, grassy path.

'That's your row,' he said.

I looked down the ragged line of tottering headstones, their inscriptions faint or obliterated.

'The best way,' he said, 'is to find a new grave with the number nice and clear, and work it out from there. Good luck, mate.'

My family couldn't afford a headstone so their names and the grave number were on a plaque at the foot of the grave. The guide left me and I started to search.

I had never known my grandparents, so it was my mother who was on my mind. Whenever I tried to remember her, wartime London emerged. The city was a landscape of monotones: shades of grey, brown and black with the occasional splash of colour from the red double-deck buses, their winding staircases open to the elements; trams grinding and lurching on silvery tracks that snaked through the city; everyone in hats; the city men, a uniformed army in their suits, detached collars, ties, overcoats and bowlers, swinging their weapon of choice, the rolled umbrella; the smell of tobacco, horse dung, and coal smoke; the acrid dampness of London's greasy fogs that slid and swirled down the streets or, when there was no wind, settled like a vast saturated blanket over the metropolis; the cries of street vendors, and the rag-and-bone man on his horse-drawn cart with his garbled call, which I could never understand. And deep below ground, the rattle and sway of the Tube trains with their smoke-filled carriages, and the fear of falling on to the tracks and landing on the deadly middle rail where, I was warned, I would end up like a piece of burnt toast.

Somewhere in that city, in that distant time, I recalled seeing a young woman whom I believed to be my mother, a shard of memory that, true or false, would remain with me for the rest of my life.

She was standing in a large room with a tiled floor. I think it was a kitchen but couldn't be certain. Through a window, I could see snow falling. The woman wore a loose blouse, half-open, revealing large breasts. She had blue eyes and blonde hair framing a full, plump face. Smoke curled upwards from her cigarette. She looked at me, threw back her head, and laughed. I looked down and saw that cigarette ash had fallen into the cleavage between her breasts.

I don't know how old I was but, since I can recall nothing before that time, I was probably very young. The vision of this young, blonde, blue-eyed woman was powerful though not shocking. She sounded happy and that made me happy too. She seemed familiar, someone close to me, and I suppose that is why I thought of her as my mother. Who else could she be? Then she vanished. It was as if she had been swallowed by one of London's fogs, never to be seen again.

No one ever spoke of her and perhaps that middle rail, which haunted me, had something to do with her disappearance, an unspeakable fate. But my memory of her survived, and her mortal remains, if I had it right, were somewhere in this jungle of a cemetery.

As I walked along the row looking for her grave, London in the 1940s stayed with me. The period evoked other memories, notably of my father who, with no one else around, became the central figure in my limited universe. Looking back over seventy years, much is lost and not all that returns has value. But certain events remain clear, sufficient to begin the story with my father, and when the past refused to lie down and die, enough to end it with my mother.

## HERTFORDSHIRE, 1943

'THERE YOU ARE GOVERNOR,' SAID THE DRIVER MAKING A sweeping motion with his hand as if he owned the place. 'St. Dominic's Priory, Ponsbourne Park. Mother Bernadette runs a tight ship the locals say, so your young lads will be in good hands.'

We'd stopped at the top of a steep hill and below stretched a valley of fields and woods. The only building was a large grey stone house surrounded by lawns, beds of rhododendrons, and clusters of pine and cedar trees. Shafts of sunlight and shadow, driven by the fast-moving clouds, chased each other over the mansion's slate roof and tall brick chimneys.

'I'm sure they will,' my father said to the driver. He gave my hand a reassuring squeeze. I glanced at my brother Maurice and saw a flicker of alarm cross his face.

The taxi went slowly down the hill, turned into a curved driveway, and stopped at the convent's main entrance. A mournful March wind, raw and sodden, cut into us as we climbed out of the car.

My father picked up our suitcases and rang the doorbell. It clanged loudly and a nun opened it so quickly she must have been waiting on the other side. She motioned us in and said the sister in charge of admissions would be with us shortly. She walked off down a long corridor while we sat in the entrance hall and waited. There was a large crucifix on the wall opposite and a painting of Jesus over the entrance, showing his exposed heart surrounded by gold rays. On another wall was a glass case of small stuffed birds. Down the hallway, I could see a statue of the Virgin Mary and more religious pictures. The only sound was the squeak of the departing nun's shoes on the polished floor. Then, as it faded, I heard the steady tick-tock of a clock but couldn't see where the sound was coming from. There was a strong smell of incense and floor wax. Maurice, who was only five years old, moved closer to my father.

'I don't like it here Daddy,' he whispered. 'I want to go home.'

My father put his arm around him. 'It will be fine Maurice, just you see, it will be fine.'

I said nothing, transfixed by the solemnity of the place yet feeling uneasy. Home? Where was home? My gaze returned to the picture of Jesus. The heart seemed too large for his chest and so lightly attached it could break free and float upwards, with his gold halo, at any moment. Was it actually beating? I wrenched my head away. Maurice was crying, a soft, breathy sniffle, trying to control himself but failing miserably. My father cleared his throat and the sound echoed down the corridor.

Staccato steps, squeaking shoes, rustling skirts, and the rattle of rosary beads came from the far end. A tall, thin nun swung into sight, moving at pace. She had a commanding air, a person used to ordering people around, and being obeyed. Was this Mother Bernadette who 'ran a tight ship?' I wasn't sure what that phrase meant but it didn't sound good.

My father rose to his feet. Maurice stopped crying for a moment and stared at her.

'I am Sister Joseph,' she announced, 'and I will be showing the boys the school.'

Why did this woman have a man's name? Did it mean something special, different from a nun with a woman's name? I suddenly felt tired and wanted to cry too. But it wouldn't help my father to have two bawling boys to deliver to the nuns. At the age of seven, I was only sixteen months older than my brother but I already felt a sense of responsibility.

Sister Joseph led my father to a desk and gave him a sheaf of papers. 'Please read and sign these.' She paused. 'You have an unusual name.'

'It's French,' my father replied. 'I grew up in the Seychelles islands, which of course are British, but my family is descended from the original French settlers.'

He sat down at the desk and began reading. In the silence, the ticking of the mysterious clock seemed louder than before. Finally, he took out his fountain pen, signed the papers, and handed them to Sister Joseph.

'You may come and see the children in three months' time,' she said. 'They are in good hands and will have a proper Catholic upbringing, of that you can be sure.'

My father put away his pen and it was time to say goodbye. Sister Joseph took a step backwards but continued watching us with a cold, clinical interest while my father kissed us. I felt his rough cheek and smelt the familiar shaving soap and tobacco. The wool of his tweed jacket was warm from his body and I wanted to nestle in the crook of his arm. But, as the older son, I knew that I should restrain myself and set an example to young Maurice, as well as make a good impression on Sister Joseph who looked as if she didn't favour that kind of thing.

Maurice clung to my father's hand, his small pink knuckles turning white with the effort. My father bent over him, whispering encouragement.

'Everything will be all right Maurice,' he said. 'I'll be back soon.'

Three months didn't sound like 'soon', but what else could he say?

He looked at me. There was no need for words. I went over and took Maurice's other hand. I pulled gently and my father managed to detach Maurice's grip. He said goodbye to Sister Joseph, and walked quickly to the door. We stood still, hand-in-hand, watching.

The taxi's starter motor churned and the engine sputtered into life. The wheels crunched on the gravel and the gears grated as the driver misjudged the change. He seemed to be in a hurry, and perhaps my father was too. The sound of the engine became fainter. Then silence. I gripped Maurice's hand, small and warm, more firmly. We remained, motionless, staring at the inside of the heavy wooden door.

I could feel Sister Joseph's presence behind us. 'Follow me,' she said.

What brought us to this isolated place was the Luftwaffe. We were living with my father in a flat in south London and I never heard the bomb. The air-raid sirens were wailing as Maurice and I went to bed but I soon fell asleep. Waking at daybreak, I heard the sound of clanging fire engine bells. I went to the window that overlooked our back garden, opened the curtains, and saw a scene of great devastation. The house at the end of the garden had taken a direct hit that sheared off one half of the building. Scorched wallpaper fluttered from the surviving rooms, each with its own small wrought-iron fireplace. Some had coals in them and one, miraculously, was still burning. Water dripped from the masonry as the fire hoses splashed against the charred walls, and wisps of steam and smoke rose in a clear sky. A small group of people on the street stared at the ruin.

My father came in looking shaken.

'Are you all right?' he said, hugging us.

Our replies were lost in the folds of his dressing gown.

'No more London,' he said, 'no more London.'

I was not sure what he meant but, within a few days, it became clear we would go and he would stay.

How does a child first know when somebody is his or her 'father' or 'mother'? Usually, I suppose, the relationship becomes clear through the actions and words of the parents, often using the third person. Hugs and kisses at bedtime… 'Mummy will take care of that… Daddy will be home soon.' Perhaps, in an occluded past, it was our experience too, but my memory does not reach back that far. It was more likely that my father entered my consciousness later through a direct intervention, possibly when one of our guardians announced: 'Your father is coming to see you tomorrow.' I knew then who he was, but I did not yet know anything about him except that he was our protector, the man who, in the absence of a mother or any other relative, decided where we should live and who would look after us.

By the time he dropped us off at St. Dominic's, I was beginning to have a clearer impression of him. The only way I can explain this evolution is through the small and disconnected incidents that preceded the London bombing, fragile scaffolding for a father-son relationship but all that I have. These incidents, some little more than anecdotes, have endured over the years, and are surprisingly precise and visual. What connects them is that they revolve around my father, a man without a wife and often absent, bringing him closer to me and defining the bond between us.

My first memory of him was at a boarding house in the Midlands, in a place called Raunds, near Northampton. I am not sure why we were there, but it is possible that it was early in the war and we were evacuated from London in advance of the anticipated German onslaught. Raunds was a shoemaking town and the smell of burning leather and coal smoke hung immovably over its factory chimneys and narrow streets. The owner of the boarding house, a thin, pincer-faced woman who never seemed to smile, acted as our guardian. While the smell of burnt leather filled the air outside, boiled cabbage held sway inside.

What I remember of my father was a single visit. Our room had a big double bed and was heated by a gas fire that was operated by dropping shilling coins into a meter. My father had a cold and before we went to bed he hung up his sodden handkerchiefs in front of the fire to dry. As they gently steamed, he talked about the importance of dressing warmly in winter.

'Do you know what I wore under my shirt when I first arrived in Scotland?' he said.

We shook our heads.

'The *Glasgow Herald*!' he said with a laugh, 'a newspaper! It was winter and bitterly cold. I had arrived on a ship from the Seychelles, which is a very warm place, and didn't have the proper clothes. My landlady took one look at me and said, 'Wrap the *Herald* around your chest, under your shirt, until you can buy some wool underwear.'

He leaned forward and turned his handkerchiefs around. 'She told me you should always wear wool next to your skin though I must say that newspaper was pretty good too.'

We slept on either side of him and as we settled down he put his arms around us and held us close. He liked us to massage his head. His hair was straight, thin, and slightly oily from the pomade he used. It smelled like the inside of a barber's shop. After a while, my arms grew tired and comforted by the warmth of his body, I fell asleep. The next day he was gone, leaving us once more with the sour landlady and Raund's unpleasant smells. It was not clear when we would see him again.

At a different time, I remember going with him somewhere in a large car with tinted windows and wide running boards. We may have still been in Raunds, or perhaps we were in another town with another guardian. Several other people were in the car and I suppose they were my father's friends. I think we were going to the races but all I recall is being carsick. My father asked the driver to pull over and sat beside me on the running board, holding my hand, as I threw up into the gutter.

One summer, we were on a farm. I saw green fields for the first time and smelled the freshness of the earth after rain and the raw odour of cow dung. Around the farm was a rich panorama of meadows, cows, sheep, chickens and pigs, flowers, muddy tracks, winding lanes, and thatched cottages, a world utterly different from the dead colours and the smoke of the cities. It was all new to me and maybe that is why it remains so vivid. Every morning, an old man walked into the cowshed close to the farmhouse carrying a three-legged stool and a bucket. He selected a cow from the stalls and led it out to a concrete stand. He sat down on the stool, adjusted the bucket, grasped a teat with a large, calloused hand and began milking. With my father at my side, I loved watching the old man's slow and measured movements and listening to the hiss of the hot milk as it hit the inside of the bucket.

I have a photograph which I think was taken on that holiday. My father had written a date on it: 15 August 1939, which meant that I was three and a half years old at the time. For some reason, Maurice is not in the picture although I suppose he was with us. My father is in a sports jacket and plus-fours (trousers cinched four inches below the knee and worn with long socks), and is carrying a raincoat and a small jacket over his arm. He is wearing a white open-necked shirt, its collar is pulled out and folded over the neck of his jacket collar. I am dressed in a woollen two-piece outfit that ends at the knees (minus fours?), and sandals. I am holding his hand and the top of my head barely reaches his elbow. I look rather solemn but he is smiling.

The longest we lived in one place before going to St. Dominic's was when my father left us in the care of two elderly women, Evelyn and Kitty Linder, early in the war. They were sisters who lived together in Buckhurst Hill, Essex, a London suburb. The house, a mock Tudor of red brick with a timber frame and leaded-pane windows, was in a quiet street. The Linders had never married but they liked children and as time went by, we began to think of them as family. We even started calling them 'Auntie Evelyn' and 'Auntie Kitty' and they didn't seem to mind. But my father did. On one of his visits, he must have heard us speaking to the Linders this way.

'They are not your aunts,' he said sternly, taking us aside. 'You should call them both Miss Linder. That is the correct way.'

The Linders were well off and had another house on Canvey Island, in the Thames estuary, which became a sanctuary for us all when the bombing of London started in earnest. Much of the island was below sea level and protected by dykes built by Dutch engineers in the seventeenth century. We lived in an octagonal thatched house, modelled on the original dwellings of those industrious men. Around it was an orderly garden tended by Henry Linder, Evelyn and Kitty's brother. Like them, he was unmarried, and rarely came to London, preferring to live on Canvey Island. He was a morose and distant figure, straight as a rifle barrel, with iron grey hair, parted in the middle and slicked back, and fierce, bristling eyebrows. The only thing that softened his appearance was a small toothbrush moustache, which reminded me of Charlie Chaplin.

When we first arrived, Evelyn took us aside and told us that Henry had been gassed and badly wounded on the Western Front in the Great War. His injuries still caused him pain, she said, and this made him grumpy and short tempered. In the evenings, he would sit by the fire, smoking and listening to the radio about the news of another war. I wanted to talk to him, to hear his war stories, but he did not encourage conversation.

One evening, he caught me staring at his damp, hand-rolled cigarette, which, when he took it out of his mouth, had a silver thread of spittle hanging from it. He looked at me intently for a moment and I felt a tremor of fear.

'There are two kinds of smokers, lad,' he said, not unkindly, in his gravelly voice, 'wet smokers and dry smokers. Well, as you can see, I am a wet smoker.'

I relaxed and went on with my knitting. Henry relapsed into silence but continued to look at me as if he, too, wanted to talk. It was always like this, a moment of hope that ended in a puzzling silence. He didn't talk much to Evelyn and Kitty either.

I am not sure how long we lived on the island. Time was like the fog that rolled over the water meadows, mudflats, marshes, and canals, a nebulous, intangible substance. We lived entirely in the present, the future as opaque as the past. Two elderly ladies orchestrated our daily lives and made sure we were safe, comfortable and as happy as possible. Once a week, it was bath night. Kitty, the youngest and liveliest member of the Linder trio, heated two large kettles on the hob and mixed the hot water with cold in a galvanised tin bathtub set up in the middle of the kitchen floor. I went to my first school, a one-room schoolhouse with a pot-bellied stove and a dozen desks with old-fashioned inkwells.

Our playground was Henry's garden and the island. We roamed the mudflats and myriad channels that drained water from the low-lying land into the estuary, wondering where the smugglers used to hide their kegs of brandy, rum, and whisky. We picked heavy, fragrant mushrooms from the meadows enriched by cow and sheep dung, and struck up a friendship with some of the local children. Maurice told me later that he remembered one of these 'friends' beating me up while he watched feeling helpless. I have no recall of the incident, perhaps an early example of what became a habit of consigning really bad memories to oblivion.

From time to time, my father turned up, with his rolling gait, wafting the scents of shaving soap and tobacco in his wake. He kissed us, shook hands formally with the Linders, and took us out for a meal. Sometimes he would bring a present, a toy, a pack of playing cards, or a book and ceremoniously hand it over. My present for him, a red wool scarf (Evelyn had taught me how to knit) was still a work in progress. He never stayed overnight, and was off again before nightfall.

Exact dates rarely make an impact on a child's memory. But there was one that I could pin down precisely because it involved a numerical coincidence. The number seven is a lucky number for many people; in this instance, it brought me mixed fortunes. On 9 February 1943, I had seven of my milk teeth taken out under a general anaesthetic by a Canvey Island dentist. I felt nauseous when I woke up and spat blood and saliva into the sink. The dentist explained he had used gas to knock me out and that it was normal to feel sick afterwards but the effects would soon wear off. When Evelyn arrived and took me back to the house, there was a birthday cake with seven candles on the dining room table.

Returning from school one day, Maurice and I lingered in the garden watching Henry light his bonfire. Weeds and brushwood were stacked high but with great precision so that the fire would burn easily and safely. He had a large box of matches in his hand and went around the bonfire, lighting it low down in several different places. We watched the flames leap into the darkening sky before going inside and up to our rooms to do our homework. My bedroom window was open and I could just see part of the fire, which was red with heat, but I couldn't see Henry. The smoke was mixing with the fog and swirling around the house. I liked its smell, the smell of autumn, that made being inside the warm house so appealing.

I pulled my head back in. Smoke seeped into the room, carrying with it a new, unpleasant odour. I shut the window and went to Maurice's room to tell him it was time for our high tea. We went downstairs and sat at our usual places. Evelyn came in with a large plate of scrambled eggs on toast. She was about to put it on the table when the door burst open and Kitty ran into the house, her face white and frozen.

'Oh Evelyn, it's Henry!' she gasped. 'He's fallen into the fire.'

Evelyn almost dropped the plate. She recovered, put it down on the table and steadied herself with both hands on the back of Maurice's chair. She moved to the door and I stood up.

'No!' she shouted, something I had never heard her do before. 'Kitty, stay with the boys. I'll go.'

We sat still, nailed to our seats, while Kitty collapsed into a chair, her eyes fixed on the door. We heard a muffled cry and then Evelyn was back. Her spectacles were smudged, her hands and sleeves were grey with ash, and strands of her hair, normally bound in a neat bun, had broken loose and fallen over her face. She looked around for a moment, picked up the heavy black telephone, and dialled.

'There's been an accident…'

She turned to Kitty and motioned her to take us out of the room. When I looked back the woman I knew best in the world was bent over the telephone, alternately talking and sobbing. I knew then that I would not be talking to Henry about sharing his experience of being gassed, or hearing any of his war stories.

We moved back to the Buckhurst Hill house and a day or so later my father arrived. Evelyn asked Maurice and me to go out and play in the garden. I came back in a few minutes later to fetch a tennis ball and heard my father and Evelyn in the next room talking in low, earnest voices. I had a feeling that our lives were going to change again.

And they did. A week or so later, Evelyn said that my father was coming the next day to take us away. She offered no explanation but I could see that she was upset. The last night was like so many before it. She came into my room, kissed me good night, and turned off the gas lamp. As I lay there, with the covers up around my chin because there was no heat in the bedrooms, I watched the mantle slowly lose its heat, glow red, then orange, and dissolve into the darkness.

When my father arrived the next morning, he told us we would be moving into a flat in Morden on the other side of London. He tried to make it sound like an exciting adventure where we would all finally be together in our own place and we could learn to swim in an indoor pool close by. But I didn't want to leave the Linders. When we said goodbye, both Evelyn and Kitty were on the edge of tears and so was I. We had hardly settled into our new home when the German bomb landed on the house at the bottom of the garden. Within a week, we were on our way to Hertfordshire.

All this time, there was no sign or mention of our mother. It would take St. Dominic's Priory, where my father had just left us, to bring out into the open what I already instinctively knew. Every Sunday, after mass and lunch, we went to our classroom to write our weekly letters home. Sister Agnes, a short, bad-tempered woman with a sallow face, was in charge. One Sunday, probably a few weeks after we arrived, I felt her looking at me as I wrote. I kept my head down. I knew by now it was important not be noticed if you could manage it. Then I heard the swish of her habit and the tinkle of rosary beads. I took a peak. I couldn't see any of the nuns' punitive instruments, a leather strap, rubber truncheon, or a bamboo cane, within her reach. A good sign.

She stopped at my desk and extended her left hand with its gold wedding band (proof of her marriage to Jesus she had told us), and picked up my letter as if it were the Devil's work.

'Why are you writing, "Dear Mammy and Daddy"?' she asked softly. Like most of the nuns, she was Irish, and we were used to the lilt of their voices that could carry a sense of menace as easily as warmth.

'Because you told us to, sister,' I said obediently.

She glowered. 'Lord have mercy on us! How old are you?'

'Seven, sister.'

'Well, it's about time you knew that you don't have a mother, is it not?'

'Yes, sister.'

'What does your poor father think when he receives a letter like that?'

'I don't know, sister. Shall I cross out "Mammy"?'

'Are you being insolent?' she hissed.

'No, no, sister,' I said, bending my head.

She folded the letter and tore it into four neat pieces. She went over to Maurice's desk and did the same with his half-finished letter.

'Your poor father!' she said, walking away.

Afterwards, Maurice and I walked back to the dormitory together. I thought of mentioning what had happened but, when I looked at him, I could see he was lost in his thoughts and kept silent. The only difference now was that, on letter-writing day, we dipped our steel-nibbed pens into the inkwells on our desks and wrote, 'Dear Daddy,' followed by a comma and a new paragraph.

From time to time, my father came to see us. Infrequent and unpredictable though his visits were, I looked forward to them. But

I couldn't help noticing that the other children were met by a full complement of parents and their mothers embraced them with a perfumed, feminine warmth that we were denied. Sister Joseph would tell us that he was arriving on such and such a day, usually, but not always, a Saturday or a Sunday. 'Make sure that you are clean and put on your Sunday clothes,' she'd say, 'and be ready for him in the hall.' We always got there well ahead of the appointed time and sat quietly, staring at the large crucifix and the picture of Jesus with his bleeding heart. The clock, which I still had not located, ticked away the minutes as I listened for the crunch on the gravel outside that grew to mean more and more as the years went by.

Finally, the taxi arrived. The bell rang and Sister Joseph, who had been hovering, opened the door. My father, dressed in a suit and wearing a trilby hat, walked in, his face lighting up when he saw us. He kissed us and held us close, a moment of bliss, a sunburst of happiness, as brilliant as the golden rays that shone down on Christ's head over the altar in the chapel.

Our routine was to go to a café in Newgate Street Village, the nearest town, where we drank mugs of sweet tea and gorged on stodgy buns and cakes. After we could eat no more, my father slowly filled and lit his pipe. He sat back, puffing contentedly. The blue smoke spiralled upwards, rich and fragrant, filling the room.

Then it was time to return to the school, the moment I dreaded. I can see us now, two small boys in their Sunday best, walking along the driveway, my brother on one side and me on the other, each of us holding firmly on to a large, warm, masculine hand. I remember my father's walk, his right foot splaying out while the left hit the ground dead straight. He pitched and rolled a bit, perhaps from his time at sea or possibly because one leg was shorter than the other. He was very attentive and affectionate. 'By Jove, you don't say!' was a favourite phrase he used to punctuate our chatter. I could see that he was as sad as we were when it was time to go; that was comforting and helped sustain me until the next visit.

In my childish eyes, he had changed. He had progressed from being 'my father', a distant figure who came and went, to the 'Dear Daddy' I wrote to every week. 'Mammy' of course was no longer in the picture, if indeed she ever had been, except as a name on a piece of paper. We only had a father, and that was that. I accepted the situation but I retained my memory of the woman whom I thought was my mother, not through any conscious decision but because it was so vivid.

I often wondered how Maurice felt. It would have been easy to ask him, and the perfect time would have been when we were alone after the letter-writing incident. But that moment passed and perhaps it was because we both knew she was no longer a presence in our lives, although she must have been at some point, however brief. We sensed that she had gone forever. This tacit agreement not to discuss our mother would continue, undisturbed, for decades. What clinched it was the fact that my father never mentioned her, even when he had been receiving our 'Dear Mammy and Daddy' letters for weeks, and we took our cue from him. Children don't always need words; an absence of words can be enough.

## 2

WE WERE WITH OUR FATHER IN A TAXI ON THE TOP OF THE
hill overlooking the school. It was four years later and I was eleven
and my brother ten. The war had been over for two years, and we
were leaving St. Dominic's Priory for good. As the taxi slowed, I
turned and looked back.

'You'll miss the sisters and your friends,' said my father.

'I don't think so,' I said.

I wouldn't miss a thing but I would remember more than I
wanted to.

I looked at Maurice, sitting on the other side of my father. What
was he thinking? His long face, as smooth and as unresponsive as
stone, revealed nothing. At some stage, it had all been too much
for him and he did 'a bunk'. Late one autumn afternoon, he slipped
out of the school grounds and disappeared into the woods only to
return cold, wet, and hungry several hours later, a hero to those of
us of the same mind but less daring, or perhaps less desperate. He
was tougher now, but more enclosed—a wary ten-year-old veteran
who didn't talk much.

The car began to pick up speed and the school disappeared
from sight.

We took a train to London and, after a long ride on the Tube,
got out at Woodford Station. We walked up Snakes Lane, a broad
street with trees on each side and large houses set back behind privet
hedges and rhododendron bushes. Woodford was familiar because
it was close to Buckhurst Hill where we had lived with the Linder
sisters. For a moment, I thought we were returning to them and
perhaps to their house on Canvey Island. We had a long summer

break ahead of us and the idea of being back with them, beside the water, was exciting. But when I asked my father, he shook his head and smiled.

'No, we are going to another house, or rather a flat in a house, owned by a friend of mine. She is a very nice Scottish lady and I am sure you will like her. Her name is Edith Ross and she teaches at Woodford County High School for Girls.'

'What does she teach?' I asked.

'Domestic science,' he said. 'She is a marvellous cook so no more school food. There is also a big garden where you can play and I can grow vegetables.' I could see he was happy, and began to wonder about Edith Ross. She didn't sound at all like the Linder sisters.

'Is she going to look after us?'

My father hesitated. 'You could say that. We will all be together...'

'What shall we call her?' I said, remembering the confusion over names with the Linders.

'Just call her Edith,' he said, 'she likes to be called by her Christian name.'

'Will you be there all the time?'

'I certainly will,' he said cheerfully. 'I'll have to go to an office during the day but I'll be home every evening.'

Home. The word had become familiar because the nuns and the kids at St. Dominic's used it all the time. 'You'll be going home soon,' the nuns would say near the end of the term. 'I can't wait to get home,' my friends often said, anticipating their departure. 'Home' for my school friends was somewhere they went every time they left St. Dominic's, and it was always the same place. Even the nuns had a 'home', the convent, as well as a maternal figure to take care of them, Mother Bernadette. What it felt like to have a conventional home eluded Maurice and me because we always went to other people's homes, places that were clearly not ours. But what my father was describing as we walked along Snakes Lane, sounded different from anything I had ever experienced, or at least could remember experiencing. It seemed evident that this unknown person, Edith Ross, was responsible for the change. Who was she? What was she like? My father obviously liked her but would she like Maurice and me? A thought crossed my mind.

'Is she married?'

My father smiled. 'No, she is not.'

We turned into a long driveway lined with rhododendron bushes in full bloom, a cascade of red, blue, yellow and white flowers. The driveway led up to a large, four-story house. On the steps, was a woman, neither young nor old. She was dressed in a tweed jacket and skirt with a pale pink blouse and wearing a pearl necklace. Her silver hair was cut short and teased into loose ripples close to her head.

My father put down his suitcase and introduced us to 'Edith'. She shook our hands, and gave us a warm smile, revealing perfect white teeth. My father kissed her on the lips and they held each other close for a moment. I was embarrassed because I had never seen him behave that way. He looked different, too. He appeared younger, more handsome, in his well-tailored three-piece charcoal grey suit, maroon tie, and polished shoes. His face was suntanned from working in the garden, highlighting the contrast with his blue eyes. His hair was thin and greying but neatly cut, pomaded, and brushed straight back. I had never thought of him being French, although he did speak English with a slight accent, but perhaps this was his French side. He seemed more carefree and dashing than the elderly, staid father I had come to know. Was this how he had been as a young man?

Edith stepped back looking flushed.

'Do come in, boys,' she said, reaching down to help us with our suitcases. She led us into a spacious hallway and up a wide staircase to the second floor.

'This is our flat. The landlord and his family live on the ground floor, and there is another tenant on the floor above us.'

Her accent was very posh, very English. We had once spent a summer holiday in Scotland and I was familiar with the Scots accent. Edith did not sound Scottish at all.

I looked up and down the stairwell. Everything was open, inviting familiarity and perhaps the sharing of secrets that would not normally be shared.

'Mr and Mrs Dunning are a nice couple,' she said, pointing downstairs. 'They have a twenty-year-old son and an eighteen-year-old daughter. You'll like them.'

She didn't mention the tenant on the top floor, and I didn't ask though I was curious.

'Here's your bedroom,' Edith said, opening the door to a large room with a bow window, a dresser, a bookcase, and two single beds. We dropped our luggage, and she took us along the corridor to the next room.

'This is your father's room,' she said, with a slight emphasis on the word 'father', 'and mine is at the end of the corridor.'

It was clear that Edith was not a 'guardian' like the Linder sisters and others had been. There was no doubt that she and my father were fond of each other. Were they planning to get married? If they did, would we have a 'mother' after all? Well, a stepmother. Did that mean my real mother was dead?

Edith showed us the bathroom, living room, dining room and kitchen. The flat was nicely furnished, tidy, and spotlessly clean. I wondered if everything belonged to Edith, or did we have some things mixed up with hers? We had brought our clothes with us and not much else. What I recall are a collection of empty pipe tobacco tins, given to us by my father after he had put the tobacco into his leather pouch. They were small but attractive, with a picture of a stag set against a background of green and gold. On the lid, 'Exmoor Hunt', the brand's name, curled over the stag's head. I remembered that we used them in a game with toy soldiers, the old lead kind, on the floor of our bedroom.

Much easier to recall was a book that my father had won as a school prize for Latin in the Seychelles in 1903 when he was thirteen. It was *The Exploits of Brigadier Gerard* by Arthur Conan Doyle, an action-packed collection of stories woven around a fictional French hero, Brigadier Etienne Gerard of the 3rd Hussars, during the Napoleonic Wars. He is a wonderful creation: brave, dashing, vain, boastful, and not the brightest lantern in the cavalry lines, but thoroughly human. My father's copy was a first edition published in London in 1899. It had a maroon cover, fine binding, smooth, heavy paper, and twenty-four evocative and beautifully executed illustrations by W. B. Wollen, a well-known Scottish painter. Once I got into a story, I couldn't stop and finished it under the covers with the aid of a torch.

'I am sure you'll want to see the garden,' Edith said at the end of the tour. 'Am I right?' We nodded shyly and she led us back down the staircase and out through the front door to the garden at the rear. The garden was really two gardens. Directly behind the house was a large, rectangular lawn with a path running down one side of it and flower beds along the other. At the end was a barn. The path made a sharp left turn and led into an equally large orchard and vegetable garden with a greenhouse at the far end.

'There's a wood not far from here,' said Edith, 'it's a great place for you to go and play with your friends.'

'We don't have any friends,' I said quickly.

Edith looked embarrassed. 'Of course, how silly of me,' she said. 'But when you go to your new schools, I am sure you will make lots of friends.'

'Do you know where I am going to school?'

'Your father didn't tell you?' she said. 'Well, you'll be going to Wanstead County High School, which isn't too far away, and Maurice is going to the Woodford Primary School up on the High Road. Both are good schools and I am sure you will like them. And they are day schools, so you'll be home every evening.'

It was settled. This flat, with my father and Edith here all the time, was going to be our home. It was too early to grasp the meaning properly but it certainly felt different and comforting although my brother and I were always wary when good fortune came our way.

Edith left us to explore and went off to prepare the supper. When we came back in, my father was sitting in an armchair, smoking his pipe and reading a newspaper. He looked comfortable and settled, almost as if it was his place, not Edith's.

When Edith called us into the dining room, which overlooked the garden at the back of the house, I was surprised. Arrayed over the polished mahogany table were cork place mats with hunting scenes on them, two sets of cutlery for each setting, crystal glasses, silver salt, pepper and mustard pots, and a vase with yellow roses in the centre of it all. Edith motioned us to sit down, with my father at the head of the table, and went out to the kitchen.

A few minutes later, she returned carrying a fish and potato pie with a golden crust. She placed it carefully in the centre of the table. Maurice and I stared, transfixed. The pie steamed gently, a fragrant, mouth-watering dish and invited instant attack but Maurice and I restrained ourselves, instinctively knowing that to do otherwise would be wrong. Self-restraint had been something we had learned, not always the easy way, at the convent school.

Edith, who had the dinner plates in front of her, began to serve, first for my father and then for us. I was about to dig in but there was a problem. Which set of cutlery to use? The outer set was smaller than the inner, and the knife, with its slightly curved blunt-edged blade, didn't look like a knife at all.

'Those are for the fish, John,' Edith said gently. 'The others are for meat, and the smallest knife is for butter.'

I looked down again and something caught my eye. On the knives, forks, and spoons, 'St. J.' was engraved on the handles.

'Look!' I exclaimed, picking up a fork, 'are these our initials?'

My father and Edith exchanged glances. I looked at him but he seemed at a loss for words.

'They are, they were a present to your father,' Edith said quickly. 'Now, boys, do start, I'm sure you're famished.'

Hunger was one of the unwanted memories that I carried with me from St. Dominic's and Maurice and I needed no second invitation to tuck in to the pie. After we had had our fill, Edith returned to the kitchen and came back with a steamed suet pudding, studded with sultanas. She also brought a small jug filled with syrup made from sugar cane. The pudding was surprisingly light and tasty, especially when doused with the golden syrup. I couldn't remember ever having eaten a meal as good as this one. Edith seemed gratified by our appetites and glanced at my father who nodded approvingly.

As she started clearing away, he bent down and whispered to us that we should help her with the dishes. We went into the kitchen and Edith gave us tea towels to dry up. He returned to the living room for another pipe. He already seemed to be the master of the household.

When we were in bed, Edith came in with mugs of hot cocoa, put them down on the bedside table between us, and wished us good night. I sipped the cocoa and a feeling of well-being swept over me. I looked over at Maurice. He was already asleep, breathing steadily. It was hard to grasp how quickly our lives had changed. Would they change again, as they had done so often in the past?

I finished the cocoa and switched off the light. I closed my eyes and fell asleep. I dreamt I was walking along a familiar corridor, from the lavatory to the dormitory. It was pitch black and I could hear the wind howling outside. A door opened and I felt a rush of cold air. I turned and saw a dark cloaked figure framed in the doorway. The head was shrouded in a heavy black veil but there was no face. My stomach churned. I panicked and started to run. Then I heard a voice that I thought belonged to the nun in charge of the dormitory.

'Walk!'

I slowed down, my heart beating painfully. I went into the dormitory and walked towards my bed but, standing in the way, was Sister Agnes. What was she doing there? I had never seen her in the dormitories before. Her lips moved. 'You don't have a mother, a mother, a mother...'

I snapped awake, sweating and confused. Where was I? Maurice's rhythmic breathing steadied me as the room came into focus. I stiffened again. There was a thud on the wall behind my bed. Someone was on the landing, muttering. I heard footsteps and the scraping of metal against metal. A door slammed on the top floor. Silence. I snuggled down into the bed and fell into a dreamless sleep.

## 3

MY FATHER GOT UP EARLY EVERY WEEKDAY MORNING AND travelled across London by Tube to an office in the War Department in the western suburbs. He always left the house impeccably dressed. He told me later that his well-cut suits were made by Jewish tailors in the City of London, and he wore shirts with detachable collars (two came with every shirt), fastened by studs in the back and front. His shoes were highly polished, waxed and buffed lovingly by hand. The final touch was a bowler hat on his head and rolled umbrella in his hand.

Occasionally, he would visit a port to inspect ships' engines, but most of the time he was in London. In the evening he sat and talked with Edith about his day, mainly gossip about his colleagues and money matters, salaries, benefits and pensions, adult talk that floated over my head. It did not sound as interesting to me as I imagine his earlier life at sea had been. He had shown me postcards of ships he had served on as an engineer, and a World War I medal for service in the Mediterranean. But he seemed content and it was becoming clearer than ever that our wandering days were over.

During the weekends he spent more time with us than he had done in the past. He bought us fishing rods, and showed us how to catch fish in a large pond not far from the house. He was more used to sea fishing, he said, which he had learned as a boy with the Creole fishermen along the great coral reefs that ring the Seychelles islands in the Indian Ocean. But he knew what he was doing and joined in our delight when we hooked a fish no matter how small it was. In the garden, we helped him clean out the weeds between the banked rows of potato plants, and picked tomatoes and green beans. I asked him once why didn't he grow flowers as well as vegetables.

'If you could eat them,' he said with a smile, 'I would.'

He astonished his neighbours by planting a sizeable plot with Virginia tobacco seedlings. Where he got them and how he made them grow he never revealed. London's climate was completely different from Virginia's, but the plants shot up with amazing speed, sturdy and green, to the point where they towered over him. By the end of the summer, the leaves were golden and we helped him strip them off the plants, take out the central spines, and lay them out on a work bench in the barn. When they were dry, he dribbled a mixture of glycerine, honey, and rum over them, and rolled them tightly into cigar-shaped plugs wrapped in cellophane. The next step was the 'pressing.' We did this by taking a plug, tying a piece of cord around it and attaching the other end to a doorknob. We pulled the cord tight by walking slowly towards the door until we reached it and the cord ran out. The plug was then tightly bound. After three months, they were rock-hard. My father took off the cord and cellophane and shaved the tobacco into fine flakes with a razor blade. He rubbed the shredded tobacco between his palms, and put it into a large tobacco jar. In the evening, he taught us how to pack his pipe and we'd take turns lighting it. As the match burned down, clouds of pungent smoke billowed into the living room while he settled back in his armchair with a blissful look on his face.

Later, he went into making wine from parsnips that he had grown in the garden and from wild elderberry flowers. During the night, I sometimes heard a muffled explosion in the barn and, in the morning, we'd pick our way through shattered glass and puddles of liquor to check the survivors. When my father deemed the wine ready for drinking, we all had a sip and universally declared it was delicious, which it was. A glass of parsnip or elderberry, pale gold in colour, would accompany his evening pipe.

On Sunday mornings, while Edith was preparing the lunch, a joint of beef or mutton (our weekly meat ration), along with vegetables from the garden, my father took us to mass at the local Catholic church, St. Thomas of Canterbury, which adjoined a small Benedictine monastery containing about a dozen monks. When I asked my father if Edith was going to join us, he said she was not a Catholic. Like many Scots, he explained, she was a Presbyterian. I did not know anything about Presbyterians except that they were Protestants. At St. Dominic's, we knew from the nuns that all Protestants ('Proddy Dogs' to us) could never go to heaven. Instead, if they led good lives, they were destined for limbo, that strange celestial transit lounge where they would spend the afterlife waiting for an onward flight that never arrived. I failed to form a clear idea how much Edith's religion meant to her because she never talked about it. All I knew was that, while we were at church, she was cooking lunch.

It was a long walk to the church, up winding Snakes Lane to Woodford Green and then along the High Road. But there was no other way. We had no car and the buses didn't run on Sundays.

While I had bad memories of St. Dominic's, I was still a practising Catholic, regularly attending confession and taking communion. Maurice wasn't. He appeared to have abandoned four years of religious teaching and practice the moment the convent's door closed behind him. However, for some time, I forced him to go through the motions with me, which meant going to confession on Saturday evenings and taking communion at Sunday mass.

The Sunday mass was sung by the Benedictine monks. The slow and beautiful cadences of their unaccompanied voices chanting the ancient Latin prayers, was a new and surprisingly emotional experience. I shut my eyes and let the rise and fall of sound wash over me. While my faith was slipping away, the centuries-old ritual of the Latin sung mass, accompanied by the smell of incense, was extraordinarily powerful and made a lasting impression. As the mass reached its climax, the priest consecrated the host, turned towards the congregation, and raised it above his head for everyone to see and venerate. Picking up a gold tray filled with wafers, he moved down to the altar rail. People began to get to their feet and walk down the central aisle. I nudged Maurice and stood up. My father was at the end of the pew so I waited for him to go first. But he didn't move. Finally, he rose and stepped into the aisle, letting us pass.

'Go ahead, boys,' he said.

We made our way to the altar. As I knelt down at the rail, I peeked under my arm to see if he was following us. He wasn't. He had gone back to his seat and was kneeling, his head bowed.

This pattern was repeated the next Sunday, and the next. As I was returning from the altar on the third occasion, with Christ's body stuck like chewing gum to the roof of my mouth, I caught my father's eye. He looked embarrassed and turned away. As the weeks went by, it was clear that he was never going to join us at the altar rail. He never came to confession either. Initially, I thought he was going at another time but, after a few weeks, I changed my mind. All this was puzzling because the rules that the nuns had taught us were clear. If you did not go to confession, a prerequisite for taking the holy sacrament at Sunday mass, your soul would be in danger. Further, if you died unshriven in that state, you would go directly to hell and burn forever. My father seemed to be a good Catholic, yet something was wrong.

As we walked home, no longer holding his hands because we were getting too old for that sort of thing, I occasionally thought of asking him. But I felt the same reluctance as I did when I thought of quizzing him about my mother, and said nothing. Instead, when we were alone, I asked Maurice, the youthful apostate, what he thought.

'Dunno,' he said, not looking up from his comic.

Edith was on her summer break from teaching and seemed eager to get to know us. She was with us every day and readily answered any questions that came into our heads. One night, I got up to go to the lavatory. The house was peaceful. I opened the bathroom door, switched on the light and recoiled. On the sink was a glass of water with a set of teeth in it. Perfect white teeth. I turned away, did my business, and left without looking at the teeth again—until the next morning when I saw them in Edith's smile. Since she was so friendly, I asked her if many people had false teeth.

'Goodness yes,' she laughed. 'When I was in my early twenties, I had gingivitis, a gum infection, and the dentist recommended that I have all my teeth out and dentures instead. My three sisters did the same. In fact, it was quite fashionable in those days.'

The living room mantelpiece was covered with family photographs and one day Edith came in as I was looking at them.

'They are mostly my family,' she said. 'This one,' she pointed at a portrait of a tall, sombre man dressed in a morning coat with a top hat on a small table beside him, 'is my father.'

There were several pictures of her mother, including a portrait and a group photograph showing her with her four daughters, and several female servants. There was also a photograph of a large stone house in Newcastle where Edith and her sisters had grown up.

'Are you really Scottish?' I asked.

'Oh yes, I was born in Dundee and my surname couldn't be more Scottish.'

'But you don't sound Scottish.'

'That's because we moved to Newcastle when I was a child,' she said. 'My father, like yours, was a marine engineer and he got a job in charge of the Tyneside shipyard. My sisters and I went to English schools and we lost our Scottish brogue.'

Her eldest sister went into the civil service, she continued. The second stayed at home to look after their father when their mother died, while Edith and her younger sister became schoolteachers.

'Are any of them married?' I asked.

'None so far. After the First World War, there were not a lot of young men around,' she said. 'Also, my father was a very strict man and didn't approve of us bringing male company home.'

I wondered about Edith. She was the second youngest of the sisters but she was not young, sort of middle-aged though a good bit younger than my father. Perhaps she would be the first in her family to be married?

There were only a few photographs of my father. The most striking was with a few of his shipmates, all in white tropical uniforms, sitting on camels in front of the Sphinx and Pyramids in Egypt. Some of his friends were slumped in their saddles, two had cigarettes in their mouths, and one had his tunic open at the neck. In contrast, my father sat straight-backed, his uniform immaculate and tidy. He was holding the reins loosely, looking confident and relaxed. His pipe stuck out of the side of his mouth at a rakish angle.

I hadn't seen the photograph before but he had told me the story that led up to him being on top of an Egyptian camel. It was near the end of World War I when he was on the SS *Mooltan*, sailing through the Mediterranean in a convoy escorted by two Japanese destroyers (Japan was an ally in that war). Among the 550 passengers and crew were two elderly college professors. They were worried about the ship being sunk at night and decided the safest thing to do was to move their bedding up on deck and sleep in a lifeboat. The rest of the passengers stayed in their cabins.

One moonless night, a German U-boat, evading the escorts, surfaced and fired a torpedo at the ship hitting the mid-section. The impact blew the professors out of the lifeboat into the water. The ship started taking on water and sinking slowly. Fortunately, a British warship came alongside and the sailors hauled the half-drowned academics out of the water while the rest of the passengers and the crew disembarked in an orderly fashion before the ship went down. My father said he had lost everything but at least he was safe and dry. The warship dropped the crew off in Alexandria where they received new clothes and had a week's leave.

'Have you seen these pictures of your family in the Seychelles?' Edith said.

I had seen a few but not the ones on the mantelpiece. Two sepia, slightly mildewed prints were especially striking. In the centre of each photograph was a formidable looking elderly woman in a black dress with a high collar and long sleeves. Her hair, parted in the middle, was pulled tightly back. She had a strong, square face, a stern expression, and looked vaguely familiar. She was sitting in an armchair in front of a flight of steps leading up to the terrace of a house adorned with palm fronds and tropical plants. In one photograph, five men stood beside her. The two oldest were on either side, each with a hand on one of her shoulders. Two more adults and a teenage boy sat at her feet. All the men were dressed in tight-fitting three-piece suits, stiff collars, some with bow ties, and several of them had moustaches. The other picture was identical, same place, same matriarch, but this time, seven women of varying ages, all in long dresses, surrounded her. In neither photograph was there a ghost of a smile.

'The old lady looks like Queen Victoria,' I said.

'She's your grandmother,' Edith replied, 'and those are her fifteen children. I think it was taken in the early 1900s, judging by their Edwardian clothes. Can you find your father?'

I looked closely. Some of the moustachioed men looked quite old, especially the pair flanking my grandmother. The man on the far right who, like the others had a hand on the shoulder of the brother next to him, stood slightly apart. He was young, darkly handsome with an air of uncertainty about him, as if he did not quite belong there.

'Him,' I said.

'Very good, John,' Edith said with a smile. 'Here he is again, but some years later, when he had become an engineer and was with the P&O Line.'

She pointed to a photograph of a group of men, all in naval uniform. My father was at the back, and this time his dark looks stood out against the collection of bluff English faces. He appeared different, more French, in fact rather like Brigadier Etienne Gerard of the 3rd Hussars. Just as we were leaving the living room, I spotted something and stopped. Edith looked at me inquiringly.

I pointed to an object on the floor next to the fireplace. It looked like a double coconut but several times the normal size, dark brown in colour with a tuft of coarse fibre in the cleft. The nut was highly polished, which added to the suggestive shape that triggered the kind of sinful thoughts the nuns at St. Dominic's Priory instructed us to confess to the priest.

'What is that?' I asked.

'It's a *coco-de-mer* nut,' said Edith shortly. 'You father brought it back from the Seychelles. I'm not sure why.' She looked at her watch. 'Now, John, I had better get on with my chores.'

I later discovered that the *coco-de-mer* was unique to the Seychelles islands and, with the nuts resembling a woman's pelvis and buttocks complete with pubic hair, were reputed to have aphrodisiacal qualities. I could see why Edith did not like having the nut around. As I was learning, she did not regard sexual matters, along with other taboo topics like religion and, I sensed, my mother, as being suitable subjects of conversation in her household.

One afternoon Edith took us downstairs and introduced us to Mr and Mrs Downing. He was a well-built man with a military moustache and a ruddy complexion. He greeted us boisterously and said we could have the run of the garden and the barn as long as we didn't burn the place down. He laughed, and so did we. His wife, a tall, thin woman with a streak of white in her grey hair, smiled but said little. Back upstairs in our flat, I asked Edith where Mr Dunning had fought in the war.

'He didn't fight,' she said. 'He had a different kind of war.'

'Different?'

'He was interned on the Isle of Man. You see he was what they called a Brown Shirt, a member of the British Fascist Party that supported Hitler and Mussolini.'

'How long was he there for?'

'Five years.'

'Is he still a fascist?'

'I don't know but he has been very helpful to us and he is, as you can see, a friendly type.' She lowered her voice. 'I think we should keep what we know to ourselves, don't you? Let's treat it as a family secret.'

I wanted to ask Edith about our upstairs neighbour. However, I was beginning to feel that, if she didn't offer to discuss someone, or something, I should not press her. I don't know how I arrived at this notion because I had asked her about her teeth. But she was so kind and caring that I didn't want to show ingratitude by over-stepping the line.

That night, as I lay in bed, my mind drifted back to the family photographs. My father's mother and Edith's father, in their old-fashioned clothes and their stern looks, seemed remarkably similar even though they had grown up in countries thousands of miles from each other, speaking different languages, and going to different churches. My father told me he always spoke French at home and had to learn English at school. Yet, it was hard to imagine him in a French family, growing up as a Frenchman. To me, in spite of his accent, he had always seemed as English as everyone else.

While concentrating on him, I had barely noticed that my mother was missing from the family gallery. But, as I grew drowsy, I thought about her. Had she also grown up in a large French family amid the coconut groves on those remote tropical islands? Somehow, that idea did not square with my memory of her. She seemed as 'English' as my father had always appeared to be. But, since he was, or had been, 'French', perhaps she was too? In that case, was I also French? And what did that mean? I couldn't speak a word of the language and knew nothing about France, let alone my parents' distant homeland. Perhaps one day, I would go there.

## 4

THE SUMMER ENDED, I STARTED HIGH SCHOOL IN THE NEXT town, and Maurice went off to the local primary school. By this time, we had settled in and established a steady routine. Our four years at St. Dominic's continued to haunt me, but less and less as time passed.

Life in immediate post-war Britain was austere, simple, and circumscribed, and was taken for granted. In our flat, we shared one bathroom and had no refrigerator, dishwasher, washing machine, dryer or television. There was a single telephone, the old, heavy, black Bakelite kind (I can still remember the number: BUC 0982), and the 'wireless' was our only form of electronic entertainment. We had no car, nor money for travel. Food and clothing were still rationed. On weekends, my father worked in the garden, and we played in the open air until the sun went down. Edith cooked, washed and mended our clothes by hand and, occasionally, we all sallied forth to the cinema, followed by a modest meal in a modest restaurant. It wasn't very exciting but for Maurice and me it was home, and that was just fine.

Neither Edith nor my father made any effort to introduce us to our neighbour on the top floor. Still, I met her anyway one morning when Edith and Maurice were visiting the doctor. I was on the landing when she came out of her flat and ran down the stairs.

'Hello young man,' she said, taking the cigarette out of her mouth. 'Who are you?'

I shyly introduced myself and stared at her. She was young and wore a bright red sweater and a short grey skirt. She had full breasts, a thick waist, stocking-clad legs, and high heels. But it was her face that riveted me: blonde hair, pale blue eyes, and dark red lips. I could smell her perfume and felt strangely excited.

'Well, it's nice to meet a neighbour at last,' she said cheerfully. 'Not something that seems to happen very often around here.' She looked at her watch. 'God, I'm late! Must be off. We'll meet again, John.'

She skipped down the stairs with remarkable agility for a woman on the heavy side, cigarette smoke trailing behind her.

I stood there for a moment, shaken. I went to the living room and sat down. The odour of cigarette smoke, so common in a house where everyone smoked, had faded. But I could still smell her perfume. I hadn't thought of my mother for some time, but this woman, whoever she was, brought her back.

A few days later, Maurice mentioned her at supper. He had apparently run into her the same way. My father looked up from the haddock he was meticulously filleting, his face clouding. He and Edith exchanged glances.

'She is not a very nice person,' said Edith primly. 'She drinks and has loose morals.'

'Oh,' said Maurice, looking at me for help.

'I met her too,' I said. 'She seemed all right. What is her name?'

'Miss Fenton,' Edith said shortly. 'By the way, how did the rugby match go? I know you were looking forward to it.'

The line had been drawn. This was where Edith's tolerance stopped. Miss Fenton's drinking did not surprise me. I had heard her muttering and cursing late at night when the house was silent and once I heard a man's voice.

During the school holidays, Edith often sent us to the shops to buy groceries and other necessities. On a crisp, cold December day, she gave me a short list, food ration coupons, and a ten-shilling note to buy some lamb chops, bread, cheese and butter. I liked these little expeditions because I would end up in the sweet shop where I could buy copies of *Wizard* and *Rover*, my favourite comics, some boiled sweets, and a bottle of Tizer (the 'Appetizer'), a ruby-coloured fizzy drink.

The butcher's shop was crowded. Three large men, with ruddy faces and wearing blue and white aprons, sliced, chopped, boned and skinned whatever their customers ordered, stopping only to take swigs of tea from steaming mugs that sat on the wooden counter amid entrails, blood, and chicken heads.

I picked up the chops Edith had ordered, turned to leave, and saw a familiar face. She saw me at the same time.

'Why John,' she said a little breathlessly, 'it is you, isn't it?'

'Yes Miss Linder, it's me.'

'My, how you've grown, it must be over four years since you left us.'

By this time, we were out on the street. Evelyn Linder was as I remembered her. Her hair, pulled back and tied in the familiar bun, was a little greyer, and her face more lined, but that was all. She looked at me closely with those gentle grey eyes that I knew so well.

'It's so nice to see you.' She hesitated. 'Do you have time for a cup of tea? There's a little café along the High Street, not far from here.'

It was my turn to hesitate. Edith expected me back as soon as my errands were finished and I wanted to go to the sweet shop.

'That would be nice,' I said politely.

We went into the café and she ordered a pot of tea and some scones.

'I'd heard that you and Maurice had been evacuated to a boarding school in Hertfordshire,' she said, 'so it's a real surprise to see you here in Woodford. Are you living here?'

I told her we had moved to Woodford recently. I said that neither Maurice nor I liked the boarding school but things were much better now because we were living with our father and going to day schools. I did not mention Edith because I didn't know how to describe her connection to us. 'We are all living with our father in her flat' didn't sound the right way to describe a guardian. All our past minders, like the Linders, had lived in houses and my father had never lived with them.

'Are you still in Buckhurst Hill?' I said.

'I am, and Kitty is there too. She will be thrilled to hear that we have met after all this time. Do you remember the house?'

'I do, and the one on Canvey Island. I loved it there.'

'We were very sad to see you and Maurice go,' she said. 'But it wasn't your father's decision, it was ours. We felt you were getting too old for us and the time had come to move on.'

I was surprised, and a little disappointed, but I said nothing.

Evelyn chatted on about Kitty and her other relatives. Her family was like Edith's—full of unmarried women with false teeth. We had finished our tea and scones, and time was moving on. An idea came to me, but how to put it? In the end, I blurted it out.

'When we came to live with you, did my father say anything about my mother?'

'No, John, he didn't,' she said slowly. 'Of course I didn't ask because it wasn't my business, although I have to admit I was curious. Has he told you anything about her?'

I shook my head. 'When we were at St. Dominic's, Maurice and I wrote him letters every week and for a time we wrote "Dear Mammy," as well as "Dear Daddy" because the nuns told us to do it. He must have eventually told the nuns because they stopped us writing that way. But he never said anything to us. He doesn't seem to want to talk about her.'

'Perhaps she is dead and he doesn't want to make you unhappy?'

'Maybe. She could have been killed in the Blitz, a lot of people were, weren't they?'

She looked at me thoughtfully. 'We didn't see your father very much when you were with us. He was travelling a lot and then the war and all that went with it made life difficult. We knew little about your family except that he was from the Seychelles and had been at sea for a long time.'

'How did you meet him?'

'My oldest brother, whom you never knew, had a ship chandler's business called Hall and Hall. When your father left the sea, he became a travelling salesman in the business and they met that way. One day, he asked my brother if he knew anyone who could take care of two small children, and that's how you came to us.'

'When was that?'

'Late 1940, the war had started. You were four years old and Maurice was three.' She paused. 'Are you worried about your mother?'

'Not really but, recently, I have been thinking about her.'

'Do you remember her?'

I fiddled with my teacup. What should I say? I couldn't tell her I remembered a virtually bare-breasted woman, smoking and laughing in an abandoned way, a sexy sort of woman like Miss Fenton.

'I have a vague memory,' I said cautiously.

'Perhaps it's best not to think about the past,' she said gently. 'So much happened during the war. But it's over now and you've got your whole life ahead of you.'

I suddenly felt I had to leave. I know Evelyn was trying to help but it was all too confusing. I didn't want to talk about my mother, my father, or anybody else any more. Back on the street, she gave me her address and telephone number and I promised to stay in touch. We shook hands and, as we parted, I thought I saw a trace of sadness in her eyes. I turned and walked away without looking back.

I bought my comics, sweets, and Tizer, and calmed down. On the way home, I thought about the conversation with Evelyn. I was surprised how much I had remembered without any real effort. Just her presence had been enough but our new life was so full and pleasant perhaps she was right and it was best to forget about the past.

A few days after Christmas, Edith said she and my father had a surprise for us. Maurice and I were in the living room, listening to our favourite weekly radio programme, *Dick Barton, Special Agent,* a swashbuckling figure, supported by his faithful comrades, Jock and Snowy, swatting evil wherever they found it. The door opened and Edith came in with a tray of drinks. There was sherry for her and my father, who followed her, and lemonade for us. They sat down and Edith lit up one of her Passing Cloud cigarettes, a special brand in a lovely box with a painting of a sunny sky and a single, silky white cloud on the lid.

'Well boys, we have some very good news,' my father said. 'Edith and I are going to get married in the New Year. So let's have a toast.'

We raised our glasses and they kissed. I was not surprised. You would have to have been in a coma not to see it coming. The only surprise was that it hadn't happened earlier. When it did happen, I had mixed feelings. I was embarrassed because I was at the age when any public display of affection was embarrassing. I was also beginning to feel resentful but wasn't sure why.

We were not invited to the wedding ceremony but we did go to the reception, which was held in a hotel. I remember little except that my father offered me Barsac, a French dessert wine, which I drank as I drank Tizer. He was in his expansive French mode and told me how his father had insisted on all his children drinking wine at dinner on La Plaine, the family plantation in the Seychelles.

'I didn't like it,' he said, 'and since I was one of the youngest—number thirteen to be exact—I sat down the far end of the table where I thought he couldn't see me. When the servant came by, I asked him to slip some water into my wineglass. The next thing I heard was a crash at the other end. It was my father's fist on the table. "Never put water in your wine!" he roared.'

My trouble at the wedding party was that I put wine in my wine and talked too much. The next day, I woke up with a brain-splitting headache but, later, could boast, truthfully, that the first time I got drunk was at the age of twelve at my parents' wedding.

Nothing really changed except that my father moved down the corridor to join Edith in her bedroom, and it was decided that we should all go up to London to have a family portrait taken. The sitting was a carefully staged affair in a studio, and the photograph, I suspect, was touched up before it was presented to us. Maurice and I, wearing our new school blazers and ties, stood behind Edith and my father. Edith sat bolt upright, her mouth pursed, looking rather prim, but my father, in his best suit, was relaxed, a smile on his face.

The photograph joined the other family pictures on the mantelpiece, uniting the de St. Jorres and the Rosses, if not by blood at least by marriage. Later, I took a closer look at the photograph and felt uneasy. Our group, so confident, conventional, and self-contained, was flawed. Somewhere in the dark backdrop was a metaphorical prisoner-in-the-attic, a ghostlike figure central to all our lives: my father's first wife, the mother of John and Maurice, and Edith's predecessor.

## 5

FROM TIME TO TIME, RELATIVES FROM THE SEYCHELLES VISITED us. Out of our vast, sprawling family from those tropical islands, came a steady stream of aunts and uncles, nephews and nieces, cousins (close and many times removed), and friends from other French planter families.

They spoke perfect English and bore a strong family likeness, notably blue eyes, with a faint circle around them, and long upper lips, and they tended to be sallow from a lifetime in the tropics. They were at ease in Britain where some of them had studied and nearly all of them had visited from time to time, but there was no mistaking their 'foreignness'. It was over 150 years since my Norman ancestors had settled in the Seychelles, and almost as long since they had become subjects of the British crown but, in their hearts, they were still French. They slipped in and out of the language with my father, occasionally throwing in a phrase or two of Creole. Overall, they were a friendly, convivial crowd, and showed a lively interest in Maurice and me. They were especially gracious to Edith and treated her as if she had been a long-standing member of the family although she had just arrived.

I came to know some of them well, in particular Michel Lemarchant, an old friend of my father. They had grown up on adjoining plantations; they swam and fished together along the coral strand that lay on their doorsteps; and they went to the Jesuit school in Victoria, the colony's capital. A short, rotund man with a neat moustache, Michel had a ready laugh and always brought us presents. When he and my father were alone together, they spoke in French. During one of his visits, I caught something that gave me the first clue, flimsy though it was, to the family mystery that had been with me for as long as I could remember.

We had finished lunch, an Indian curry prepared by my father who had learned the basics from Indian sailors during his seafaring days. Maurice and I were in the kitchen helping Edith clean up the devastation he habitually left behind him whenever he cooked. I went to the dining room to pick up some plates and heard voices in the living room. It was my father and Michel. I had started to learn French at my new school and understood just enough to pick up something I heard Michel say as I was about to return to the kitchen. It sounded like: '*Et alors, Grace, où est-ce qu'elle est?*' What caught my ear was not the French phrase but the word 'Grace', pronounced the English way in the middle of a French sentence. I stopped. My father answered but he lowered his voice and I could not hear what he was saying. Still, the conspiratorial tone convinced me that he and Michel were talking about my mother. I had no evidence that her name was Grace. But, somehow, it seemed just right.

Not long after that incident, I was with Mark, my best friend from school. He lived nearby and often came over to our place because our garden was so much larger and more interesting than his own. He was a tall, gangling boy with freckles, tangled brown hair that looked like dead gorse, and a relaxed, easy-going manner. I had first noticed him at school when he was entertaining a group with an unusual feat. He opened his mouth, shot out a long, narrow tongue, much like a snake's but with a single point, and delicately probed the inside of his nostrils—a riveting achievement.

We spent most weekends together and felt at ease with each other. On warm, sunny days, a favourite spot was an old wooden bench in the orchard where, taking a rest from our games, we would sit and yarn. Much of the talk was about our plans for the future, fuelled by the popular boys' adventure books and comics of the day. We talked about travelling the world, exploring unknown lands, fighting our way through dense jungles, and trekking across endless deserts. We were entering that romantic period, on the cusp of puberty, still innocent in many ways, dreamy and idealistic. Then, one day, the conversation turned personal.

'Why do you call your mum, "Edith"?' Mark said.

'Because she is not my mum. She's my stepmother.'

Mark gave me an inquiring look.

'Where is your real mum?'

Maurice and I had developed our own way of dealing with that question, which occasionally came up at school. Without discussing the matter, we simply arrived at the same solution, independently of each other. 'She is dead,' we said in a matter of fact manner, as if we talking about a pet cat or dog. But on this occasion, with Mark peering at me expectantly, I suddenly and unaccountably changed the script.

'She ran off with a younger man,' I said nonchalantly. 'My father was a good bit older than her and, after we were born, she met this chap. He was about her age, and rich and handsome. They fell in love and took off, leaving my brother and me with my dad.'

Mark looked at me in astonishment. 'Gosh, I had no idea. Do you still see her?'

'No, she vanished,' I paused. 'It was a long, long time ago.'

'Would you recognise her if you bumped into her in the street?'

'I doubt it,' I said. Miss Fenton's carmine-lipped smile and the waft of her perfume came unbidden into my mind. I felt myself reddening and blundered on. 'I'm sure she wouldn't recognise me or Maurice. It all happened when we were little kids.'

'Do you miss her?'

'How can you miss someone you don't know?'

I was in too deep. Time to get out.

'Let's go fishing up at the pond,' I said, jumping to my feet. 'You can use Maurice's rod.' As we went into the house, I realised I had adopted Edith's diversionary tactics, something I had begun to resent when she did it.

When I later thought about the story I had told Mark, I felt stupid. What if he started telling my friends at school, including kids who had already heard the other version? I would look like an idiot. And if they challenged me ('Hey, Jorrie, is she dead or what?'), what would I say?

Later I realised why the story had popped out. I had been having fantasies about my mother that were mixed up with romantic daydreaming about rescuing damsels in distress, notably one who looked remarkably like the pretty girl with golden curls in my class. The scenario about my mother running off with a handsome lover was not the only one. Another imagined a sudden illness afflicting my mother after Maurice's birth, ending tragically in a deathbed scene with a grieving husband and two small, bewildered children at her side. But it was hard to beat the yarn I had told Mark. After all, my mother had made a dramatic choice, love for a man over love for her children. What could be more romantic than that?

It wasn't long afterwards that Maurice and I began to call Edith, 'Mum'. I can't remember who suggested it but I was tired of explaining the relationship. Mark and all my friends had mothers—divorce and single parenthood were rare in those days—whom they called 'Mum'. So, although the change wasn't accurate, at least we would be like them. Uniformity was the thing. Having a complicated French name and being a Roman Catholic was bad enough but calling a parent by her first name was distinctly weird. Mark must have noticed the change but he said nothing, nor did he spread my fevered story about how my mother disappeared among my school friends and, for those small mercies, I was thankful.

Edith was delighted with the change of title because it consolidated her position as the mother figure in the most public way possible. I, too, was happy with it—for a time. It certainly simplified matters as my circle of friends grew and it pushed us out into the mainstream of British life in the late 1940s. Later, I would come to regret it because, by anointing Edith as 'Mum', I felt I had betrayed my real mother. I cannot say that I was desperate to find her or unravel her story at that stage, but I felt a swelling resentment with my father and Edith for denying her existence. In fact, it was resentment, a negative force perhaps but a force all the same, that helped keep my mother's memory alive. Meanwhile, as time went by, the wall closing off the past was rising, brick by brick, and I, as a passive observer, was one of the bricklayers.

Our lives had settled into a pattern, defined as much by the small things as by the large. Everything had its place. Apart from the elaborate settings on the dining room table, there was a special knife for the butter, a special spoon for the marmalade, and yet another for the jam. There was also a code for second helpings when guests were present. Edith, choosing her moment carefully, would whisper to us, 'FHB' (family hold back), or 'MIK' (more in the kitchen). Conversation, avoiding the topics we already knew were too close to the bone, focused on politics (the iniquities of the Labour government and the trade unions), the importance of a good steady job, savings, and pensions, and gossip about relatives and neighbours. I noticed that my father and Edith often talked about people who had visited us in a critical, and, at times, derogatory fashion.

Edith was the dominant force in all this although my father also cherished order, middle-class morality and, most important, to be seen to be doing the right things. But, what if Maurice and I had been with our real mother who I sensed was not like Edith at all? How would she have shaped our lives? I was too young and too preoccupied with my new life to dwell on such a hypothetical situation, but it did cross my mind.

After a year in Woodford, our lives suddenly changed when my father got a government job in Singapore, then a British colony. We travelled the slow way, on a troopship that took a month to get there. Edith, who had taken over our education, put us into a British army school but, after fifteen months, she decided we were falling behind and needed to go to a better school back in England.

Maurice and I boarded another troopship and sailed home by ourselves. When we arrived, Edith's younger sister met us and took us to Colchester Royal Grammar School in Essex. It had a small boarding establishment and we settled back into the sort of school life we knew well. However, unlike St. Dominic's, Colchester was a good, secular state school, and we both thrived. Our travels and the sheer passage of time were separating me from my childhood and all that went with it. By the time we returned from Singapore, my father and Edith had elided into being my 'parents', that common collective noun which obscured any anomalies or mysteries, and brought us into the mainstream. Nevertheless, if I needed reminding of my missing mother, Edith's presence and my father's silence were enough.

My father's contract in Singapore ended a year later and they returned to England. But they did not go back to Woodford, which was strange. Edith, I knew, wanted to return to teaching at her old school where she was well liked and where she had many friends. Instead, they settled in Ealing on the opposite side of London. Maurice and I also wanted to be in Woodford because we had friends there, too, and it was closer to our new boarding school. It was a baffling decision. But we did not question it, and neither Edith nor my father offered an explanation.

Two years later, my father retired and we finally moved back across London to Buckhurst Hill, the town next to Woodford, where Maurice and I had lived with the Linder sisters. They bought a semi-detached house—the first home they had ever owned—a small car, and a television. Edith returned to teaching at the Woodford County High School for Girls and my father spent much of his time in his garden. The flow of Seychelles relatives resumed and, when I was in my late teens, a cousin dropped off a copy of a family tree that he had painstakingly put together.

My father showed it to me briefly before going out to tend to his tomato plants that had taken a pummelling in a thunderstorm.

I forgot about it for a few days but caught sight of it one morning on the dining room table. I was alone in the house and decided to take a closer look.

When I spread it out, it covered a third of the table. Elegantly sketched on thick parchment-like paper was an actual tree outlined in black ink, the trunk and branches coloured brown with a crayon. The tree was vast with branches of thinning width reaching out to the four corners of the paper. At the trunk were our pioneering ancestors who left France in 1740, and settled in the French Indian Ocean island of Ile de Bourbon (now Réunion). The trunk then bifurcated and developed myriad branches, large and small. Clustered in them were dozens of Jorre de St. Jorres, the full family name, many with melodious and archaic French Christian names, such as Melicourt, Zelomire, Polyphile, Corentine, Aricia, Eudoxie, Félicien, and Mathurine.

The detail was impressive. The names of family members, spouses and children, with their dates of birth, were carefully recorded. Starting at the bole of the tree, I checked my early ancestors who moved successively from Ile de Bourbon to Ile de Maurice (now Mauritius), and finally to the Seychelles where they were among the first French families to settle permanently. Moving up the tree, there was my purist wine-drinking grandfather, Jean Armel Polyphile Despilly Jorre de St. Jorre, and his intimidating-looking wife, Emilie Fleurot, whose photograph sat on our mantelpiece. And there, dangling from several branches that covered a good quarter of the space, were their fifteen children and the short-lived sixteenth, a boy who had died in infancy. More branches shot out in all directions bearing dozens of grandchildren.

There were aunts, uncles, and cousins, many of whom I recognised. Each name was in a rectangular box with room for the spouse's name below, preceded by *Marié à*, for a wife, and *Mariée à*, for a husband. If a couple had no children, there was a notation after the individuals' names: *Sans descendance*. All the entries were typed, making them easy to read. I returned to my grandfather and grandmother and ran my finger out along the branches. Sixteen kids merited a lot of tree and it was some time before I found my father, 'Louis George Jorre de St. Jorre'. Moving past him, on two small branches almost off the page, were Maurice and me. I returned to my father, and saw that he, like all the others, had his box. Below his name was the customary *Marié à*. But the space below for a wife was blank. Confused, I looked around at the other entries. Every box seemed to be complete. Except ours. George had no wife, and his two sons had no mother. She had fallen out of the tree, if indeed she had ever been in it, and disappeared.

How could that happen? I took a closer look. Thirteen of my grandparents' sixteen children had their spouses clearly listed. Most of them had children of their own, but even two daughters, who were childless, shared their boxes with their husbands. The three exceptions were all male. One was the child who had died as an infant, and another was described as dying as a bachelor. Then, all alone, was my father, the man with two clearly documented children but no spouse.

Why had my cousin done this? Presumably he had been in contact with my father who kept in touch with many of his Seychelles relatives. Had my father told him not to mention his wife's name? Or had my mother been originally listed and then removed at a later date? If so, by whom?

My father was the obvious person to ask. But my mother was a taboo subject, and his steadfast silence had always deterred me from confronting him. So, what could I do? If I could find the author of the family tree and talk to him, perhaps he could help solve the mystery. But he was in Mauritius and, even if I could get his address and write to him, would he be likely to explain my mother's absence? I doubted it. He would surely check with my father before telling me anything. Nevertheless, this discovery strengthened my determination, one day, to delve further.

# 6

THAT DAY TOOK SOME TIME COMING. MEANWHILE, I WAS growing up and becoming more independent and critical. My resentment of my father increased not only over his secrecy about our past but also for his and Edith's views on just about everything else. In this, I am sure I was no different from countless rebellious British teenagers in the 1950s, except that one of my complaints had a long history. I grew tired of my parents' endless talk of money and financial security, their refusal to accept change, or even try to understand what was going on in the modern world, and their hypocrisy over culture.

I had started listening to jazz at night on a small radio in my bedroom and the more I heard the more I liked it. When I told my parents, they denounced it out of hand as 'not real music'. Only classical music was 'good music', they said, the rest was rubbish. But I cannot remember them ever listening to classical music themselves, either on the radio or going to a classical concert. They seemed to have no interest in buying a record player or collecting records. They often mentioned how important it was to read 'good books', that is the great works of literature, yet there were virtually no books of any kind in the house.

Looking back, I realised that a veneer of arrogance coated my youthful rebellion. I had begun to think I was superior to them. Then something happened that stripped the veneer away, an incident that marked Maurice and me for life, albeit in different ways, and revealed a side of my father that complicated my feelings for him.

We did not often go on holiday as a family but this particular summer, my parents thought it would be nice for all of us to spend a couple of weeks on the Cornish coast where we could swim, sail and fish. I was about to begin my final year at school, so I suppose they felt this might be the last chance for us to go away together.

Maurice and I had bicycles and went everywhere on them in the days when the roads were far less crowded and dangerous than they later became. We often rode back to Colchester from Buckhurst Hill after a school vacation, a fifty-mile journey, while our luggage went ahead by train. We had also done some long trips in southern England, together or with friends, staying at youth hostels and pedalling far and wide.

Edith booked us into a small hotel in Coverack on the southern Cornish coast, and Maurice and I set off on our bikes. It was a five-day trip, stopping overnight in youth hostels, with our parents following by train. The weather started out fine but deteriorated as we cycled farther west. We stopped for breaks throughout the day and, on our third day out from London, we were sitting under a hedgerow in Devon when Maurice said he thought there was something wrong with his front brake.

We pulled the bike over and studied it. One of the rubber pads was missing so that when he applied the brake, the metal casing, which had held it, closed on the wheel but failed to stop it moving. The other pad was in place but had little effect without an opposing pad to put pressure on the wheel and make it stop. That pad was loose and, since I could see no point in leaving it there, I pulled it off, leaving the two metal holders. I squeezed the front brake lever, and the pieces came together evenly on the wheel, slowing its movement, but not holding it firmly, and making a screeching sound.

I can't remember exactly what I was thinking. Perhaps we did plan to stop at a cycle repair shop and have new pads fitted. Or maybe we didn't. The result was the same, we cycled on without doing anything. As the older brother—I was then seventeen and Maurice was sixteen—I realised later what I should have done, namely had the brake repaired.

That evening, we stayed near Dartmoor, an ancient granitic plateau in south Devon, and planned to cross the moor the next day. It is a forbidding place, a bleak, rugged, treeless expanse of moorland featuring rocky outcrops known as tors, peat bogs, ravines, and powerful streams. It was traditionally a place for hunters, pursuing stags, and for the hunted, escaped convicts from the Dartmoor Prison, which opened in 1809, built by, and for, French prisoners-of-war during the Napoleonic Wars.

Dartmoor holds a special place in the English imagination, a tract of land rich in myths and legends. Pixies, trolls, a headless horseman, and the 'Beast of Dartmoor' (a large cat or, possibly, an equally large dog) are reputed to have haunted the moor. Even Satan is said to have paid a visit in the seventeenth century after an unusually fierce thunderstorm.

Dartmoor's isolation, desolate appearance, and its fortress of a prison made it an appealing backdrop for literary adventure. Arthur Conan Doyle was especially fond of the moor. He set several of his Sherlock Holmes stories there, notably *Silver Blaze*, where the dog famously failed to bark in the night, and *The Exploits of Brigadier Gerard*, where that dashing French cavalry officer, my childhood hero, was one of Dartmoor Prison's first inmates.

While we were having breakfast at the youth hostel, it started raining. It did not particularly worry us because we had yellow oilskin capes and were used to riding in the rain. However, as we climbed on to the top of Dartmoor, some 2,000 feet above sea level, the sky became darker, the wind, blowing in from the Atlantic Ocean, picked up velocity, and the rain fell like lead. I have no recollection of how long we were on the moor but I do remember how desolate it was. We saw few vehicles and no other cyclists or any living soul. I also remember the descent.

After what seemed like an eternity, the road started to go down in a series of long, sweeping curves towards Tavistock, our destination. I stopped pedalling and cautiously applied the brakes. I knew from experience that back brakes are often treacherous in wet weather, especially if you apply them too harshly. You need to use them carefully in conjunction with the front brakes to counter skidding as you slow down. The wind, which had been steadily in our faces, now veered as we took the curves, buffeting us from the sides as well as from the front.

I was leading and was about halfway down when a glistening yellow blur shot past me. It was Maurice going twice my speed. I shouted but the wind blew the words back into my mouth. I tried going a bit faster but found it hard to take the next turn. I sped down a straight stretch, leaned into the curve, and saw him.

He was sprawled in the gravel on the outer rim of the bend, his bike about twenty feet from him.

Oh God! Was he dead? Had I killed my little brother?

I took the bend and gradually pulled on to the side of the road. I leapt off the bike and ran back to where Maurice lay. He was groaning, his face a mask of blood and his right knee gouged and bloody. It was raining harder than ever, great bolts of water hitting the ground with a percussive force and spitting gravel in all directions. I could see deep gashes below his right eye, and white bone beneath the tattered flesh of his knee. I sat down beside him and held his hand, as I had done at St. Dominic's, staring at the door that separated us from our father years ago.

I leaned over and asked Maurice if he was all right. Of course he wasn't all right, but I didn't know what else to say. We were both soaked and shivering. He had stopped groaning and looked at me, the rain pouring down his face and mingling with the blood on his oilskin cape. He muttered that he wasn't too bad but couldn't move. I got up and looked up and down the road but it was empty. His bike lay there, twisted and smashed.

'Your bike is a bit of a mess,' I said, walking over to it. Stupid. Who cared about his bike? But I suppose I was in shock. As I was turning back to him, I saw the car. It was coming slowly up the hill from Tavistock. I jumped into the middle of the road and started waving. It stopped and a middle-aged man got out. I told him what had happened. He nodded in a matter-of-fact way, went to the trunk of his car, and pulled out a travelling rug.

'It's important to keep him warm,' he said, wrapping the rug around Maurice. 'I'll get an ambulance from Tavistock and we'll have him out of here and into hospital in no time.'

I thanked him and he turned his car round and drove back down the hill. I sat beside Maurice and told him help was on the way, that he would be better soon, and then we'd do a lot of swimming and fishing. He said nothing as the cold rain streamed down, cleaning his wounds but deepening the pain. He closed his eyes.

My next memory is waking up in a hospital bed with Maurice in another at my side. He was propped up on the pillows with a bandage covering half his face, and his knee, also heavily bandaged, was raised above the covers in a kind of sling. I felt exhausted but was fine. They'd kept me in as a precaution for shock, and I was relieved when I heard Maurice talking normally. He said he had tried to control his bike but that sharp bend had been too much. He had gone into a skid and the bike tipped over dragging him along through the granite gravel that lined the road. He did not say anything about his front brakes but, of course, we both knew what had caused the accident. And I knew who was to blame.

I looked up. My father was coming towards us. He was walking fast, his right foot splayed out as ever, and his face as dark as the rain clouds over Dartmoor. He looked angry and anguished.

'No more bicycle,' he said, his voice quivering. He sometimes lost his plurals in English when he was upset and translated literally from the French. 'No more bicycle.'

He glanced at me and went over to Maurice's bed. He leaned over and kissed him on the small piece of forehead not covered by bandages. He took Maurice's hand and held on to it. This was the father whom I remembered from my childhood. I regretted being so critical of him. He was, after all, a good man deeply attached to his children.

After that moment in the hospital, my mind is a blank. I do not know how long we were in there, how we got to Coverack, about eighty miles away, how our bikes were delivered, or what happened to the good Samaritan who had saved us and sacrificed his travelling rug. Edith joined us and we did have our holiday by the sea although Maurice spent most of it recovering in the hotel. What I never forgot were the scars. Maurice carries them on his face; mine are internal.

## 7

IN MY LAST TERM OF SCHOOL, I APPLIED TO UNIVERSITY College London, and was accepted. Shortly after my interview in London, my headmaster called me into his study and said he thought I should apply to Oxford. I could not see much point in doing so because I was content with London but, in those days, you didn't question your headmaster or indeed anyone in authority. He suggested New College, Oxford; I took the exams, had an interview and, to my surprise, was accepted. I wasn't an exceptional student but, with three decent A levels and an O level pass in Latin (on the second attempt), that was good enough, and Britain's welfare state took care of the cost. Little did I know it at the time but my headmaster's desire to boost his school's Oxford and Cambridge successes influenced my life in a way that I could not imagine.

Going to Oxford meant that I would do my two years of compulsory National Service before university. When I joined the army, I knew the trick was to get a commission and not serve either in the United Kingdom or Germany, a fate which would mean menial work and boredom. My luck held. I joined the serried ranks of National Service officers and was sent to Singapore, going the way I knew well on a slow-moving troopship. I was assigned to a Malay regiment, an archetypical imperial military unit with indigenous soldiers and British officers operating 'up-country', meaning in the Malay Peninsula. We first shelled the jungle, somewhat aimlessly, then patrolled in it, searching for elusive CTs ('Communist Terrorists'), a task that involved neither great danger nor opportunities for martial glory. Meanwhile, Maurice finished school and went to Durham University to study mining engineering with a National

Coal Board scholarship, which meant he was exempt from military service. When my time was up in the army, I returned home and went up to Oxford.

It was there, amid the medieval quadrangles, the narrow, cobbled streets, and the age-old rhythms of college life, that the train of events leading to a showdown with my father over the mystery of my mother was set in motion.

One afternoon during my last year at Oxford, my senior history tutor, an avuncular, pipe-smoking medievalist, took me aside and asked if I might be interested in 'government service abroad', after I finished my degree. If I were, he said, he would put me in touch with 'the appropriate people'. I had little idea about the future except to delay the moment when I would be obliged to choose a career and get one of those steady, safe jobs with a good pension that my parents urged me to seek. My immediate plan was nothing of the sort. Instead, it was to go to Spain, teach English, travel around Europe, and sample life beyond the confines of my English middle-class upbringing. However, I did not want to disappoint my tutor, so I thanked him, and waited.

Among the distractions and pleasures of student life (Oxford was a relaxed and easy-going place in those days), my mother flitted in and out of my consciousness and occasionally came into full view when I confided in a close friend and told him the story. I felt that, one day, I would search for her but, while the relationship could not have been closer—that of a mother and her child—the odds against finding her could not have been longer. I was confronted by a total lack of oral and documentary evidence, an implacable parental silence, and the quasi-Victorian mores of a repressive social era. Hard to imagine now in this interconnected, know-everything-about-everybody age, but that's how it was. Meanwhile, I had other things on my mind.

Within a week, I received a letter from a section of the Foreign Office called the 'Coordination Staff', inviting me for an interview with Sir Charles Woodhouse, a retired admiral. The meeting seemed to go well in the sense it did not go badly. The admiral, a small, trim man with a moustache and a genial air, greeted me in a large office overlooking Green Park. I had looked him up in *Who's Who* before arriving and knew I was in the presence of a hero of the Battle of the River Plate, a successful naval action against the German navy in the South Atlantic early in World War II. The battle ended with the scuttling of the German battleship, the *Graf Spee*, and the suicide of its commander. Woodhouse had commanded HMS *Ajax*, one of the three British light cruisers involved, and went on to become an admiral.

It was more a conversation than an interview, relaxed and unspecific. I knew I was dealing with some part of the Foreign Office because that august organisation's seal was embossed on the top of the letterhead and 'Foreign Office' appeared under 'Coordination Staff' on the right. Coordinating what? The admiral did not offer an explanation.

I am not sure why I failed to ask him about the job, but I suppose it was that I imagined he assumed I already knew—otherwise why would I be sitting in front of him?—and no explanation was necessary. And if that wasn't the case, wouldn't I look stupid for *not* knowing? On his side, he was probably under orders not to divulge much this early on in the recruitment courtship. It was all very British and typical of that era: a decent reticence on the part of both parties, subtle signals going back and forth, certain assumptions based on education, military service, and family background, a nod and a wink and, I say, what filthy weather we're having.

The admiral did, however, describe the path ahead. There would be another interview with him, followed by the Civil Service Selection Board examination (a battery of writing, intelligence and group tests, plus more interviews) and, if all went well, a final interview with several members of the 'Service'. Sir Charles asked me to write to him if I continued to be interested in that still vague formulation—'government service abroad'—and we could move on to the next stage.

I did, took the exam, passed it, and returned for the final interview. On this occasion, I sat in front of a quartet who did not match my idea of what British diplomats looked or sounded like. They were younger than the admiral and less benign; hard-nosed types who looked as if they had been around. The admiral sat at the end of the row and said nothing, no longer commanding the fleet or even a single ship.

The interview focused on my background, interests, and general knowledge of international politics. At one point, the man on the opposite end of the row to the admiral was about to ask me a question when he stopped short.

'Excuse me, St. Jorre,' he said, 'but might I ask you what that red mark is on your forehead?'

Confused, I put a hand up to my head. Then it dawned on me. I was spending the summer, a particularly hot one, driving a car for a small livery company. Being short of time, my boss had allowed me to use one of the cars to drive to the interview. I was wearing my tight-fitting chauffeur's hat and, when I tossed it into the back of the car before going in, it had left a red weal across my forehead.

I explained all this and there was a rustle of interest from the quartet, followed by a flurry of questions. Who was I working for? How did I get the job? Who was I driving? Who were the other drivers? *Really*, how interesting. Had I done other jobs like this?

I told them I was currently driving the stars of stage and screen to the Pinewood and Elstree film studios, and my co-drivers were three former London bus drivers. I then reeled off my other vacation jobs: a postman at Christmas; a bricklayer's mate on an East End building site; a tutor to the indolent son of a wealthy, aristocratic family; picking potatoes and strawberries in Essex with a group of international students; a kitchen porter, cashier and security guard in Butlin's holiday camp at Clacton-on-Sea; working in a fruit canning factory in Suffolk; a night porter at Liverpool Station, and so on.

The reunification of Germany was forgotten. There was a surprising surge of interest among my interrogators. They wanted to know more about these not uncommon student activities and were clearly impressed by my range of experience among England's labouring classes, which seemed like a foreign country to them.

In September 1959, I received a letter from the 'Coordination Staff' saying, 'It is desired to offer you prospective long-term employment, subject to a probationary period of three years, at a starting salary of 755 pounds per annum gross.'

No one had told me what I was going to be doing, or for whom I would be working, and the letter maintained that well-bred silence although, by this time, I had my suspicions, which were soon confirmed. I accepted and pondered whether to tell my parents that I was about to join an organisation, which had two names but did not officially exist: Her Majesty's Secret Intelligence Service (SIS), more familiarly known as MI6. The job was to recruit spies and run them from under diplomatic cover in British embassies around the world.

Our masters encouraged us to tell our parents the truth, albeit in the strictest confidence. That posed a dilemma. Would my father and Edith, so conventional, so proper, be happy and proud to have a son who was a spook? Or would it embarrass them? Britain, after all, did not officially spy on anyone, and spying was hardly a respectable profession. Would they understand, or want to understand? In the end, I decided to keep it simple and say that I had joined the Foreign Service, my official cover. On reflection, my decision was not entirely altruistic because it contained an element of payback. My father had his family secret and now I had mine.

He and Edith were still living in their small suburban house in Buckhurst Hill. There was an equally small garden at the back, and an old World War II air-raid shelter, a damp, rank concrete bunker under a pile of earth. Beyond was a boundary fence and the open tracks of the London Underground's Central Line. The Tube trains rattled by day and night, a constant reminder of how far these two elderly people had descended from their grander beginnings.

With the job offer came a sheaf of vetting forms to be completed 'with the utmost care'. At home, I spread them out on the dining room table and started to go through the questions and the request for supporting documents. I saw immediately that I would need help. I went to the living room where Edith and my father were watching television.

'They want to see my birth certificate,' I said.

Edith, who looked after the family's documents, went upstairs and came down with a rectangular piece of paper in her hand, which I had never seen before. I returned to the dining room with what might seem to be a run-of-the-mill document in most households but was, for me, nothing of the sort. It represented a shaft of light illuminating a hitherto impenetrable past.

Entitled 'Certified Copy of an Entry of Birth', I learned that I had been born in the subdistrict of Kensington South in the Royal Borough of Kensington at Princess Beatrice Hospital. There were a series of boxes, under different headings, and each box had an entry, written neatly in black ink. Moving from left to right, were my date of birth and the name of the hospital, my two first names, my sex, and my father's name, given as 'George Louis de St. Jorre', the abbreviated, anglicised, and first-names-reversed version that he used in Britain. Most of which I already knew. The next box, however, stopped me in my tracks.

Under the heading 'Name, surname and maiden name of mother', it read: 'Grace Rose de St. Jorre, formerly Islip.'

I sat back and stared out of the window. It had taken me twenty-four years to learn my mother's name. How ridiculous was that? But at last I had it, and her maiden name too. There was also an address, 67 West Cromwell Road, Kensington, given as our residence. My father's occupation appeared under a special heading, but there was no such provision for mothers, presumably on the assumption that women in those days, especially mothers recorded on birth certificates, could surely be nowhere else but the home. My hunch that my mother's name was 'Grace', culled from the conversation between Michel Lemarchant and my father several years earlier, had been on target. This small victory reinforced my belief, admittedly without much logic behind it, that the bare-breasted, laughing woman in my childhood memory could only be my mother.

Grace Rose, such pretty names, presumably English although they could conceivably be French. However, her maiden name, Islip, surely could only be English. Driving to Oxford on the London road, I had often passed a sign to a town called Islip but had never gone there. Is that where my mother and her family came from? Who were her parents? Did she have brothers and sisters? I suddenly wanted to know a lot more. What did she look like? In her youth, had Grace Rose Islip been an English beauty with satiny skin, rosy cheeks, and highlights in her wavy hair? I always assumed she had curly hair because I did, whereas my father and Maurice had dead straight hair. Could there be a photograph hidden away in Edith's stash of family documents?

I put the birth certificate to one side and concentrated on the form. I was able to answer most of the questions about my father without difficulty. I knew his date of birth, 21 October 1889, and the place, La Plaine St. André, Mahé, the family plantation in the Seychelles, his profession, his last job, and his date of retirement. But when I came to questions about his marriage, I was at a loss. I looked further down and saw that the next batch of questions concerned my mother and there, apart from her first names and maiden name, I had no answers.

There was only one person who could fill in those blank spaces. I got up and went back into the living room.

'How is it going?' said Edith brightly.

'So far so good. But there are quite a few questions that I need help with.'

'Let me come and see what I can do,' said Edith starting to rise.

'They concern my mother,' I said. There, I had mentioned that taboo word, the word that had come to signify Edith, not Grace. It was so out of line, that I felt it was akin to saying 'shit' or 'fuck'.

'Oh,' Edith said, sitting down again. She turned to my father. 'George, you had better do it.'

My father slowly got up out of his chair. He looked as if he were going to the scaffold but I sensed that he knew there was no escape. Having worked for the government, he knew the importance of official forms; hiding the truth was unacceptable. I followed him to the dining room. I had grown tall and filled out and could easily look over his head of thinning grey hair and his stooped shoulders. For the first time in my life, I felt I had the upper hand.

He sat down opposite me.

'What do they need to know?' he said.

'I have her full name from my birth certificate but I don't know her date of birth.' There was no need, at this stage, to grapple with what to call the woman we were discussing. He knew whom I meant.

'April 18th, 1907,' he said.

Eighteen years younger than him, effectively from a different generation.

I wrote down the date and moved on.

'Her parents' names?'

'Charles Victor Islip and Lucy Peagram.'

I checked the spelling of 'Peagram', and wrote the names down. The next question was closer to the bone.

'The date of your marriage?'

'March 31st, 1934.'

It was a relief to bend my head and write. When I glanced at him, I could see that he was defensive and embarrassed. I had come a long way from the days of my childhood dependency on him and the days when I longed to see his rolling figure, feel the rasp of his cheek, and massage his scalp. I felt a twinge of guilt. He looked so miserable, so trapped. We ploughed on.

'I have to explain what happened to her because I need to explain who Mum is,' I said. That didn't sound right. It would have been easier if I could have said 'who Edith is' but, by this time, 'Edith' had disappeared from the family vocabulary. She was simply 'Mum' and thus, to all intents and purposes, our mother. I felt as if I was learning a new language.

I could see this was particularly hard for him, especially if my youthful fantasy of Grace taking off with a young lover and abandoning him and his children were true. He didn't answer.

'Did she die?' I prompted, playing it safe and still avoiding giving her a name or a title.

'No,' he said flatly. 'We were divorced.'

There it was. 'She died young', the standard answer that Maurice and I gave so often when asked about our missing mother, was false. So were my romantic fantasies about the deathbed scene and the grieving relatives around it.

My father was looking down at the table. Apart from all the unhappiness that may have surrounded the divorce at the time, I sensed that the religious fallout had inflicted more lasting damage. He was a devout, if imperfect, Catholic, and the nature of that imperfection was becoming clearer. The divorce would explain why he had never gone to confession or taken communion with us when we went to mass together on Sunday mornings in Woodford. Divorce without a Papal dispensation—something he was unlikely to have—was a mortal sin. It ruled out taking the sacraments and marrying again, and the penalty was clear: hell and its eternal flames.

Of course, you could remarry anyway but that would mean you had abandoned the Catholic faith, something I felt sure my father would never do. But he *did* remarry and then appeared to try to square his conscience by going to mass but not to confession and communion, not an arrangement endorsed by the Vatican. It was clear that he and Edith had not been married in a Catholic church. Perhaps Edith had organised a Presbyterian wedding, or they had a civil ceremony in a registry office? I idly wondered which the Catholic Church would consider more heinous and put my money on anything endorsed by the heretical Presbyterians.

I assumed that my father had made the decision not to bring us to the ceremony. Was it because it would be embarrassing to have two young children there inviting awkward questions about our past? Or perhaps because we would understand how far he had fallen from a state of grace? If that were the reason, it would be ironic. By sending us to St. Dominic's, he had ensured that we were well-schooled in Catholic dogma and able to recognise a sinner when we saw one.

I glanced at the next question.

'I need to include the date of the divorce,' I said.

'December 31st, 1947.'

So Grace had been alive when I began to think seriously about her, but where was she in the years between the separation and the divorce? She could not have remarried, unless she had done it bigamously. I did a quick calculation. We arrived in Woodford in July 1947 so six months separated our arrival and my father's marriage to Edith. I had always wondered what they were waiting for. Well, now I knew. However, solving that mystery posed another one. Why had the divorce taken so long? Twelve years had passed since then. Was she still alive? Would my father know? I was about to ask him when I realised it would be best to stick to the form for the time being. He was providing information frugally, as if he were under interrogation and had a lot to hide, as I am sure he did. Only one question remained that related to his marital status.

'I remember you and Mum got married in early 1948,' I said, 'but they want the exact date.'

'January 3rd,' he replied.

Fast work! Just three days after the divorce came through.

He was sitting with his back to the window that looked out over the garden at the rear of the house. I glanced over his shoulder and saw his runner beans, supported by bamboo canes, swaying in the wind. His love of this garden, and his passion for the individual plants that he coaxed so expertly out of the heavy London clay, touched me. My earlier feeling of being in command evaporated. Instead, I felt embarrassed, an unwelcome intruder in a place he had never wanted to revisit or have me see. I realised how painful these questions were, forcing him to dredge up memories that he had spent twenty years or more burying, never expecting to disinter them.

Yet these forms had to be completed properly and Grace, now centre stage instead of in the wings, was, after all, my mother. Questions continued to churn in my brain. Grace would have been forty years old when the divorce occurred. What would a woman of that age, at that time, with that history, do? Did she have any skills? Did she work? Had she remarried and had more children? Did I have another brother or a sister out there?

'If there is nothing else,' he said, standing up. 'I'll leave you to it.'

He was right. The government's appetite for information about my mother and his past was satisfied. I had learned a lot and was ready to stop. But there was one more question I simply had to ask. I hesitated for a moment, finally having to choose a word from the new family lexicon to describe her.

'Is Grace still alive?'

'I don't know,' he said, shaking his head.

'Well, that wraps it up.' I scanned the form, a little ostentatiously. 'Thank you.'

As he left the room, I pushed the papers away and sat back. Grace could easily be alive—she would only be fifty-two years old—but nobody seemed to know. Or care.

# 8

ABOUT SIX MONTHS AFTER THIS EPISODE, MY FATHER HAD A stroke. I had just arrived in my first post, the Congo, a country that was falling apart in post-independence chaos. His stroke, according to Edith, had not paralysed him but had restricted his mobility, damaged his eyesight, and left him depressed. Since his life was not threatened, there was no chance of compassionate leave to return to the UK to see him. When I finally did manage to get away, I went home for a few days to see how he really was and do what I could to comfort him.

On the flight home, I mulled over how I could track down the woman I now thought of as Grace. I would have a good opportunity to talk with my father again but this time I had no convenient way of broaching the subject. Yet, if I did, would he be likely to peel back the layers of secrecy that had congealed over the years? I doubted it. His whole attitude in our single discussion had been negative. Why would he open up now? Still, it was worth a try.

Meanwhile, there was nothing stopping me looking for her on my own and I had begun to think about ways of doing it. I knew her full name, date of birth, marriage and divorce, her parents' names, and less important, an old residential address. A good start although I needed time and, since I would only be in London for a week, the sleuthing would have to wait.

As I walked in the front door, I braced for the worst. Nevertheless, I was shocked to see how much my father had aged and how frail he looked. He had difficulty reading, he said, but he could watch television although everything was a bit blurred. He also had diabetes that seemed to run in the family with one of his brothers in the Seychelles losing a leg to the disease. But he brightened up when I mentioned his garden. He could still grow his vegetables although he had to hire a local youth to do the digging and weeding.

'Last winter, I thought I would try growing mushrooms in the garage,' he said. 'I heard how you do it on one of my gardening programmes on the wireless. It's all done indoors. You spread the seeds on sheets of flannel, give them plenty of water, and leave them in the dark.'

'No earth?'

'No earth,' he said cheerfully, 'and no light.'

'And…'

'By Jove! It worked. A wonderful crop and they had a very good flavour. Ask Mum. Just as good as the wild ones in the fields.'

'How about the tobacco plantation?' I asked.

'Those days are over,' he said, smiling slightly lopsidedly. 'I am sure the local tobacconist is happy. That's where I go now.'

When I talked to Edith after he had gone to bed, she said he had good days and bad days.

'He is bitter about the treatment he got in hospital,' she said. 'He thinks the doctor who treated him gave him the wrong medicine the day after he arrived. He said he could see normally after the stroke but, the next morning, his sight was blurred and has been that way ever since.'

'What do you think?'

'The doctor told me he had a second, milder stroke during the night. It often happens apparently, and it affected his sight. But he is stubborn and refuses to believe it.'

'Any other effects?'

'The diabetes doesn't help because he cannot eat some of the things he likes. Someone told him that garlic was good for him, so he chews a clove a day.'

'What can be done?'

'Not much. He spends more time in his armchair than he used to.' She paused. 'And he prays.'

'Prays?'

'With his rosary, in a sort of whisper. In French.'

I had thought of asking Edith's advice about raising the subject of Grace with him, and quizzing her too. But imagining him sitting by the fireplace, counting off the 'Hail Marys' and 'Glory Bes' on his rosary as he recited the prayers in his old language, the language of his ancestors, killed the impulse. It was not the time to rake the ashes of a broken marriage or the divorce. Fear of eternal damnation, I thought, was enough for him to handle for the time being. I would soon be leaving for Kenya, a new assignment that promised to be exciting. I felt I should wait until he had settled into his more limited life before asking him to dig into something that was not London clay.

Edith was full of Maurice's news. After graduating, he began working for the National Coal Board in the collieries of the Midlands. He had also got married to a young woman he had met in the Lake District, and a baby was on the way. A week earlier, a mining company had offered him a job in the Yukon, Canada's most western territory, and he was thinking of taking it. Edith was not so happy about Maurice's favourite sport. For someone who was currently spending a good part of his working life in the bowels of the earth, he filled his leisure hours climbing forbidding rock faces to reach Britain's highest mountain peaks. But that was Maurice, a tough young man who believed in a physical challenge—he had completely recovered from the bike accident—and a bit of a loner. I promised Edith that I would visit him and his wife before leaving England.

Back in Africa, time passed in a blur of travel, work, and pondering the future more than the past. I spent two more years there, with varying amounts of time in Kenya, Burundi, Togo, and Somalia. My masters in London then decided that a change was in order and told me that I would be going to the Lebanon to learn Arabic.

I had one home leave and spent a few days with Edith, who had retired from teaching, and my father. She said there had been little change in his health. His garden was still the centre of his life and he rarely left the house by the front door. His Seychelles relatives and friends still came to see him. He liked the gossip and listened patiently as they complained about the depressed prices of copra, cinnamon, vanilla, and patchouli, and what they saw as the deterioration of the family plantation under the direction of one of my uncles.

I asked Edith about my father's morale.

'A little better,' she said. 'He seems to have accepted that he will never fully recover and is reconciled to the way he is.'

'Does he still pray?'

'Yes, usually in the evenings.'

'What about church?'

'After the stroke, he used to go fairly regularly, but now hardly ever. I told him I was happy to drive him whenever he wanted to go but he said he was fine.'

Every time I arrived at the house, I promised myself I would get to grips with my father about Grace's fate and start a serious search for her. And every time, I left without having done either. I hadn't forgotten her and I knew, one day, I would make a sustained effort to find her. I was young and life was full so it was no surprise that the present and the future were more compelling than the past. However, I would discover that the past could exert its own kind of compulsive power. Meanwhile, things were not getting any simpler because, halfway through the Arabic course, I decided to quit MI6 and drift.

I had been programmed all my life and being free and footloose for a while was an enticing prospect. It was the 1960s, after all, and it seemed the right thing to do. The limited world of the 1940s and 1950s that I had grown up in had given way to a brighter, more expansive universe. London, the city I knew best, had become prosperous and vibrant. Drivers weaved in and out of the clogged traffic in trendy little cars; women wore miniskirts and took the pill; free love was in, meaning, if you and a willing partner wanted to do it, you did it; the songs of the Beatles and the Rolling Stones filled the airwaves; old houses were converted into fashionable modern flats; new plays, films, novels, even clothes and furniture seethed with rebellion against the old order; the young were at the centre of the universe, or so it seemed, the old shunted away into the shadows; time-encrusted social taboos were discarded like cracked china; the chiaroscuro tones of old London that I remembered from my childhood ceded to the bright colours of a confident future. 'You never had it so good,' trumpeted a political slogan of the day. World War II and its dreary, exhausted aftermath were forgotten. London was swinging and it was cool to be British.

From Beirut, where I had resigned from MI6, I went to the Greek isles, and moved slowly westward ending upon a Spanish one, Mallorca. In a small mountain village overlooking the Mediterranean, I bought a simple stone house at a knock-down price, a house that became a retreat and a home. The whole setting could not have been more different from the England I had grown up in or more remote from my past and its mysteries. Yet, ironically, it turned out to be the place where the search for my mother would take several dramatic turns.

Running short of money, I turned to short-term survival jobs beginning in Madrid where I gave private English lessons. When that dried up, I bought an old French car, a Peugeot 403, from an American serviceman for fifty dollars and drove it to London, with his original Virginia license plates front and rear. Nobody, including the officials at three different borders—Spanish, French, and British—seemed to mind. Perhaps the spirit of the 1960s had affected them too.

In London, I met a young Canadian broadcaster who had a radio job pending but, needing some immediate cash, was selling small fire extinguishers for a Mr Singh, a Mauritian Sikh, who lived in the suburbs. George had sold things before and, helped no doubt by his well-modulated radio voice, was good at it. Over drinks in a pub in the West End, he said he could do with some help off-loading Mr Singh's stock so the good man could move back into his living room with his family. At present, he could barely get in the door because boxes of fire extinguishers, stacked from floor to ceiling, were in the way.

From the pocket of his threadbare brown overcoat, George pulled out a small, shiny aerosol tube, painted bright red and topped with a snazzy little plunger. On it was printed: 'Evanex Dry Powder Fire Extinguisher'.

'Very sexy,' said George, caressing the metal casing. 'People love touching it.'

Next came a one-page flyer, which he had produced himself. It featured a new government regulation concerning fire safety in shops and small businesses. The key phrase, highlighted in red, was the need to 'provide and maintain fire-fighting equipment in an accessible position.'

I looked at George. George looked at me. 'Well?' he asked.

'It doesn't say anything about fire extinguishers,' I said.

George shrugged. 'Leave it to the punters' imagination.'

'Like a bucket of water or sand?'

'Too much imagination. Anyway, nobody would think about that when they see this.'

Out came a yellowing, wrinkled clipping from the London *Evening Standard*. Entitled 'Evans the Flames', it showed an elderly man in rimless spectacles, who looked remarkably like Mahatma Gandhi, engulfed in flames. A young man was spraying him with a white powder from a small canister. The accompanying story explained that the burning man was Mr Evans, a seventy-seven-year-old Welsh inventor, who had developed a fire extinguisher that never failed. The inventor doused himself with paraffin, set himself on fire, yet walked away unscathed. The trusty Evanex dry powder fire extinguisher, wielded by his son, had saved him.

'Powerful shit, eh?' said George. 'We'll sell like bastards.'

Well, we did and we didn't. London was a washout and I even tried selling around the Woodford-Buckhurst Hill area, keeping a wary eye out for Edith or people I knew, and off-loaded a few. The Welsh coal-mining valleys, however, were something else. On the home turf of 'Evans the Fire,' as the Welsh affectionately dubbed their compatriot, we finally sold like bastards.

When George started his radio job, I looked around for something else. I had moved out of the family home and was staying with friends in Kensington but I visited my parents from time to time. I could see they were embarrassed by my wayward behaviour and once overheard them worrying that I had gone the way of my slothful Seychelles relatives who, according to my father, were congenitally lazy. They rarely finished anything they began, he said, and invariably ended up on the family plantation, watching the coconuts fall, ordering the labour around, and gossiping with the other French families. 'It's in their blood,' he concluded darkly.

But I wasn't ready to settle down. It was a measure of the unprecedented economic prosperity and the social giddiness of the times that I assumed I could continue to fool around a bit longer, pretty sure that another promising career lay within my reach whenever I chose to make the move. Hubris, of course. But those were heady times when young people, especially those lucky enough to have been to university, really thought they could do anything and get away with it.

I looked around for another temporary job and found one through a personal advertisement in the *Daily Telegraph*. It offered 'abundant travel and well-paid part-time work in Germany'. Just up my street, I thought, as I went for the interview in Wimbledon. Harry, the group leader, and two other young potential salesmen were waiting. Harry was about my age, wore a smart navy-blue suit and a burgundy tie, and spoke with a mid-Atlantic accent though he was undoubtedly a Londoner. He sat us down and gave us the pitch. He was, he said, a book salesman, a veteran of the campaign to enlighten American troops in Germany by selling them encyclopaedias. He had returned to England to recruit a crew and hoped we would join him.

'It's a piece of cake,' he said. 'We only work in the early evenings and lunchtime on weekends. That's when the families are home and you can get the signatures of both husband and wife on the contract. For every sale you make $50. One sale is enough to cover travel, accommodation and food for a week. Anything after that is pure profit.'

He paused, picked up a glossy publicity sheet and spread it out. It displayed a large picture of a bookshelf, lined with encyclopaedias. On top was a vase of roses.

'The Grolier Encyclopaedia International,' said Harry. 'It comes with the bookcase—oak or rosewood—but not with the vase and flowers. They'll often ask you about the flowers but don't laugh. It's a good talking point—takes their minds off the money side of things.'

'What about work permits?' asked one of the aspiring salesman.

'That's the beauty of it,' said Harry, getting into his stride. 'We enter Germany as tourists and travel around as tourists. We only work on the bases and they're American territory so the Krauts can't touch us. No visas, no permits, no taxes. Just greenbacks, in your hand, as soon as you've made a sale.'

Harry said it didn't matter if we knew nothing about selling, he would train us on the job in Germany. All we had to do was to get ourselves to Stuttgart. He would meet us there and we would set out on an adventure that would make us amazingly rich, amazingly quickly. After all, what American family could resist the lure of education for their children so appealingly packaged in the Encyclopaedia International? The pitch sounded familiar but his enthusiasm washed over me like a warm tide.

'When do we get the books?' I asked.

'No books,' said Harry with a grin. 'It's all done from this sheet. I've sold dozens of sets but I've never seen the books.'

I telephoned him later and said I was his man. Could I bring my car? 'By all means,' Harry said. 'See you in Stuttgart.' He gave me the name and address of the man who headed the sales force in Germany. 'He started just like us,' he added, 'and now he's a millionaire.'

I went home and broke the news to my father and Edith who shook their heads in despair. They probably felt that their fears about the Seychelles malaise were turning out to be true. It was particularly hard for my father who had often boasted to relatives and friends that his oldest son would one day be an ambassador. He didn't know that MI6 officers never reached that exalted height and were perpetually embedded in the lower echelons of embassies and Whitehall. But since I had quit, it was all academic anyway. Moreover, I felt I had to lead my own life the way I wanted, not the way my father and Edith would have chosen. I didn't stay the night as I usually did because I was eager to get away. Had I known what was coming, I would have stayed longer. I packed a bag, tossed it into the battered but reliable Peugeot, and set off for Dover.

Once in Germany, I travelled with Harry and two others—a former London policeman and a Cockney lad from the East End— the length and breadth of the country. We spent the days on the autobahns and the nights trawling for sales on the bases. The promised fortune proved elusive. Over a period of six weeks, I sold just enough books to survive.

The night the telegram came, I was in a German jail. We had been on an American army base in Kassel, near the East German border, tramping up and down stairwells and knocking on doors, when a swarm of American military policemen appeared and arrested us. They handed us over to the German police and we spent several hours in a cold and draughty cell.

It wasn't the first time it had happened and we knew that it was pure harassment, a way of preventing us from selling any more books that night. However, that was all they could do, as Harry had predicted. The MPs had no legal grounds for stopping us working but they went after us all the same, and the Germans, good NATO allies, were happy to join in.

When we finally got back to the inn where we were staying, the landlord handed me the telegram.

DAD VERY ILL STOP PLEASE COME HOME STOP MUM

## 9

I DROVE BACK TO LONDON AS FAST AS I COULD AND JOINED her at his bedside. He had suffered another stroke that felled him. He couldn't speak but he recognised me and, when I held his hand, I felt the warmth that I remembered as a child, and a faint pressure. When we left the hospital after our daily visits, Edith put on a brave face but I could see that she was close to tears. I would make some comment about him looking better and she would politely agree. We understood the rules and played the game.

We received an urgent call from the hospital early on a peerless May morning. It was Sunday, bright and cloudless, with a hint of apple blossom in the air, the kind of day in which it is marvellous to be alive, the kind of day my father loved to spend in his garden. After his first stroke, he spent as much time out there but did less. He would potter around for a while and then stand motionless, gazing at his haphazardly planted vegetables, as if his devotion would encourage them to grow.

We were the only visitors in the hospital where the normal activity of dealing with illness and death seemed suspended. Our footsteps on the polished linoleum sounded louder, and the smell of disinfectant more astringent than usual. Edith moved ahead of me, her bronchial lungs wheezing. It was painful to see her straining to confirm what we both already knew.

A nurse was waiting for us outside my father's room. She opened the door and Edith gazed at him lying on the bed with his eyes closed. Her face crumpled. She let out a strangled cry, and rushed out. I remained, finding it hard to tear myself away. A Catholic priest had given him the last rites a few days earlier, removing his sins if not his guilt. His death had been expected. I looked down at his sunken, waxen face. They hadn't put his teeth back in. He had never liked them; too uncomfortable, he said. So, perhaps they had done him a favour. I leaned down and kissed his still-warm forehead.

For a moment I didn't feel pain, rather loss and nostalgia for my childhood. I remembered his arm around me when I needed to feel his presence, like the time I sat on the running board of the big car and threw up my lunch. Or when I clung to his hand as he took Maurice and me back to St. Dominic's after one of his visits. The few happy days of childhood were always associated with him, when he appeared out of nowhere and spent time with us, and the not-so-good-to-awful times when he was absent. For the moment, the frustration and resentment I felt over his attitude towards my mother were forgotten.

When I was in Germany, not long before I received Edith's telegram, I had a dream about him. He was sitting in his favourite armchair, wearing a suit and tie, and puffing on his pipe that bubbled with tar-laden spittle but, as always, created a cloud of fragrant smoke. He was talking about his childhood in the Seychelles, roaming free on the plantation and fishing in a pirogue off the blinding white beaches, and his years at sea, travelling around the world. He had been relaxed, chatty, and open, not the way he really was but the way I wanted him to be.

When he retired from his government job, he came home, quite proud, with a formula thank-you letter on an official letterhead, signed by some time-serving flunky, and a Parker fountain pen in his pocket. It seemed that after years of struggle, the rewards, such as they were (his government pension was a hundred pounds a year), had come too late. As it turned out, he only had a few good years of retirement before his first stroke.

It was quiet in the hospital room, dappled with light from the spring sunshine. No one disturbed us. Edith was surely still in the building, alone with her grief and leaving me with mine. I looked around but there seemed to be no personal possessions. That was how I remembered him, a man who travelled light through life. I took his hand and held it as I had done as a child although now my hand enclosed his rather than the other way around. His palm was calloused and the warmth lingered, a fading link between us.

As a small boy, when I first became aware of death, my father was the person I immediately thought of. I felt terrified and stricken contemplating his end, which I assumed would come well before my own and was thus more real. I had reached an age when I felt that crying, whether in private or public, was a childish lack of control, a sign of weakness, to be avoided at all costs. But I made an exception for my father. 'The day my Daddy dies,' I said to myself, 'I will cry.' And I did.

Then I felt a strange, almost shameful feeling of relief, tinged with excitement. A good cry has a purgative effect. But it was much more than that. I was thinking of my mother, in the room with the tiled floor and the snow falling outside, the woman who now had a name, an age, a lineage, and a brief marital history. Neuroscientists believe that while the essence of childhood memories may remain true, the details change over time, as I am sure many of mine did. But an exception was my sole recollection of Grace. I believe that scene remained pure and unchanged over the decades and, as I became fully aware of my father's death, Grace's image was stronger than ever.

I looked down at him and regretted that I had not tried to supplement the information he had reluctantly provided when I joined MI6. For some time, I believed that, given the right moment, we could continue where we left off, awkward though the whole business had been. The right moment never came, but, even if it had, I finally realised that he would never have told me anything that I did not already know. So complete was the barrier separating his two marriages, it was as if he had never known his first wife and the mother of his children. The past for him was not merely dead; it had never happened.

I placed his hand on the bedcover. He was gone and Grace's story had gone with him. It would mean starting from scratch. Still, the situation had changed in an unexpected way. My father's end, it slowly dawned on me, was my beginning. I felt sad but I also felt liberated. I was suddenly free to explore my own history. The metaphorical wall blocking off the past was breached. It was time to get serious and begin the search.

How to go about it? Edith was the obvious person and I felt none of the inhibitions that I had with my father about questioning her. I could also enlist Maurice's help. But he was in the Yukon, Canada's far, far west, and unable to come over for the funeral. And, even if he had been closer, I sensed he would not be interested. Sixteen months younger than me, he almost certainly had no memories of our mother. In all the years growing up together, we had never talked about her, a fraternal silence that mirrored the paternal one, so I could not be sure. The best thing would to be to let him know my intentions and see how he reacted.

The funeral was presided over by an Irish priest in the parish church. There were six of us present—two Seychelles cousins, a dear old couple who lived in the house next door, Edith and me. After leaving the sea, my father had made few friends and his surviving shipmates were scattered. Having been born into a huge family, he left with just four relatives to see him on his way.

At the cemetery, two gravediggers stood by with shovels. Edith had brought freesias and put them in a vase at the graveside. My father's name on his birth and baptism certificates was 'Louis George Jorre de Saint Jorre'. He dropped the first 'Jorre', presumably for sake of convenience because the name was already a mouthful, but then for some reason he reversed his first names. He always signed his name, 'George L. de St. Jorre', and he was always called 'George'. Edith was horrified to discover this anomaly after his death, fearing that the confusion might cause complications with his will. Wrongly, as it turned out; death rectified the matter. On the black-bordered death certificate, and the tombstone in front of us, my father's name appeared in the correct order and in full. 'In Loving Memory of Louis George Jorre de St. Jorre. Died 16th May 1965 Aged 75 Years.' A simple end to a complicated life.

After the funeral, we drove home and Edith went upstairs without a word. I was preparing a pot of tea in the kitchen when I heard her crying softly. After a few minutes, she came down wiping her eyes and for a brief moment we embraced, awkwardly because that was my way. She went into our tiny living room and I brought in the tea. I sat down in my father's favourite armchair, assuming, without thinking, the male role of head of the household. On the table beside the chair were two pipes, a packet of pipe cleaners, his familiar brown leather tobacco pouch, softened with age and pungent with the oil of tobacco, and a box of Swan Vesta matches. I reached out and touched the pouch. This was his place after Sunday lunch. He would light his pipe, puffing hard to get it going, and tune the radio to his favourite gardening programme. Settling back in the chair as spirals of blue smoke rose up to the ceiling, an aura of contentment settled over him. A man at peace with himself, you would think, with nothing on his conscience.

I turned to Edith.

'Mum, what happened to Grace?' Clumsy, but I couldn't stop myself.

'I really don't know,' she said quietly, taking it pretty well considering the timing. 'I felt it wasn't my business. Of course, I knew about the separation and that he had to look after you and Maurice.'

'Did he leave any papers? Marriage or divorce certificates, that sort of thing?'

She looked at me sadly, fingering the pearls around her neck. I felt the knife turn in the wound. Never a tall woman, she seemed to have shrunk since the moment the hospital called.

'He destroyed everything to do with your mother,' Edith said slowly. 'He never talked about what had happened, and I didn't ask him.'

While I had become used to his stubborn silence about his former wife, I was shocked at the intensity of his determination to obliterate all traces of her. Not confiding in Edith was one thing but destroying critical documents, like his divorce papers, was another, especially for someone who had such a great respect for authority and the law. Did he assume he would never need the documents again? Clearly, he did. Or, he simply didn't care. A pattern was developing. Perhaps Grace's name had originally been on the family tree and he had erased it, for here was a man who would stop at nothing to hide or obliterate the evidence. A murderer could not have been more diligent in covering his tracks.

The next morning, when I came down to breakfast, there was a surprise. On the dining room table, neatly laid out, were my father's engineering certificates, diplomas, and the Marine Engineer's Manual for 1932, two World War I medals, his rosary and Catholic missal, and a small pile of yellowing photographs of his Seychelles relatives, dating back to the middle of the nineteenth century. Among all this was a scrap of paper that looked as if it were torn from a pocket diary. Dated 4 December 1955, it was headed 'Jeddah'. Below, he had written: 'I have just finished *The Power of Positive Thinking*, the greatest book I have ever read. I feel a good deal better and happier and, above all, stronger in my belief in God and our Lord Jesus Christ.' The date rang a bell. He had gone to the Seychelles by ship that year and must have stopped at the port of Jeddah in Saudi Arabia on his way through the Red Sea.

I fingered the rosary. I could still remember the prayers the beads represented from my time at St. Dominic's Priory although it was years since I had recited them. My father had used that rosary to the very end, whispering the prayers in French—*Je vous salue, Marie, pleine de grâce, le Seigneur est avec vous...*' and '*Gloire au Père, au Fils et Saint-Esprit...*' One object stood out in the sense that it had not belonged to him. It was a silver chalice on a wooden stand, about four inches tall with two delicate handles, rather like a miniature trophy. It was slightly dented, highly polished, and engraved: 'J. A. St. J. April 5th 36.'

Edith came in. 'I'm sorry,' she said, 'that's all there is. I may find something else when I go through everything but I doubt it.'

'What is this?' I asked, holding up the silver chalice.

'Your christening cup,' she said, looking slightly embarrassed. 'I found it the other day, wrapped in tissue paper, in one of his drawers. It was badly tarnished, so I cleaned it up. It's yours now.'

'Do you know where I was christened?'

She shook her head. I put my arm around her shoulder and gave her a hug. Still tentative but an improvement. A death in a family can have unexpected results. I felt free and perhaps Edith and I were becoming closer.

She went out to prepare breakfast, leaving me staring at the meagre collection on the mahogany table, which gleamed with her insistent polishing. That table and a few other pieces of good furniture had been with us since we first moved in with Edith in the Woodford flat on that sunny summer's day many years ago. The furniture had travelled with us as we moved from house to house, even to Singapore and back, familiar objects that reminded us of a more affluent past when we lived on the right side of the train tracks. My father's life was there: his career, his religion, and his ancestors. But, unsurprisingly, there was nothing on the table to recall the woman who had borne him two sons and disappeared off the face of the earth.

AFTER THE FUNERAL, EDITH DECIDED TO SELL THE HOUSE
and return to her native Scotland. We went in her small car, which
my father had never learned to drive, and took our time. As we
drove over the green hills, with their dry stone walls and placid
sheep, and through the slow-paced towns and villages, I thought of
asking her help in looking for Grace. But I could see that she was
still upset by my father's death and decided to wait. Also, I sensed
that she did not know any more than she had already told me, a
mistake that would have unexpected consequences.

Back in London, I needed to get a real job and tramped around
Fleet Street, talking to the major newspapers to see if anyone would
hire me as a correspondent and send me back to Africa. Some of the
news editors I talked to made sympathetic noises about liking people
who had resigned from the Foreign Office, as well as having some
knowledge of the 'Dark Continent', but no one offered me a job.
Not surprising, I suppose, since I had not written a published word.

Meanwhile, I checked the London telephone directory, and
found four 'Islips' listed. I wrote to them all explaining my quest.
A story in one of the London evening newspapers piqued my interest. It concerned the Salvation Army helping a mother, separated
from her son during the war, find him and facilitate an emotional
reunion. The organisation had a special research department, the
article explained, dedicated to searching for missing people. Off
went another letter.

A friend recommended me to the Oxford University Press and
I had a series of interviews that led to an offer of a position in
the Middle East. I can't remember the title but it was essentially a

salesman's job. I hadn't distinguished myself peddling fire extinguishers or encyclopaedias and didn't think I would be much better with OUP's more upscale products. Nevertheless a job was a job. I was about to take it when fate took a hand and swung me in a different direction, setting in motion a new career and, through that career, a startling development in the search for my mother.

One damp November day, I was walking across the courtyard in front of St. Paul's Cathedral when I caught sight of a newspaper billboard. 'SMITH DECLARES INDEPENDENCE', it read. Ian Smith was the leader of the white minority in the British colony of Rhodesia. Britain was decolonising rapidly in Africa and the process had reached Rhodesia's northern border with the recent independence of Zambia. Fearing that Britain would grant independence to Rhodesia, where the vast majority of the population was African, Smith decided to go it alone. The crisis posed a dilemma for Harold Wilson's Labour government. If negotiations failed, military force should, in theory, be used to crush the rebellion, as it had with so many other colonial revolts. However, Smith and the white colonists were not the usual black or brown colonial subjects but British 'kith and kin', as they described themselves. Smith himself was a decorated RAF Battle of Britain fighter pilot, with a scarred face to show for it. Wilson ruled out military force. Rhodesia's Africans, backed by the independent African states, were bitterly angry and demanded action. It was a big story, a story that, in the journalistic jargon I would soon learn, had 'legs'.

I had a good friend at the *Observer* who had been the paper's Africa correspondent when I was in the Congo. He said this was a perfect opportunity to earn my spurs as a freelance. Do the Fleet Street rounds again, he advised, but, this time, tell them you are going out to Africa under your own steam. Make your base in Lusaka, Zambia's capital, where you can report on Rhodesia, Zambia and Malawi. Then beg, borrow, or steal the money for the airfare. I returned to Fleet Street and, when I said I would take care of myself, I picked up accreditation and telex credit cards from three national newspapers, including the *Observer*. Four days after seeing that billboard at St. Paul's, I was 30,000 feet above the Sahara, heading south.

I had not forgotten Grace but my new life put the search on hold. When I left London, I had not received any answers to my letters to the various Islips, or from the Salvation Army. I arranged for a friend to send my mail on to me and the replies slowly caught up with me. Three Islips wrote, politely and regretfully, saying they knew nothing about my mother or her family. The fourth never responded.

The most interesting letter was from the Salvation Army. It was signed by 'Brigadier Bramwell Pratt, Investigation Secretary' and came with a form soliciting details of my missing mother. The brigadier assured me of his desire to be of service, 'hoping thereby to relieve your anxiety'. He cautioned that it 'would be wise to read our Notes of Guidance before completing the details in order to be assured that your request comes within the scope of our usual procedures.' Apart from a registration fee of two pounds, there would be no charges. However, the Salvation Army felt sure it could count on my 'generosity in a further contribution at the conclusion of our endeavours should your circumstances make this possible.' Fair enough.

I completed the form, enclosed the fee, and mailed it in Lusaka's main post office, wondering if it would ever arrive. But it did and, in a surprisingly short time, I had another letter from the Salvation Army saying that a Major Read had been assigned to my case. The letter pointed out that if my mother were found, her consent would be required for me to get in touch with her. 'However, you may rest assured that every endeavour will be made towards a renewal of contact between you and your relative,' the letter continued. 'Our desire is to try and alleviate your anxiety as soon as possible.'

It was nice of the Sally Army to be so solicitous of my mental state and in such quasi-Dickensian language. I wrote to Major Read, acknowledging his letter and giving him my Zambian address, but I never heard anything more and assumed that the Salvation Army had failed to find any information about Grace.

Meanwhile, my editors in London kept me busy as their attention shifted from crisis to crisis and country to country. After making periodic reporting trips to Salisbury, Rhodesia's capital, for almost a year, Ian Smith's government banned me from re-entering the country and I moved north to Nairobi, Kenya. I was still writing for a collection of newspapers and magazines, with the *Observer* as my main customer, and learning my trade, the journalistic equivalent of my father's apprenticeship in the Glasgow shipyards.

However, my learning curve, I had no doubt, was much more fun than his had been. The *Observer*, the paper I wanted to join, was using me more frequently as a 'fireman' (nothing to do with fire extinguishers), sending me all over the continent and even up to Aden in the Yemen, whenever a big news story broke. The travel, the adrenalin charge that came with chasing a major story while trying to stay ahead of the competition, even the danger that was endemic in most African stories, and the feeling of satisfaction seeing the results in print combined to produce a powerful, intoxicating experience, like a junkie landing a fix. It was hard to think of anything else.

Eventually, the *Observer* put me on a contract and I dropped my other publications. The foreign editor, the man who, for the last two years, had been at the end of the cable and telex messages whose face I had never seen and whose voice I had never heard, agreed that I should return to London to discuss the future. First, however, I decided to make a detour. The Seychelles were within reach and, since my father had spent the first twenty years of his life in the islands, this was a good chance to see the place where he had grown up, and spend time with my relatives. While I expected to learn more about him, I did not expect to discover anything new about Grace.

In those days, there was no airfield, so I went the way my father and our family had always gone, on a British India Company ship. The journey began curiously. The ship sailed from Mombasa so I reserved a sleeper on the overnight train from Nairobi. I walked along the platform looking at the names on the carriage windows and soon found mine. There were four berths in each compartment and I was surprised to see that I was in the company of three other de St. Jorres. I had relatives in Kenya but none of them that I knew had our name. I boarded, went to the compartment, and met three sallow, down-at-heel men, two in their twenties and the third much older. They were as surprised as I was.

We introduced ourselves and they said they were going down to Mombasa to look for work. They were foremen, working on white-owned farms, and had been up-country for many years but now, with an African government in control and the white farmers pulling out, work was scarce. They were part of Kenya's small poor white population, a sad group of misfits in a rapidly changing country. They had been born in the Seychelles and grew up there. Our kinship was a mystery because although we shared the same unusual name, we couldn't trace any family connection between us. All we knew was that our origins lay in those distant islands and that, long ago, we must have had a common ancestor.

I boarded the British India steamer in Mombasa and over the next three days had plenty of time to think about where I was going and what I might find there. I knew the outlines of our history from the family tree and what my father and various Seychelles relatives had told me. The pioneer was my great-great-great-grandfather, Jean François Marie Jorre de St. Jorre, an early entry on the family tree, who sailed from Mauritius, with his family and slaves in 1790, to start a new life in the Seychelles. The islands, thought by some to be the original Garden of Eden because they were so fertile and beautiful, were uninhabited, and the idea was to make them French before Britain made them British. The settlers were given land and planted cinnamon, patchouli, vanilla and coconuts. They built simple but elegant houses from hardwood cut from the tropical forest, and did their best to recreate eighteenth-century France in a place that had as much in common with the mother country as the Amazon jungle. During the Napoleonic Wars, the islands changed hands several times. The British fleet sailed in and the French governor fired a few token shots from a small cannon in front of his official residence before he hauled down the French flag. A deal was quickly struck with the invaders. The British obtained food, water and repairs for the ships, and hoisted the Union Jack over Government House. The French settlers kept their land, language, religion, slaves, and even their governor. A month or so later, the ships weighed anchor and, as the last sail disappeared over the horizon, down came the British flag and up went the French *tricolore*. Until the next time. But the defeat of Napoleon at Waterloo put an end to this unusual *pas de deux*. In 1815, the Seychelles finally became British and remained so for the next 161 years. The durable French governor, who had endeared himself to his conquerors, became the first *British* governor of the islands.

The French plantation owners behaved as if little had happened although they were now all British subjects. They continued speaking French, held on to their slaves, imported their wine from France, sent their children to Catholic schools, and maintained their patrician ways. But, during the slumbering, uneventful years of the nineteenth century, their fortunes slowly declined. The slaves were freed and the plantation economy began to match the torpor of the tropical climate. Britain paid scant attention to a remote speck of empire that had little economic or strategic value, and the more energetic and enterprising sons and daughters left for Europe, Africa, North America and Australia. Among the by now thoroughly mixed population, the old families were still known as the '*grands blancs*'.

However, when my father came along in 1889, some of them were not particularly *'grands'* nor uniformly *'blancs'*. While my relatives talked proudly about *le sang pur de la France*, flowing through their veins, the reality was somewhat different.

Shortly after dawn on the fourth day out of Mombasa, the soaring peak of Morne Seychellois appeared on the horizon. A large granite outcrop, Mahé, the principal island, rises majestically out of the turquoise Indian Ocean, forest-clad and encircled by white coral beaches, fringed with palm, pine, takamaka, and casuarina trees. Standing on the deck, I felt the damp heat and smelt the scent of frangipani flowers. It was a spectacular sight and made me wonder why anyone living there would ever want to leave, especially for a place like Glasgow where my father had spent five years as a marine engineer apprentice in the grimy, clamorous shipyards of Edwardian Scotland.

An immigration officer boarded the ship and looked at my passport.

'You must be George's son,' he said with a smile. 'Your *Tonton* [Uncle] Abel is down there.'

I looked over the ship's rail and there, bobbing up and down in a small boat, was an elderly man in a white shirt, long khaki shorts and a broad-brimmed straw hat. He waved and I waved back. Abel introduced me to his brother-in-law, Paul Chenard, and we drove in Chenard's car along the palm-fringed coast road to La Plaine St. André, the plantation that my great-great-great-grandfather had founded. The house, built in the mid-nineteenth century, faced the ocean but was set back at the end of an avenue, and framed by two tall breadfruit trees. It had a steep roof, and the broad, shaded veranda that I remembered from photographs, though the house was smaller than I had imagined. Waiting for us on the veranda, with coffee and cakes, were my two Aunt Léonies.

One of them was Abel's wife, who had been a Chenard (Paul's sister) and was now a de St. Jorre. The other was Abel's own sister, who had been a de St. Jorre and then, having married an Englishman named Woodley, was no longer one. I had never met Abel's wife but I knew the other Léonie well. She and her husband had lived in Kenya but when he died, she returned to the Seychelles. My father's youngest sister, she was close to him in age and affection, and I first met her when she visited us in London. Unlike Abel and his wife, who had never left the islands, Léonie was a woman of the world.

I spent almost two months with my uncle and two aunts at La Plaine and during that time Léonie became my mentor and cultural interpreter. We had always got along well and, being equally familiar with the outside world and the islands, she helped me ease into the old plantation lifestyle that Abel and his wife preserved as best they could.

During those lazy days, I often wondered what it was like for my father growing up in a large family on a plantation where the rituals and rhythms of daily life had changed little during more than a century. And how had such an upbringing formed his character? He had played among the palm groves where I took my early morning walk. He fished along the coral reefs with the Creole fishermen, went to mass on Sunday with his family (they had their own front row seats), and learned to drink his wine at the table without putting water in it. Every Sunday afternoon he and his brothers climbed into a large pirogue at the beach in front of the house and two Creole plantation workers paddled them to Victoria. They spent the week at school in the capital and returned home the same way on Friday afternoon.

The Seychelles side of my family intrigued me. Here I was in one of the last enclaves of French colonial plantation life, witnessing the terminal days of the old order. The elements of a system that had endured for almost two centuries were still in place. A British governor, who wore a plumed pith helmet on ceremonial occasions and got around in chauffeur-driven Rolls Royce, was still in charge, and a Swiss bishop, head of the Catholic Church, still wielded enormous power. The only way to reach the islands, a thousand miles from anywhere, was by ship from Mombasa or Bombay, a three-day journey either way. Tourism was virtually non-existent. The sole car rental firm had a single car, a Morris Minor, and I hired it.

The old house creaked with history. At the back, the bell that summoned the slaves to work was still there. During my grandfather's time, some of the plantation workers lived under the house and when they got drunk and rowdy on a Saturday night, he used to stamp on the floor to shut them up. Linking us with the past was a giant tortoise, a long-lived species indigenous to the islands. As children, my father and his brothers and sisters had sat on its back. It barely moved during my stay and did not seem to mind when I sat on it too. I felt like part of their lives at times, living among uncles, aunts and cousins, who had grown up with my father in this remote place and accepted me fully as a member of the family; at others, I saw myself as an intruder from another planet.

Many stories emerged. There were tales of ancestors and their child brides who had pioneered the settlement of the islands, of buried treasure, of scandals and bitter feuds with other families and within our own. When I arrived at La Plaine, I was put in the *pavillon*, a charming guesthouse that was built in the style of the main house and close to it. It had a living room, a bedroom and a bathroom. Every morning, a Creole cleaning woman would arrive and polish the floors with a coconut husk, rubbing it back and forth with a naked foot until the dark wood gleamed.

One day, when Léonie and I were alone, she told me the story of the *pavillon*. After my great-grandfather's first wife died, he took a second, a widow who appeared to be a beauty. Until the wedding night. When she undressed, my great-grandfather was horrified to discover that much of what had attracted him—hair, bosom and buttocks—was false. In a fury, he tried to throw her out. She refused to budge, saying she was now the chatelaine of La Plaine St. André and had as much right to it as he did. So, he moved out and built the *pavillon* as close to the big house as he could. He lived there until she finally left the plantation and he moved back into the main house.

As for the poor white de St. Jorres whom I had met on the Mombasa train, Léonie told me that my grandfather had a brother, one of whose sons had married a Creole woman while other members of that branch had 'drunk their land'. The men on the train were from this side of the family, in effect my cousins many times removed. Léonie made it clear the subject was taboo on our side of the family, and her account was the first and only time I heard about it.

Léonie also told me about her brother Marcel, who had always been a mystery figure to me. I had seen his name on the family tree where he stood out as the only one of my fourteen uncles and aunts who had never married. Marcel's entry was simple and unambiguous: *mort célibataire*, a dead bachelor. One day, Léonie, out of earshot of Abel and his wife, announced that we were taking a trip to the other side of the island—to visit Marcel.

'But he's dead!' I said, astonished.

'Not yet,' she said smiling. 'As you will see, he is very much alive. Your father used to send him a card every Christmas. He was fond of him and kept in touch after...' she hesitated, 'after the trouble.'

As we drove over the central spine of Mahé, with its dense tropical foliage and steep winding road, I wondered who had killed off Uncle Marcel on the same family tree that omitted my mother but included her children. We arrived at a smaller replica of La Plaine, shrouded in palm and casuarinas trees. The door opened and a tall, strongly built, handsome man, with a head of thick white hair, stepped out. He was my *Tonton* Marcel and he was eighty-seven years old. Just behind him was an attractive light-skinned Creole woman, some twenty years younger, who was introduced to me as *'Fille.'* Léonie greeted Marcel and his lady warmly and we had a pleasant lunch with a lot of reminiscing about my father, his youth on the islands, and the scattered brood of de St. Jorres around the world. *Fille*, whose real name was Marie, although no one called her that, spoke only Creole. She served us but did not sit down at the table, hovering attentively in the background. She would occasionally catch my eye and give me a shy smile.

On our way home, Léonie told me the full story. Marcel, while still living at La Plaine, had fallen in love with *Fille* and begun an affair. The family professed shock, although sexual liaisons across the colour line were common enough as was clear from the Creole population that ranged from coal black to light tan in colour. What had been exceptional in Marcel's case was that he refused to abandon the girl when the family presented him with an ultimatum: give her up or leave La Plaine. He left and built a house on the opposite side of the island.

'A little while ago, Marcel fell ill and thought he was going to die,' Léonie said. 'The priest came and asked him if he had anything to confess. "Yes," said Marcel, "I have lived with this woman for forty years, I've had three children by her, and I never married her." "Well, my son," said the priest, "you'd better marry her now." And Marcel did. Then, to everyone's surprise, including his own, he made a full recovery.' Léonie looked at me with a wry smile. 'I'm not sure whether he regrets his decision.'

One afternoon, Léonie took me to visit another of my uncles, Henri. As with our trip to see Marcel, she did not tell Abel and his wife. *Tonton* Henri lived in a small, attractive house on a plot of land adjacent to La Plaine and on the edge of the Indian Ocean. I knew two of his daughters, Maryse, who later married the German consul, and Danielle, who was to become a dynamic foreign minister of an independent Seychelles in the years ahead. Henri and his wife had fond memories of my father and were gracious and friendly. They never mentioned Abel or La Plaine.

Maryse later told me the story. Henri managed La Plaine on behalf of the family for forty years, and she, her two sisters and her brother had grown up on the plantation. But then Abel and another brother conspired to get rid of him because they wanted to take over the house and the plantation for themselves. Abel worked for the cable and wireless station in Victoria and, as part of his campaign to rally the family against Henri, he sent a cable to my father in London urging Henri's ouster. He signed it 'Marcel', who held my father's proxy. My father, who knew nothing about the plot, gave his assent, and eventually Henri was forced out. So bitter was the feud that he could not bear to look at the old house whenever he passed it on his way into town. When he was dying, Abel came to see him. Henri told his wife to send him away.

As my stay came to an end, I felt that I understood my father's character better than I had before. In some ways, he had grown in stature. He was a more educated man than I had thought and was much admired by his family. (My cousin Maryse found another book prize that he had won at school, this time for geography, and gave it to me.) Abel's wife remembered how handsome and accomplished he looked in his naval uniform when he had returned to see his mother in the 1920s. He was a pioneer in a way because most of our relatives seemed content with staying put, lulled by the slow pace of island life, the humid, spice-scented air, and their privileged position.

However, I also saw what family feuds in the Seychelles could do to anyone embroiled in them. While my father used to criticise some of his relatives behind their backs, especially if they didn't work as hard as he did, I did not think he was vindictive like some of his brothers clearly were. Then I thought of Grace and wondered if I was wrong.

A few days before I boarded the ship back to Mombasa, I decided to tell Léonie about my hopes of finding Grace. I would have done so earlier but, knowing how close she had been to my father, I was uncertain how she would react. However, as I was preparing to leave, I realised I might never see her again.

'I knew about your mother,' she said quietly, 'but we never met. George and I used to write to each other a lot and once he sent me a photograph. I think it's time you had it.'

She went to a jewellery box and returned with a tiny, faded black-and-white snapshot, barely three and a half inches by two and a half inches in size. It was of my father and mother, taken in London in the mid-1930s, Léonie said, probably around the time of their marriage. It looked as if they were in a park or botanical garden with tall trees and a fountain in the background. My father was wearing a blazer, his open-necked shirt folded down over the collar like the one on our farm holiday. Grace had on a light-coloured dress and her hair was parted on one side and pulled across her forehead. She was standing close to him, her head barely reaching his shoulder. My father was smiling but Grace looked more serious, giving the unknown photographer a rather intense stare.

This was the first picture I had ever seen of my mother and the excitement of the discovery matched the moment when I had first learned her name. Moreover, since a Seychelles member of my family was helping me, perhaps more of my relatives, who had grown up with my father, could do the same thing. The photograph was not much of a portrait and Grace's expression was unrevealing although I sensed vulnerability in that small figure and a certain reticence. Was she a little wary of my father? Was she having doubts about their relationship? Was this *really* the woman of my memory, the laughing blue-eyed woman with ash between her breasts? There was no way of knowing. It came down to an act of faith, and I believed it was.

I HAD COVERED THE NIGERIAN-BIAFRAN CIVIL WAR FOR THE *Observer* and, when I returned to London, a publisher commissioned me to write the history of the conflict. I spent a few days with Edith in Scotland and thought again about pressing her further on Grace but came to the same conclusion as before, that the well was dry, so what was the point? Returning to London, I loaded up my car with everything that I would need for the book and drove down to Barcelona where I took the overnight ferry to Mallorca.

The drive from Palma, the capital, to my mountain village was a familiar one. A narrow ribbon of grey, the road weaves across the plain, ascending slowly through almond orchards and olive groves. It circles a small town featuring a church with a minaret, recalling the time when the Moors ruled this land, and crests a hill. Another bend and the Mediterranean appears, this time of year a foam-flecked swath of winter grey, but in summer a deep, ethereal blue that softens the glare and cools the landscape. The road follows the coast through stony fields of gnarled olive and carob trees and then begins to descend in slow, sweeping curves. One last swoop and there is the village, perched on the top of a small hill in a valley and walled in by a great arc of mountains on all but the seaward side. The houses, with their stone walls, red-tiled roofs and green shutters, appear to lean on each other, old friends weary with age, as they climb up the steep hill to greet the church. A graveyard, guarded by tall cypress trees, shares the summit with the church and accommodates generations of farmers and fishermen and their families.

At this point you can see everything—the mountain range clear and sharp against the sky; the countless terraces, sculpted from the living rock by the Moors centuries ago to nurture the precious olive trees; the occasional ancient, weather-beaten *finca*, high up on the mountain side; and the magnificent sweep of the pine-clad coast, fading away in a purple haze. I drove along the main street, up a short hill, and parked the car. The large iron front door key was in the geranium pot where I had left it. The lock squeaked as I turned the key and the heavy wooden door needed a shove to open it. I stepped inside and inhaled the mixture of smells that I had grown to love: the linseed oil on the wooden beams; the dry, fusty odour of straw from the mattress stuffing; and a faint scent of jasmine, a reminder of hot summer days when the stone walls retained their warmth well into the night. It was a long way from Buckhurst Hill. I was home.

My daily routine began with a walk to the village post office to check the mail. The weather was becoming colder and wetter and, one morning as I left the house, a storm had lurched inland from the sea and was battering the island. As I walked down the hill to the village, clouds raced over the mountain ramparts, water spouted from gashes in the rocky walls as blood does from head wounds, and mud ran down the village paths. On the high terraces, the wind thrashed the olive trees into a frenzy. The branches, supported by their sturdy trunks, fought back, their green and silver leaves quivering in the rain.

I opened the door of the village barber shop, which doubled as the post office. The mail lay on a marble slab among shaving brushes, cutthroat razors, scissors, combs, and bottles of *eau de cologne*. It was usually difficult to find your own letters because they were often mixed up with other people's. But, on this particular morning, I had no trouble. Right in front of me was a single item, a plain blue envelope addressed in an unfamiliar hand. Postmarked 'Bournemouth', it had been originally sent to the *Observer* in London. Someone on the foreign editor's desk had crossed the address out, substituted mine in Spain, and there it was. I went into the single, smoky café in the village, ordered a croissant and a *café con leche*, and opened the envelope. The letter was neatly typed on a single sheet of matching blue notepaper.

Dear John de St. Jorre,

My husband and I have been deeply interested in your reports in THE OBSERVER, which we read every Sunday.

It has suddenly occurred to me if you could possibly be the same John de St. Jorre I knew prior to the war and you were then a small boy? If so, I knew your parents very well, and your father I recall was from the Seychelles.

At this stage I will not go into more details other than to say that, if my assumption proves correct, it will give me great pleasure to hear from you. The war years unfortunately were responsible for losing touch with one's friends. I trust you will pardon the liberty I take in writing you but, if it proves the means of renewing a friendship, which meant much to me, I will indeed be very happy.

Yours sincerely,

Joan Cooper.

Shaken, I read it again. I hadn't forgotten Grace but I can't say she was on my mind. Suddenly, unbidden and out of nowhere, came this stranger with a story to tell. It was as exciting as it was unexpected and I read it twice more, after which I knew the contents word-for-word. There was no mistaking the author's authenticity or her familiarity with my parents. There had to be more.

I rushed back to the house and pulled out some writing paper and envelopes. The Nigerian Civil War could wait for a bit. I wrote back to Joan Cooper saying that she was not mistaken and I was keen to hear what she knew about my mother and her family. Joan replied quickly and said how pleased she was that we were in contact. 'It was your mother's side of the family I knew so well,' she wrote.

Apparently, her sister, Eva, who lived in Canada, had first spotted my byline and photograph in the *Observer* and alerted Joan in England.

'I at once thought of Grace Islip,' Eva wrote to Joan, 'and maybe my imagination ran wild but I thought the photo resembled Grace, especially in the nose and mouth. One of her boys was named John. He would be about thirty-five years old. I wonder what you will think, Joan, but I guess we'll never know.'

Joan took up the story, a story that opened up a whole new world. The first revelation was that I had an aunt called Olive, Grace's older sister. My father could surely have mentioned her when I was filling out the government forms. But since there was no request for information on my mother's siblings, I did not ask, and he did not offer. He could have been a spy himself, following the cardinal rule of never revealing anything except on a 'need-to-know' basis. Anyway, an aunt's appearance was exciting news because it doubled the odds of finding someone alive.

Another discovery was that the two sets of sisters, all young, single and enjoying life in 1930s London, became good friends and spent a lot of time together and with each other's families. They also paired off: Joan was closer to Olive and Eva closer to Grace. The greatest revelation of all came at the end of the letter.

'After Maurice was born, I know your mother's health was bad,' Joan wrote, 'I think Maurice was about two years old when it was necessary for your mother to be treated for mental sickness.'

Grace recovered and went back to her old job at Negretti and Zambra, a venerable company that made optical instruments with offices in Bond Street in London's West End, where Grace was the secretary of one of the directors. However, while she was in hospital, Joan went on, 'your father, for some inexplicable reason, broke all relations with your mother and, to your mother's grief, as well as that of your aunt and grandmother, they had no idea where you were. Doubtless the strain of being parted from her children was cruel and she had another mental relapse.'

Joan emphasised how much Lucy, our grandmother, and Olive 'adored' us and wanted to look after us while Grace was in hospital. (No mention of a grandfather. Divorced? Dead?) However, my father had other plans. Joan added that she had lost contact with Olive and her family during the war and her approach to me was the first time she had been successful in locating any of us.

She ended the letter in a puzzling way: 'Doubtless, John, your mother must still be alive and nothing would please me more than to discover ways and means of tracing her.'

I wondered why Joan Cooper seemed so confident that Grace was still alive when she said she had lost touch with her and Olive so long ago? It made no sense but perhaps she was just trying to encourage me? Of course, Grace could be alive, she would be sixty-three years old, but she could also be dead. Nevertheless, whatever Joan thought, I was no longer on my own.

She and I kept up a lively correspondence as the clouds hung low over the mountains and the Mediterranean winter tightened its grip on the village. She said that my response had given her 'much food for thought' and she was certain of one thing. 'There was no question of your mother wishing to be parted from you both,' she said. The last address she had for us was 7 Crescent Road, Church End, Finchley, which was our grandmother's home. 'I am under the impression it was from there that Grace went into Friern Hospital in Barnet, just north of London.' Joan added that she had some photographs of Olive, which she would show me when we met.

The village grew quieter with my neighbours' shutters opening later and later in the dark mornings. Busy in their fields and gardens most of the year, they seemed to hibernate in the winter. I worked steadily on my book but I had plenty of time to ponder Grace and my new family. It seemed strange, at this stage in my life, to think of my mother as a person and not an image, and to say 'Aunt Olive' and 'Granny Islip' aloud. They were still strangers somewhere out there, but they were coming closer.

I also thought about coincidence and fate. Was there some unknown force at work that led to Joan Cooper sitting down one day in her Bournemouth living room and writing a letter to a man she had never met? If I had been working for MI6 or the Oxford University Press, instead of a British newspaper with a regular byline, our paths would almost certainly never have crossed. The past seemed to be stirring even though I had done nothing to stir it.

I looked forward to Joan's letters although they did not add much that was new. Until, on one glorious day of winter sunshine, another blue envelope, with the now familiar handwriting, landed among the shaving brushes and razors. In it was a nugget of pure gold.

'A couple of days ago,' Joan wrote, 'I received a letter from my sister Eva in Canada and with it she enclosed the last letter that she received from your mother, written in the summer of 1940. It is four pages long, closely typed, and you will be able to see it when we meet. You and Maurice were then obviously with your mother as you will gather from the letter.'

Unfortunately, Joan concluded, Eva had thrown out 'a very nice studio portrait of your mother' three months before seeing my *Observer* article. But the letter was a miracle and, through it, I would hear Grace's voice, not the living sound of course, but the resonance of her written words at a time when Maurice and I were still at her side.

My book was not quite finished but I decided to cut short my stay and return to England. I wrote to Joan and she told me to contact her in Bournemouth when I was in London. I arrived a week later, and was about to contact her, when the *Observer*'s foreign editor called and asked me to come into the office. When I got there, the newsroom was humming.

'You've heard the news?' he said. I had heard it on the radio, that morning. A Palestinian group had hijacked three Western commercial airliners in Jordan, and forced them to land in the desert not far from Amman, the capital. The passengers and crews had been taken off and were being held hostage. The planes were wired with explosives, ready to blow up.

'Our Middle East man is on leave. Can you go?' the foreign editor said. 'I'm sure it will all be over within a week, and you'll be back and can wrap up your book.'

It was bad timing. I was dying to meet Joan Cooper and read Grace's letter, but I did not want to let the paper down. I was returning to work for it after my Nigerian book was finished and this assignment was exactly what a foreign correspondent was supposed to do. Also, I felt a frisson of excitement, a big story in an exotic place.

'Fine,' I said. 'When shall I leave?'

'Tonight,' he said, reaching into a drawer and handing me an airline ticket with my name on it. 'Good luck.'

I called Joan and told her what was happening. She said she understood and we would meet when I returned. I also called Edith in Scotland.

'Oh, that's good,' she said, sounding relieved. 'It will keep your mind busy.'

I smiled. When my father died, I had a feeling Edith wondered if I would ever be gainfully employed again, although she never mentioned it. She did, however, once send me a birthday card with the comment, 'Let's hope next year will be better.' Hint. Hint. For her, my new life, working as a newspaper reporter, was just all right—regular salary, pension, etc.—but taking time off to write a book was a dubious diversion. She clearly did not think researching and writing a history of a complex African civil war exercised the mind in any meaningful way.

I flew to Amman and the hijack story was over in a week but then Jordan erupted as King Hussein moved his Bedouin troops into the capital for a bloody showdown with Yasser Arafat and his Palestinian guerrillas who had been responsible for the hijackings. Amman turned into a battlefield, the airport was closed, and the borders sealed. Along with about a dozen other journalists, I was trapped in the Intercontinental Hotel, perched on Amman's highest hill, with the battle eddying around us.

The situation appeared grim but had its advantages. Disaster, war and tragedy are meat and potatoes on the foreign correspondent's plate and this was the perfect story. It was a tightly focused life-and-death drama, with the whole world watching, and a limited number of hacks to report it. There were moments of danger. Food was scarce, and water for washing non-existent, so we were hungry and dirty. But it was a great story and I would not have wanted to be anywhere else.

The battle sometimes raged across and even through the hotel as the Jordanians and the Palestinians shot at each other from opposite sides. War can be hell, and it usually is, but it can also be incredibly exciting as long as you are not a casualty. Winston Churchill knew what he was talking about when, as a young cavalryman on the Northwest Frontier in India, he wrote: 'Nothing in life is so exhilarating as to be shot at without result.'

Our best vantage point was on the top of the hotel, in the night-club, which had lost part of its roof and taken some artillery fire, leaving ragged holes in its walls. One night I was up there with a few others, including Don McCullin, a renowned British photographer who had made his name photographing wars around the globe. As we lay on the floor watching the battle, he told us he had been invited to New York to give a talk to the students at Columbia University on the horrors of war. He was trying out his carefully tailored anti-war speech, using us as an audience, when a particularly spirited exchange silenced him. The barrage ended with a direct hit on a petrol station on the hill opposite, producing a volcanic explosion with flames, smoke and debris blown high into the night sky.

The silence on the rooftop of the Intercontinental Hotel was broken by an orgasmic groan from the newly transformed peacenik.

'Fucking *marvellous*, isn't it?' he breathed.

When it was finally over, I flew out to Beirut and then on to London. On the London flight, I thought about Grace writing to her dear friend in distant Canada thirty years ago with a much larger war going on than the one I had just witnessed. What did she have to say about her illness, about my father, and her two small sons? Would I really hear a 'voice' amid the written words and be able to get a sense of what she was like? What did she feel about Maurice and me? Was she planning to leave us? If so, why? Too many questions and I was probably expecting too many answers.

I called Joan from Heathrow and we agreed to meet the following day at Jaeger's Tea Room in Regent Street. I arrived just before she did and saw a small, neatly dressed woman with glasses walking to my table as if she knew me. She greeted me with a warm smile and seemed as intrigued by the encounter as I was.

'Their father was a London policeman,' she began, sipping her tea, 'but he died young. When Eva first met Grace, she and Olive were living with their mother in a basement flat in Earls Court. Lucy Islip was the caretaker of the building, so the place was probably rent-free. They had very little money but Olive was studying to become a teacher and Grace was working as a secretary.'

Joan had far more to say than she had written and I sat back and let the details of my mother's hitherto mysterious life flow. Grace, according to Joan, was several years younger than Olive, very vivacious and fun-loving. Olive was the stay-at-home type, and Grace the girl who loved to go out. Apparently, my father was also living in Earls Court at the time and Joan said she had heard that he and Grace met on the platform of the Tube station.

'Grace was fascinated by George's exotic background and often talked about going to the Seychelles with him.'

I am pretty sure Grace never went to the Seychelles and Edith did not go either although I think that was her choice. She certainly did not want to live there. I wondered if my father ever promised to take Grace with him on one of his trips and, then, for some reason, changed his mind. Could he have been ashamed of the slothful life and his squabbling relatives? Or did he feel that Grace, and possibly Edith as well, were too 'English' to fit in?

During my stay in the Seychelles, I had caused consternation when I suggested to my uncle that it would be nice to invite an English friend of mine to La Plaine for a drink. He was chief secretary in the government (second only to the governor), had been in the islands for two years, and spoke perfect French. But he had never been inside a plantation house. My uncle and aunt were initially horrified but eventually agreed. I think it was the first, and probably the last, time an English person, who was not part of our family, stepped across the threshold.

I already knew when my father and mother were married but Joan added that Olive left for Canada shortly afterwards and my father saw her off at Waterloo Station. It occurred to me, with greater force than before that, even if Grace were dead, Olive might be alive, and she would surely be a rich source of information about our past. Joan said that Olive, although not as out-going as her younger sister, was a lively person but felt socially inhibited by scars on her face caused by eczema when she was a teenager.

'We were really good friends and I was terribly sad when I lost touch with her,' she said. 'I made inquiries but all I heard was that she had gone to live with a man in Ramsgate on the Kent coast.'

Then came the bad news. Grace was hospitalised in late 1937, about six months after Maurice's birth. Joan said she felt sure it was the first time it had happened. Grace was not in for long, was discharged, and returned to her job at Negretti and Zambra. I stopped her for a moment, because I was confused. I reminded her that she had said in her first detailed letter to me that my father had taken Maurice and me away when Grace was in hospital. But apparently the letter from Grace to Joan's sister Eva, mailed in 1940, made it clear we were still with our mother.

'I'm sorry,' she said contritely, 'I must have mixed things up. You were definitely with her at least until 1940, perhaps longer.'

Not much longer, I thought. My earliest memories dated to two or three years *before* we went to St. Dominic's in early 1943, which included the short time we spent in the boarding house in Raunds, and the much longer time with the Linders. During that period, Grace was nowhere to be seen.

Although Grace was happy to be back at her secretarial job, Joan continued, she was not well. Not long after leaving hospital, she telephoned Joan.

'I feel I am losing my grip again,' she said, 'and I'm scared stiff.'

A few days later, Grace had to go back into hospital and Joan went to see her.

'I was really upset at her appearance,' she said. 'She looked sloppy and seemed to have deteriorated. She'd also lost some of her teeth that had been replaced by false ones.'

I was shocked, and I suppose I showed it.

'I didn't tell you this before because I didn't know you very well and I didn't want to upset you,' Joan said quietly. 'But I think you want to know everything, don't you?'

I did, but I hadn't realised how painful it was. When I knew nothing about Grace, a sad, even a tragic story about her would have seemed more distant, even impersonal, and hence less distressing. But she had begun to take shape as a human being, as my mother, and it made a difference. She was no longer simply the happy woman of my childhood memory, she had a face, a personality, a family, friends, and a chronology. The more real she became, the closer I felt to her.

'Yes, I do want to know everything,' I said. 'What was Grace suffering from?'

'I don't know but it was some sort of mental illness that appeared after the birth of your brother,' Joan said. 'Grace told me once that she had been walking you two little ones across a busy road when she saw a great flash of light in her head.' Joan paused, 'I'm sorry, John, I wish I knew more.'

I did, too, or did I? Perhaps that was enough for one day. I needed time to absorb what I had heard. I called the waitress to bring the bill. But then I had a thought.

'You said in one of your letters that Grace must be alive,' I said. 'I wondered what made you so sure?'

Joan looked uncomfortable. 'I probably shouldn't have said that because, as you know, I lost contact with her and Olive during the war. And so did Eva who was in Canada the whole time.' She paused. 'I just have a feeling and I wanted to give you hope.'

'I understand,' I said, 'we all need hope.'

Joan opened her bag and took out a blue airmail envelope.

'Grace's last letter to Eva,' she said, handing it to me.

We parted like old friends, linked by a confused and still murky past, Grace's thirty-year-old letter in a place where she had never expected it to be, her oldest son's pocket.

WHEN I WAS ALONE IN MY FLAT, I SAT DOWN AND OPENED IT.
It was four pages long, neatly typewritten, single-spaced on thin
airmail paper. The last three pages had small holes in them, brown
and ragged around the edges—cigarette ash?—but they did not inter-
fere with the text. The address was Lucy Islip's home in Finchley,
North London, and the date was 6 June 1940. The letter, written
when I was four and a half years old, began:

Eva darling,
    It was delightful to receive your long letter of the 18th April.
This sounds as though I have lapsed somewhat in an early effort
to reply but actually, as usual, all is not as it seems. You don't mind
a piece of paper with a hole in it, do you, my love? After all, there
is a war on!

Grace reported that she had bought a pram canopy for Eva's baby
son, André, who had already received some of Maurice's old baby
clothes. Cast-offs, it turned out, would not be the only connection
between Maurice and André though Grace, writing the letter, and
me reading it thirty years later, could never have imagined how it
would occur.

    'How are you liking motherhood now, chérie?' Grace continued.
'However much one moans and gets tired, I know we wouldn't be
without 'em, and when they love you and say and do such adorable
things, it soon puts paid to any inconveniences.'

    She went on to describe her 'great piece of news', a return to
her secretarial job. Her euphoria was short-lived because a week

later she was dismissed. 'I got the sack,' she explained, 'because Mr P.E.N. thought I was trying to slope off earlier than I should.'

However, Grace fought back.

'I just let him have it. I told him I wanted to talk to him and did so at great length and the consequence was, I was reinstated.'

I stopped. The letter was professionally typed and I had a feeling that she had written it at the office on Negretti & Zambra's time, and on one of their typewriters. She loved her job, even though the salary was only three pounds a week, plus a five-shillings wartime bonus, and she explained why. 'Typing and shorthand, compared with the humdrum of domestic life, certainly suit my temperament—I look and feel heaps better.'

It was clear from the letter that Grace, Maurice and I were all living with her mother in a rented house.

'Mum's very fed up with her landlord,' Grace continued. 'Her bedroom hasn't been straight since we had the floods during the winter cold spell. Then, last week, through the damp, the bedroom ceiling collapsed. Luckily, John was in the bath and not in his cot. They've sort of repaired it. After Ma went to the Sanitary Inspector in Finchley, he, the landlord, is behaving in a more humane way. A terrific cheek, I think, the way they take your money for the rent but don't want to look after the property.'

Grace must have sent Eva a newspaper cutting, probably from a local paper, because she refers to the incident that it described.

I just can't help but laugh about it all—I think I was too sleepy to have contracted shock. But when I think of how serious it might have been, I thank my lucky stars for my escape. An aunt once told me I'd have lots of ups and downs but, like a cat, I would always land on my feet. Here's hoping, anyway.

The fire happened in May. Early one Sunday morning, young fella-me-lad, Maurice, awoke and demanded a drink of water. (No beating about the bush with my kids!) Like an idiot, I left my candlestick on the windowsill above my bed. Naturally, what I should have done was use my electric torch. Ah yes, I see it all now!

I staggered across the bedroom, gave him his 'drink o' water', and just flopped back into bed, so sleepy that I omitted to blow out the light! The next thing I knew was that I was sitting bolt upright in bed, gazing at the flames leaping to the ceiling—awfully bright looking! Young Maurice chose to awake at the same moment, and let out an ear-piercing scream. Anyhow, with a presence of mind worthy of a better cause (than saving my skin, you follow), I controlled the situation by dashing out into the hall, grabbing a walking stick, and flinging the curtains off the wall, cleared my bed, and then rolled them up in one of the rugs on the floor. A piece of burning curtain fell between the window frames but I seized a glass of water and flung it over the flames—I quite enjoyed that! The woodwork of the window frame was charred but only one pair of curtains was burnt, and that was all the damage, except that when it was all over, I suddenly realised my hand was hurting like hell.

Mother was priceless. She was so absorbed by the events that she quite forgot she hadn't put on a dressing gown and she was floating about, just like Lady Macbeth, in a marvellous mauve satin nightie, cut in Empire Style, which Olive had made recently and didn't like.

The drama ended with firemen arriving and taking Grace to hospital where her hand was treated. Her narrative then turned to a happier subject.

I've just bought Maurice and John a trike between 'em. It's a little beauty but gosh aren't they dear! But it's worth it, 'cos they are so bucked.

She finished by sympathising with Eva's homesickness for England, though she cautioned the country was not so appealing close up. She added that she would like to go to Canada.

I thought I would ask you now if you can accommodate any refugees from England, for me and mine!? If you hear of any good jobs going and cheap dwelling houses, etc. just let me know honey, and I'll take a high dive. (Thought you'd had enough of those, says Eva!)

Lots and lots of love to you and yours—hugs for André—from all of us. As always, Grace.

The signature was written in pencil, in a clear, firm, rounded hand and underlined with a flourish.

I've read this letter many times since that first occasion in London. It sits beside me now, a little yellow and worn, over seventy years after a young, vivacious woman, who happened to be my mother, wrote it. But it has never come across as powerfully as now. Perhaps the act of copying what she had originally typed—I can see her painted fingernails dancing across the metal keys—on to a modern computer, gives it a new lease of life and perhaps a deeper meaning.

Her narrative showed her to be enjoying her young children, hard though life was with very little money in wartime London. She seemed to be living harmoniously with her mother, happy to be back at work. A young woman in her prime.

I loved her fizzle, her readiness to confront adversity, to turn it round and make light of it. Nobody was going to sack her after only a week back in the job that she adored. I wonder if 'Mr P.E.N.' knew that she was typing long personal letters on the office typewriter during office hours? If he had, would he have sacked her again?

Yet Grace lived dangerously. I had survived a fallen ceiling at the age of four, and Maurice had come through a fire at barely three. It made the German bombs that came later seem mild by comparison.

But most important were the omissions. Not a single word about my father. It was as if he didn't exist. Where was he? Was he living somewhere else? Had they split up? She talked of going to Canada, as if she were a single mother, with two young kids, branching out on her own. Her husband, by his absence, sounded like a figure in the past, someone who was no longer part of our lives. Considering how things turned out, this was ironic. It was also baffling.

Grace was equally silent about her mental state and her time in hospital. All she revealed was that she felt much better being back at work. Nothing in the letter suggested a person with serious health or marital problems. Yet she would soon be separated from her children, whom she manifestly loved and cherished, although there was no hint of how that would happen.

## 13

With my Nigerian book finished, the *Observer* put me to work on the foreign desk in London, pending an overseas posting. I had bought a flat in Notting Hill when the area was still unfashionable and funky. It cost about the price of a good car but I still needed to borrow some money from Edith in order to obtain a modest mortgage. The flat was in a nineteenth-century house that, in its heyday, had been the Spanish ambassador's residence and had recently been subdivided into eight modern apartments of varying sizes. Mine was in a section of the old ballroom, on two levels with high ceilings, and it retained many of the original features. Several floor-to-ceiling windows opened on to a wrought iron balcony overlooking a spacious communal garden. The first thing I did was to put a fuchsia plant, its delicate bell-like red, pink, magenta and white flowers in full bloom, in a large earthenware pot at the far end of the balcony. The Portobello street market, clusters of antique shops, and a slew of atmospheric pubs were a few minutes' walk away. New restaurants bloomed like the spring flowers in our garden and often disappeared with them by summer's end. Every September, the West Indian carnival descended on the area, rocking, and sometimes wrecking, the neighbourhood. The 1970s, with its boom and bust rhythms, were under way and the distance from my childhood was growing greater whether I noticed it or not.

When I did think about it, I recalled how I had grown up in old England and here I was in a different, almost unrecognisable country. Moreover, I was not simply a witness to the transformation but an active participant. The war had delayed things, with the old verities of my parents' generation remaining in place, as my brother and I discovered at our Dickensian boarding school. But with peace, everything began to move, and to move fast. In my teens, I was a beneficiary of the radical changes in education and health (both cost-free and freely accessible) under a zealously reformist Labour government. I was educated at a good state school and kept healthy by the National Health Service, all without a penny changing hands.

In the army in Malaya, serving in a Malay regiment, alongside other colonial units—Fijians, Northern Rhodesians, Gurkhas and so on—I saw the sun sinking over the British Empire. The Communist insurgency was defeated but Britain departed anyway, ending its long imperial sojourn in South East Asia by handing over its territories to their inhabitants. At Oxford, I was part of the post-war, state-educated, and state-supported wave of students who breached those ancient walls of privilege and wealth in increasing numbers. In Africa and the Middle East, first in MI6 and, later, as a journalist, it became clear to me that America called the geopolitical shots worldwide, and that Britain, bereft of empire and reduced to the status of a second-class power, obediently followed.

As all this changed, so did I. I found myself becoming more independent, more questioning, bolder, and scornful of many of the social conventions I had once regarded as sacrosanct. In a profound way, I felt like a different person, a person who could do anything he wanted, including looking for his mother. Thus I was ready to take advantage of the astonishing opportunity offered by the appearance of Joan and Eva in a way that I might not have if they had materialised earlier in my life.

I now knew my mother infinitely better than ever before. Her voice, as I had hoped, resonated through those professionally typed pages. Here she was, at last, the authentic Grace, a non-person for so long. Over the years, I had sometimes wondered if she were a drudge, a scold, even a slut, a woman who invited rejection and divorce thus giving my father a rationale to dump her. But she seemed to have none of those characteristics although I still had no idea what had gone wrong in their marriage. Was infidelity behind the break? From her letter, there did not appear to be a man in sight, not even her husband. Her delight in being a mother of two young children and working at a job she liked was unmistakable. Yet, with all this came a sense of doom. While I was still a long way from knowing her full story, I knew what happened next, and it seemed to contradict all that she was doing and thinking when she wrote that letter.

Meanwhile, I had to sort out my future with the *Observer*. I needed time to look for Grace and I wanted to write more books, which meant a regular full-time posting to some distant place would not be the best option. On the other hand, I didn't want to give up journalism or the money that went with it. This was the old *Observer*, David Astor's *Observer*, which he ran shyly but brilliantly from the quietude of his large office, a newspaper of comrades and friends that we all loved. It gave great flexibility to its writers and, while I wanted take advantage of its generosity, I also wanted to ensure that I could return.

By chance, another *Observer* foreign correspondent, who happened to be a close friend, was in London and I arranged to have lunch with him in the Blackfriar pub, a favourite haunt of *Observer* journalists that was close to the office. Gavin was a tall, good-looking man with the bearing of the Guards officer he had once been. As a foreign correspondent, he had a reputation for disappearing into a remote corner of the world for an indeterminate period, but returning with a scoop meticulously reported and elegantly written.

'Hmmm… you've just described my problem,' Gavin said in his quiet voice. 'I want to write a book, too, and I think I have the perfect solution.'

He talked at some length.

'Do you think they'll buy it?' I said.

He shrugged. 'No harm in trying.'

He pointed up at one of the Victorian mottos inscribed in mosaic tiles on the walls around the pub's ornate snuggery. Among them were 'Industry is All', 'Haste is Slow', 'Finery is Foolery', 'Wisdom is Rare' and the one Gavin was indicating.

'Seize the Occasion,' he said with a grin.

An hour later, fortified by a good lunch and a couple of pints of strong ale, we were in the foreign editor's office.

'You what?' he said incredulously.

'We want to be one correspondent,' Gavin repeated.

'And how exactly would that work?'

'We would divide the year equally, six months on, and six months off, and the paper would pay us each for that work, thus one salary a year, instead of two. During our time on, you could send us wherever you wanted. No need for a regular base, just hotels will do. What do you think?'

The foreign editor, who had been a foreign correspondent himself, was a man of few words and considerable caution. He looked at us warily.

'That's a new one on me. Do you really mean it?'

'Yes,' we chorused.

'Well, let me run it past the editor and managing editor. It may take a few days.'

We left and went back to the pub to discuss our chances, which neither of us rated highly. However, to our surprise, we received a summons to the foreign editor's office the following morning.

'They have agreed,' he said with a wry smile. 'I hope you won't regret it. The bean counters really like the idea of one less salary on the books. But I can't say I'm happy with losing a correspondent.'

Gavin and I looked at each other with the same thought in our minds. Why had it been so easy? Were we on a slippery slope? Yet we had what we wanted.

'Well, who's going first?' the foreign editor said. 'We need someone in Vietnam.'

Gavin had spent a lot of time in the country, and liked it. He looked at me and I nodded.

'I'll go,' he said.

The foreign editor grunted and turned to me. 'We'll see how things stand when you come on. It will probably be the Middle East. OK?'

'Fine,' I said, 'wherever you want.'

I went back to my desk and called Joan.

'I've just heard from Eva,' she said. 'She and her husband are coming over to England next month. You must come down here and meet them.'

I had promised Edith that I would visit her in Scotland and told Joan I would come to Bournemouth as soon as I returned. Edith had settled near the Scottish border town of Hawick. An old mill town that still made tweed, Hawick was an unremarkable place dominated by heavy Victorian buildings but redeemed by the rolling hills, moors, and scattered woods that surrounded it. Edith's modern bungalow was in a small parkland development about two miles outside Hawick. The bungalow stood on a piece of land that gave her an unimpeded view of the countryside. It was small with two bedrooms, a modest kitchen and dining room but had a large, airy living room overlooking a gently sloping meadow that ran down to a sparkling burn. On the other side of the water, a squat stone church sat on the crest of a hill. The wind blew ceaselessly and the trees along the banks of the burn were in constant motion.

The house, though new to me, was familiar because Edith did not believe in parting with her possessions. The furniture that I remember from our first days with her in Woodford, including my father's favourite armchair, was there. When we sat down to a meal, it was at the same three-leaved oak dining table, and we ate off the same dishes and with the same cutlery, embossed with our initials. A camphor wood chest, which Edith brought back from Singapore, had, in its turn, become a familiar object. The collection of family photographs on the living room mantelpiece had expanded with pictures of Maurice and me growing up, the occasional group photograph of our neat nuclear family, and Maurice and his wife and their two young daughters. The missing member, of course, was still missing but I am sure that I was the only one to notice.

This corner of the Scottish borders was a peaceful place where the tempo of life was slow, steady, and on a human scale, rather like my Spanish village. Edith had developed a small circle of friends among the locals and spent much of her time visiting them in their houses, entertaining them at her home, or joining them on excursions through the Border country, where they browsed the antique shops, visited tweed and cashmere mills, and took lunch and tea in genteel restaurants and small hotels. She had given up long distance travel but she kept in touch with old friends and Seychelles relatives by mail and on the telephone. She seemed happy and she deserved it.

I knew she missed us, particularly Maurice and his family, and I tried my best to see her as often as I could. I was the dutiful son, often remarked upon by her friends, who never forgot her birthday, invariably brought her a gift when I turned up, and wrote her regular, morale-boosting letters. Edith had always wanted to be the complete mother to Maurice and me, a fully integrated member of her husband's life and household. We wanted it, too. We needed a mother, an affectionate, caring, competent woman, who could compensate for our father's deficiencies and our fractured past, a woman who could give us stability to grow up happy and hopeful. Edith performed that role admirably.

My father and Maurice, I felt, had always been unequivocally behind her. My feelings were more complicated. While I was happy she was with us and grateful for all that she had done, I couldn't quite shed the old ambivalence. Resentment for the way she and my father had wiped the memory of Grace off the face of the earth lingered. I realised that it wasn't Edith's fault, she was simply following my father's lead and deferring to his wishes.

When I arrived, Edith greeted me warmly and I gave her one of my tentative hugs. I could never embrace her fully and I avoided kissing her. I always felt bad about it afterwards. It was mean and petty to deny her something so easy to give. But even a false intimacy suggested betrayal of my real mother and was, I discovered, a line I could not cross.

I told Edith about my new job and said I could not stay long on this visit but would be back in time for her seventieth birthday.

'That's lovely,' she said happily. 'Maurice and Dorothy and the girls will be over from Canada and they plan to stay for at least a week.'

Edith had two neighbours, both Scots, a family doctor and a vet. During my visits, I got to know them well, especially the vet. Angus was a tall, rangy man with an angular face and a dry manner. He was a Scottish nationalist of the romantic kind who could quote reams of Scottish poetry by heart and knew the country's turbulent history backwards. He always wore a dark blue tie with the date '1314' embroidered in gold, the club tie of a group of Scots who celebrated the Battle of Bannockburn, Scotland's last triumph over the English on the battlefield.

Angus kept horses and invited me to ride with him on several occasions. The most memorable outing was the 'Moss Paul Ride', a wild gallop across the moors with the men and boys of Hawick, celebrating the Battle of Flodden, a defeat by the English this time although a heroic one. Our destination was the Moss Paul pub on the Scottish-English border where large amounts of food and drink were consumed to the accompaniment of Scottish poetry and ballads. I also went with Angus on his rounds among the farms scattered in the surrounding hills and, one evening, to a reading (and more whisky drinking) at the home of Hugh MacDiarmid, the Scottish poet who had been, unusually, a party-affiliated communist and a Scottish nationalist. When they found out, each organisation expelled him for belonging to the other. Angus ushered me into the presence of the 'Baird', as he called him, with the deference customarily shown to the Pope.

One evening in the middle of my stay, Angus invited me to his home for a drink.

'I've just got a new malt,' he said, lifting up a bottle and gazing at the red-gold liquid in the light of the fire. 'It's the only whisky made on the island of Skye. It's called Talisker and I think you will like it.'

I had no doubt he was right, having sampled many malt whiskies with him. We sat and drank and Angus launched into one of his diatribes about the perfidies of the English over the centuries with their border raids, pillaging of Scotland's treasures and heritage, and annexing the country to the British crown. As he was talking, I realised that he regarded me as a Scot, or at least half one, with the living proof in the house next door. Edith's other friends in the area all clearly thought the same and I did not want to disillusion them since Edith had not done so. But Angus was a special friend and he was so passionate about England's evil deeds that I thought I had better come clean.

'Angus, I have to tell you something,' I said. 'The woman whom you know as my mother is actually my stepmother, although over the years she has become my mother, if you see what I mean. While my stepmother is undoubtedly Scottish, my real mother was English so that means I haven't got a drop of Scottish blood in me.'

Angus raised a quizzical eyebrow, studying me thoughtfully.

'Aye,' he said, slowly sipping his dram. 'But you're half *French*, and that'll do.'

I spent three days with Edith touring the Borders, dropping in to see her friends, and spending quiet evenings at home with her, playing Scrabble by the fire. Although we never talked openly about my work or my love life, I sensed she was concerned about both. I think she had accepted that journalism, although vaguely unrespectable, was better than being a bum or taking time off to write things like books. But none of it was as good as that 'government job' with its cast-iron security and long-term pension plan, which I had abandoned so cavalierly.

My sturdy bachelordom also worried her, not such a good idea, she occasionally hinted, what with 'time ticking by'. She knew little of my love life because, apart from a Danish student I met at Oxford, I never brought anyone home. The few girlfriends whom I mentioned—a Zambian, an Israeli soldier (female), and a Lebanese—had not impressed her. I think she hoped that I would eventually come to my senses and marry a nice English or Scottish girl.

Near the end of my stay, we did finally talk about the subject we never talked about. Joan Cooper had done her bit, it was time for me to do mine. After supper one evening, I brought it up.

'By the way, I am still trying to find out what happened to Grace,' I said as casually as I could. 'I'm sure you'll understand.'

It was easier calling my mother 'Grace' than risk upsetting Edith's feelings by mentioning the sensitive maternal word when it normally referred to her but, in this case, meant someone else. There could not be two 'mothers' in the same sentence, in the same house or, while my father was alive, in the same life. Edith looked upset and I felt guilty. However, if I did not raise the subject with her, I would feel bad about Grace. Guilt both ways, but only one way forward.

'Is there anyone who might have known her in the 1930s, relatives, friends, that sort of thing,' I said.

'Does Maurice want to know, too?' she countered.

'I don't think so. It's all too far back for him. We haven't talked about it although I am sure we will when he arrives.'

'I'll get my address book.'

She went to her bedroom and came back with a small pocket diary.

'One of Dad's old friends, Stanley Belcham, may be able to help, if you can find him. He worked for the Crown Agents in Westminster and your father saw him quite often.'

'I think I remember him,' I said. 'I'm pretty sure Dad took me up to the West End once or twice to have lunch with him. I believe he hired people to work in the colonies. Why would he know about Grace?'

'He may have been one of her relatives. But I'm not sure.'

Edith wrote down Belcham's address and turned the pages.

'The other person is Fernande Cook. She is a niece of your father but close to him in age and they were good friends. You probably met her when we were in Buckhurst Hill because she'd come over from time to time.'

I had seen so many Seychelles relatives come and go that I had a hard time telling one from another. Fernande, Edith said, married an Englishman named Jack Cook and they, like my Aunt Léonie and her English husband, had lived in Kenya. He died relatively young and Fernande bought a house in the south of Spain where she lived with her daughter and grandchildren.

Edith, it seemed, had gone as far as she could go and I set off for London the next day with a simple plan. First, Mr Belcham, then cousin Fernande. Andalusia, where she lived, was quite a detour from Mallorca where I intended to spend some of my time off, but worth a try. In London, I did my best to find Stanley Belcham but neither address nor telephone directory revealed any trace. I thought of asking the Salvation Army to start another search with the new information I had acquired, but decided against it after I received a letter from Fernande in Spain. She said she remembered Maurice and me well from her visits to our house and regretted losing touch with us over the years. She ended her letter with an arresting phrase, just three words.

'You must come and see me,' she wrote. 'I was there.'

Two days later I was on the road, driving steadily towards the Spanish sun.

Fernande's villa was in the foothills near Fuengirola, a safe distance from the hotels, bars, and tourists of the Costa del Sol, on a flat, high plateau of olive groves and fields of ripening wheat. In the evenings, after dinner with her daughter and grandchildren, we sat and talked on the terrace under an indigo sky embroidered with stars. Fernande was a warm, charming, and intelligent woman. Her gentle voice, inflected with the lilt of the islands, recalled the old way of life on the plantation where she had grown up with my father, my uncles Marcel, Henri and Abel, Aunt Léonie, and countless other de St. Jorres. I almost felt that I was sitting on the veranda of La Plaine again, smoking a cigarette rolled from Uncle Abel's home-grown tobacco, and listening to the steady rhythm of the surf breaking on the reef.

Like Joan Cooper, Fernande took her time and gradually eased into the story.

'I first met your mother when she was still Grace Islip, or 'Bunty' as everyone called her, and I always thought she was a sweet girl,' she began. 'She was in her mid-twenties, a generation younger than George, with blue eyes and fair hair. Her sister was lively and friendly, and about to go off to Canada. Their father had been in the Metropolitan Police but died young.'

I couldn't help wondering what my two grandfathers—the patrician French colonial planter and the down-to-earth London bobby—would have talked about had they met.

'My husband, Jack, was George's best man at the wedding,' Fernande continued. 'I borrowed a fur coat for the occasion but cannot recall the church or even which part of London it was in. But I do remember taking a wrong turn at Marble Arch, and almost missing the ceremony.

'After their marriage, we often saw your father and mother and they seemed happy. In the summer of 1934, we all went on holiday together to Ilfracombe in Devon. I was pregnant and remember being sick in the morning and longing for something sour to eat. There were cooking apples growing in a nearby orchard and George said he would see what he could do. The next morning, when I went down to breakfast, a large green apple was on my plate.

'Jack and I moved to Kenya in 1935,' Fernande said, 'but George and I continued to write to each other and all seemed well. We heard from him that you were born and then Maurice. I think it was after Maurice's birth that the trouble began. But I don't know what caused it. All I heard was that, one day, your father came back from work to find that your mother had left you and Maurice alone. You were barely three years old.'

Fernande paused.

'Do you know anything about your father's previous romances?'

I shook my head and urged her to go on.

'There was an American woman whom he had met in California on one of his sea journeys in the late 1920s, and he nearly married her. I think he was actually engaged but he broke it off rather abruptly. Later, he went out with an English Catholic girl whom he had met at Sunday mass at the Brompton Oratory in London. She was wealthy but her mother, so George told me, took an objection to his pipe. She suggested he switch to cigarettes, a suggestion that he scornfully rejected, and that apparently was the end of the romance.

'It can't have been too serious,' said Fernande with a smile. 'But I think the American one was.'

Fernande also mentioned another romantic interlude, this time with Yvonne Boullé, a Seychelles cousin, though she didn't know the details. The French families in the Indian Ocean islands did not frown on cousins marrying each other; acceptable partners were limited, and the unions reinforced the links between the old families. The only cousin-cousin marriage that I knew about in our immediate family ended in divorce, but not until the last child had been born with mental and development problems.

Finally, Fernande solved a small mystery that had puzzled me for years.

'In 1952, I stayed with Edith and your father in Ealing, after they came back from Singapore,' she said. 'I asked about Grace and was told that she was in a mental hospital and that the Islip family lived in the Woodford, Buckhurst Hill area. Edith told me she wanted to go back there to teach at her old school but your father flatly refused. The result was they stayed in Ealing for two years and Edith taught at a local school.'

What did he fear? Running into a hostile Granny Islip in the street? Being tracked down by a vengeful and possibly deranged Grace?

'I know, I know,' said Fernande, reading my mind. 'It didn't make much sense. But I never knew the whole story. If your father never spoke of your mother to you, he must have had some very good reason. I am sure he thought by leaving you in ignorance of what happened, he hoped to save you a lot of unhappiness.'

The next day I said goodbye and set off for Mallorca. The weather was hot and dry, the road trip and the ferry ride over to the island uneventful, and my house greeted me with its welcoming potpourri of ancient smells. But I couldn't get something out of my mind. What 'very good reason' could my father possibly have had for not only taking us away from our mother but also shunning any form of contact with her, and eradicating her from his past and from our present and future?

## 14

TWO WEEKS LATER, I WAS BACK IN SCOTLAND WITH EDITH who had been joined by Maurice, his wife Dorothy, and their two young daughters, Louise and Susan. On the way north, I briefly broke the journey in London where an old friend invited me for a drink to catch up on our lives and to meet his new girlfriend.

When I arrived, the pub was packed and I eventually found him at a table in the corner of the room. He introduced Janice, a pretty Jamaican girl, and went to fetch the drinks. We chatted and she told me she was a nurse working in a hospital just outside London. My friend returned and asked me how I was spending my time back in England. I briefly thought of telling him about my search for Grace but decided not to because I felt it would not interest him. On the few occasions that I had told my story to friends, I noticed that women seemed much more intrigued and sympathetic than men.

'I'm going up to Scotland for my mother's seventieth birthday,' I said. 'My brother and his family are coming over from Canada, a rare family reunion.'

We had another round of drinks and Janice looked at her watch.

'I had better get going,' she said, 'I'm on the night shift.'

'Where do you work?' I asked.

'A place you've never heard of,' she said with a smile. 'Friern Hospital.'

'I *have* heard of it,' I said quickly. 'It's probably the only hospital I've heard of outside London. I believe my mother may have been a patient there.'

'Well, if she was, she sounds all right now,' said Janice cheerfully.

She hesitated, sensing that something was amiss. 'I mean, you know, if she is celebrating her birthday at home and all that.'

'Oh yes, she's fine,' I said lamely.

Later, I kicked myself. I called my friend and asked him for Janice's telephone number. I didn't want him to think that I was trying to hit on her so I told him the truth. He said he understood and gave me her work and home numbers. The next day, I called her at the hospital and straightened out the misunderstanding surrounding my two mothers.

'I understand,' she said sympathetically. 'You'd be surprised how many people, who are separated from their families, end up here. How can I help?'

I told her about Grace and said that I had heard she was in the hospital at some stage, possibly during the war. When Grace wrote to Eva in 1940, she was living with her mother in Finchley, north London, and Friern Barnet was the nearest mental hospital. Janice said she would check the records and talk to some of the nurses who had been at the hospital for a long time. I gave her Edith's telephone number, as well as my own.

The following day, I went to my local library and, after digging around with the help of a librarian, I found a magazine article on Friern Hospital. It had opened in 1851 as the Second Middlesex County Asylum with 1,250 beds, the most modern asylum in Europe at the time. Later, the hospital expanded to accommodate 3,500 mental patients, had 'the longest corridor in Britain', and a walk through every ward took five hours. The institution later changed its name, first to the Colney Hatch Lunatic Asylum, and then to Friern Hospital. In 1941, German bombs destroyed five villas in the grounds, killing thirty-six patients and four nurses. I knew that Grace was not among the victims since she was a participant in the divorce initiated by my father six years later.

The hospital grew smaller but, near the end of the war, it still housed over 2,500 mental patients. (Was one of that multitude my mother?) Friern's most infamous alumni included John Duffy, a British serial killer and rapist; Aaron Kosminski, a Jack-the-Ripper suspect; and Dorothy Lawrence, a woman who, during World War I, dressed as a man, enlisted as 'Private Denis Smith' in the 1st Battalion, the Leicestershire Regiment, and reported for duty at the Somme front on a bicycle.

Edith was happy to see us all gathered under one roof and I knew she adored having the young girls around her and calling her 'Granny'. I liked to think that the unreserved loyalty flowing from Maurice's side of the family helped to ease any unhappiness caused by my pursuit of Grace.

Edith and the girls usually went to bed early, leaving Maurice, Dorothy and me to our own devices. One lovely evening, with the northern summer light lingering over the meadow that ran down to the burn, we poured ourselves drinks and talked. After our father died, I had written to Maurice with the details of the funeral, as well as Edith's future plans, and mentioned that I intended to look for Grace. He replied that he understood and we left it at that. I thought this was a good moment to tell him about Joan Cooper's sudden appearance and Grace's letter. Dorothy was immediately intrigued while Maurice was more guarded.

'I don't have any memories of her,' he said. 'Not a single thing.'

It wasn't a surprise. I had always assumed this was the case, but it was the first time he had said so, at least to me. We had spent a childhood together sharing a simple assumption. Since there was no mother around and no one that I can recall told us what had happened, we assumed she had died when we were too young to remember. Thereafter, during our childhood years, it seemed likely that the people around us, notably our elderly guardians and the nuns at St. Dominic's, thought the same. Finally, Edith came along and we were a whole family again. For everybody, including me for a time, the past was the past. My attitude changed with our father's death, while Maurice's did not. However, he and I, at opposite ends of the globe, seemed to have a wordless understanding that he would leave things where they were, and I would go wherever my instincts and conscience led me.

But, now we were together, he was quite ready to talk, so I asked him if he remembered hearing anything about Grace during our younger years.

'Not much,' he said. 'Once in the 1950s, when I was with Dad, we ran into one of his old acquaintances. The man asked after Grace. Unfortunately, I can't remember his name, or what Dad said in reply, so I guess it's not much help.'

He took a sip of his beer. 'When we were in Woodford, I did ask Edith once about Grace. She said she was not a very nice person. I suppose that put me off and I never asked her again, or anyone else.'

The years rolled back, and I was on the landing of our Woodford flat. There was the sexy Miss Fenton, our upstairs neighbour, all bust, blood-red lipstick, and attitude, striding along the landing trailing a cloud of perfume and cigarette smoke in her wake. At the dinner table, Edith had called her 'not a very nice person', the same phrase she apparently used to describe Grace.

I told Maurice and Dorothy about the nurse I had just met in London and the bombing raid on Friern Hospital where Grace had probably been in the early 1940s. We talked about her mental problems and our father's silence concerning her and her family.

'I think the problem for him was mental illness,' Maurice said. 'There was a stigma attached to it in those days. People were frightened of the mentally ill and didn't want anything to do with them.'

Dorothy, who had been listening intently, said: 'When I was planning to marry Maurice, my father reacted badly. He was suspicious about a mother who had mysteriously disappeared. He kept saying, "What had happened? Was there something wrong with her?" I asked Maurice but he couldn't help.'

'What did you do?' I said.

'Well, Edith said she would talk to him. I don't think your father wanted to get involved. Anyway, Edith somehow managed to reassure my dad and we went ahead with the wedding.'

Edith the diplomat, I thought, she knew how to handle sensitive problems and sensitive people. I admired the way she often stepped in when my father shied away from anything connected to my mother, unless, as in the case of the MI6 vetting forms, he had no way out.

I told them about Joan Cooper's sister, Eva, finding the letter she had received from Grace, and handed it to Maurice. After reading the first page, he looked up at Dorothy.

'A surprise for you here,' he said smiling. He resumed reading and, when he had finished, he looked up.

'It was all pretty chaotic, wasn't it?' he said. 'And sad.'

He passed the letter to Dorothy. She had barely started, when she stopped.

'André Lebel!' she exclaimed. 'We knew him and his wife in Golden, Colorado. He was a geophysicist and he and Maurice were studying for their masters degrees at the School of Mines.'

'They lived in Quebec,' Maurice said. 'We became good friends.'

'How strange that André and Maurice were the children of best friends,' Dorothy said. 'I wonder what André would have thought if he had known that thirty years earlier he'd been dressed up in Maurice's cast-off clothes?'

I suppose that, with our childhoods on our minds, it was inevitable that St. Dominic's came up.

'It was really awful,' Maurice said. 'I was hungry all the time. Do you remember "sourgogs"?'

I had forgotten the edible weed that grew abundantly in the fields around the school. But that childish name brought back the small green leaves and their sour flavour.

'I ate them whenever I could,' Maurice continued, 'and I stole berries from the nun's vegetable garden during the summer. Also,

I'll never forget being beaten by Mother Bernadette for who knows what breach of the rules.'

'And you did a bunk.'

'I don't know how old I was,' he said, 'probably eight or nine. But I remember coming out of the woods on to a road and not knowing which way to go, so I went back to the school. Mother Bernadette interrogated me and I assumed she would beat me but, to my surprise, she didn't.'

He had memories of others going 'over the wall'. Several apparently got as far as London and one nameless hero was picked up on a train somewhere in the Midlands. None of them returned to the school.

'I think the only thing Mother Bernadette was really worried about was adverse publicity,' I said. 'The convent was like that German prisoner-of-war camp not far from us, two sealed institutions full of alien people in the heart of the English countryside. A breakout from either would have been big news.'

'I don't recall having any friends, or enemies, in the four years we were there,' Maurice said thoughtfully. 'Either it was a reaction, in a continuously stressful situation, to avoid any ties with anyone or, alternatively, I was blotting out a period of my life that was uniformly bleak.'

'Well, you got your own back by abandoning Catholicism the moment you left.'

'Actually, I didn't,' he said, 'although I wish I had. It may have seemed that way but I felt guilty for years afterwards.'

Maurice finished his drink and stood up. 'I'm going to turn in.'

'Have you ever thought of going back to the school?' I said.

'Never. And you?'

'No point. Too many unhappy memories.'

Maurice went off to bed, but Dorothy lingered.

'You know John, I asked Edith about Grace a couple of years ago. I had always been curious about what happened. Maurice, as you can see, has no memory of her, and I think he wants to forget about the whole thing. But he understands why you want to find out.'

'What did Edith say?'

'That's the curious thing. She talked about Grace as if she were alive, just like you said Joan Cooper did. She seemed pretty sure. I suppose I should have asked her why she thought that way. But it wasn't really my business. I felt that I shouldn't press her if she did not want to talk about it any further.'

Near the end of my stay, I was with Maurice and his family in the garden, when Edith came to the door and said I had a telephone call. I went into the living room where the phone was and Edith disappeared into the kitchen.

It was Janice, in London.

'I've got some news for you,' she began. 'I spoke to the registrar and she said a Grace Rose de St. Jorre entered the hospital on 1 June 1942. One of the older doctors here recalled her name, because it was unusual, and thought she had been in Ward 36. Well, I found the sister of the ward at the time and asked her about your mother. She said she remembered a "Mrs St. Jorre, a tall, slim woman with ginger hair". The sister left that ward in 1951 and heard that this woman died not long after that.'

Janice paused. 'Then something strange happened. When I questioned the same sister again, a little later, she completely changed her story. The woman who could have been your mother, whom the sister now described as being short and plump with fair hair, wasn't in her ward at all. She said she remembered seeing this woman in the corridors and grounds. She also thought that this memory of your mother—if it was your mother—was quite recent.'

The story became more complicated when Janice decided to check the records herself. Grace's entry was documented with a registration number for her admission, the number of her wartime identity card, and a short note saying that she was admitted under the provisions of the Mental Health Act. There was no confusion over the date of her admission. It was 1 June, 1942.

'But the strangest thing is that there is no record of her being discharged or of dying,' Janice said. 'Not a single thing, and she is certainly not still here.'

She hesitated.

'I'm not sure how to put this, John, but your mother seems to have disappeared into thin air.'

BACK IN LONDON, I TELEPHONED JOAN COOPER. SHE SOUNDED excited and said Eva and her husband, Maurice Lebel, had arrived from Canada three days earlier. They were staying with her for a week, and I could come down any time that suited me. The next morning, as I drove to Bournemouth on the south coast, it struck me again how lucky I was to have found two sisters who had forged deep friendships with my mother and aunt in London in the early 1930s, friendships that embraced their respective families. None of them had much money but they were young and carefree, four women in their prime. Things changed in the middle of the decade. Grace got married in 1934, became pregnant with me not long afterwards, and remained in London; Joan married an Englishman and moved to the south coast; and Eva wed a French Canadian and left for Canada just before the war started. Olive, who had gone to Canada on a teacher-exchange programme, returned after a year, and found a teaching job in London. The quartet stayed in touch but distance and the war eventually separated the two sets of sisters.

Joan's house was in a quiet residential part of the town. She opened the door, led me into the living room, and introduced me to her sister and brother-in-law. Maurice Lebel, a university professor, was a good-looking man with a head of iron-grey hair and a courtly manner. After greeting me, he let his wife take over but listened attentively to what she was saying.

When I saw Eva, an attractive, silver-haired woman with dark eyes, I felt a jolt of excitement. Here, standing in front of me was the woman whom my mother had called 'darling', 'my love', and 'chérie', and loved like a sister. I sensed that I was in the presence of someone who could take me by the hand and guide me into the past as no one else could. We sat down on the sofa, side by side. Eva began talking in a calm and gentle voice and, as her story unfolded, my mother finally stepped clear from the fog of neglect and deliberate obfuscation that had shrouded her for so many years.

The Islips came from the rural Midlands of England, Eva said. They were yeoman farmers and artisans—carpenters, blacksmiths, and wheelwrights. In another of those curious coincidences that were becoming familiar, my grandfather, Charles Victor Islip, was born on the same day as my father—October 21st—but sixteen years earlier, in 1873. The two men, so different in their backgrounds, shared a determination to uproot themselves and make a career elsewhere. While my father worked his way on a ship to Glasgow to serve his marine engineering apprenticeship, Charles set off for London where he joined the Metropolitan Police Force. A cheerful and hard-working man, he quickly adapted to his new job in the tough East End.

The Peagrams were Essex people, Eva continued. Lucy, my grandmother, was born in Braintree, not far from Colchester, where Maurice and I had gone to school. Like her future husband, she moved to London and got a job as a housemaid in one of the grand houses in Grosvenor Square in Mayfair. If you have seen *Upstairs, Downstairs*, or *Downton Abbey*, you will have a good idea of how Lucy Peagram, in her drab long-skirted uniform, apron, and a starched white cap on her head, worked and lived.

'On Sundays, she would go for a walk in Hyde Park,' said Eva, 'and one day, she met Charles Islip. She was a stickler for protocol and 'proper behaviour' but, in my mind, there is no doubt that she gave her future hubby "the glad eye" and hooked him.'

After they were married, they lived in police quarters in Whitechapel where Jack the Ripper had done his grisly work a few years earlier, and the two girls were born there. In 1914, Charles was promoted to inspector and took charge of the Ladbroke Grove police station in Notting Hill Gate, a much more pleasant part of London, then and now. With the job came comfortable quarters for his family, the girls went to the local school, made new friends, and did well. Things were looking up.

Then disaster struck. When Olive was fourteen years old and Grace eleven, their father suddenly died. The tragedy left Lucy almost destitute with a pension of ten shillings a week, and she and her family had to leave the police quarters. Threatened with homelessness, she managed to find a job as a janitor of a building in Earls Court through the Women's Pioneer Group, a charitable organisation. She was given a basement flat consisting of two dark, damp rooms, and that's where the girls spent their teens.

'Grace was the more vivacious of the two,' Eva continued. 'She had expressive eyes, sex appeal, and a lot of nervous energy. She loved going out, and adored buying clothes. She had colourful tastes and sometimes overdid it. I remember her once wearing a tartan skirt and black blouse, topped off by a Tam O'Shanter hat that she'd picked up in the Portobello Road, much to Granny Islip's horror. We used to go ice skating in Richmond, and she had boyfriends.'

Grace did not sound like the type of woman I would have thought my staid father would have been attracted to, but, when he was younger, perhaps he was different. Nevertheless, his second choice, prim, proper and steady Edith, seemed far more compatible.

'Grace met George near Earls Court Tube station,' said Eva. 'She dropped something, a handkerchief or a glove, and he picked it up. They walked together to the station, that's how it began. It's strange but mother and daughter seemed to have picked up their men in public places. A short time later, George and Grace became engaged. He was lonely and wanted to settle down, have a home and children. She wanted to get away from her mother and get married. Lucy didn't approve of her daughter marrying a Catholic but admitted that being a Catholic was better than being nothing.'

The way that Eva described Lucy and Grace picking up their men in public places made the process sound disreputable. But courting was often conducted that way in the days when there were few social opportunities or formal gatherings available to those who had neither money in their pockets nor time on their hands. No debutante balls or party invitations for the housemaid and her daughter, or for the travelling salesman with a funny name and foreign accent.

While I had idly wondered what my two grandfathers would have had in common, the notion of my two grandmothers together was bizarre. The thought of that formidable French chatelaine, the mother of sixteen children, in her widow's weeds, and surrounded by her plantation, servants, and myriad offspring, sitting down with the English housemaid-turned-janitor to discuss their children's marriage made me smile.

'Grace and George were married at Our Lady of Victories Catholic Church in Kensington, and you were also christened there,' Eva went on. 'Grace wore a floor-length plum-red dress for the wedding. She looked pretty though I remember her telling me once that she did not like her mouth. "I've always had a mouth like a frog," she said.'

Olive was a bridesmaid at the wedding. Eva remembered her making a striking entrance. 'She came up the aisle in grand style, wearing a long velvet dress, and carrying a bouquet of flowers,' she said.

The image was striking. The two sisters, my mum and my auntie, walking down the aisle in long dresses. Must have been quite a sight.

Lucy Islip's antipathy towards my father went deeper than simply disliking his religion, Eva continued. Her hostility never abated, although she and my father were closer in age than the newly-wed couple. Shortly after the honeymoon, Eva visited Grace and remembered her mother being scornful about my father.

'Maurice and Eva took a *normal* honeymoon and went off to Paris,' she said to Grace, 'while you and George scuttled off to Brighton.'

The couple had different attitudes towards domesticity. 'George had firm ideas about a home—regular hours, good food, and so on,' Eva continued. 'Grace hadn't a clue about cooking but did her best under George's guidance. One Christmas, she came back late from an office party a little tipsy. George was very annoyed.'

Joan brought in some tea and cakes and we had a break as the conversation turned to Canada. I told them about my brother, another Maurice, and his family living near Toronto. Also about the strange coincidence of him and André, the Lebels' oldest son, becoming friends at the School of Mines in Golden, Colorado. Eva said she vaguely recalled André talking about an English couple whom he and his wife were friendly with, and he may have mentioned their first names. She also remembered the baby clothes sent by Grace, and even the pram canopy bought in the Tottenham Court Road.

'We were all so close in the 1930s,' she said thoughtfully, 'we could have been members of the same family. Perhaps that helped bring us together with you in some strange way, although I must say I had given up until I saw your name and picture in the *Observer*.'

Eva went back to her story, recalling the time she visited Grace in Princess Beatrice Hospital in Earls Court just after I was born.

'I had difficulty recognising her,' she said, 'she had changed so much. "How am I going to cope with a child?" she asked me despairingly. Poor Grace, she wasn't the type to have children. She couldn't handle all the domestic things like cooking, the housework, and small children. But she loved her job and I suppose that's what she should have stuck to.'

After Maurice was born, Eva remembered Grace telling her how she had felt one day when she went out to buy a birthday cake.

'She said she was pushing Maurice in the pram and you were trailing along behind. "I walked across the road and knew no harm would come to us," she told me. "I felt Jesus Christ was at my side, a presence in a long brown cloak. After that, I remembered nothing. It was a complete blank."'

When we moved to Morden, Grace was admitted to Cane Hill Hospital in Coulsdon. 'A large motherly woman called Phyllis came to look after you,' Eva continued. 'You were very calm with her but cried and became nervous when Grace was around.'

After Grace came out of hospital, she visited Eva at her family home. 'I think it was in the summer of 1939, just before we left for Canada,' Eva said, 'and either you or Maurice was with her. She told me about her experiences in the hospital. The most frightening thing was that she had been coming back through the barrier to sanity, a sort of halfway stage, but the nurses did not understand. One of them hit her with a bunch of keys. There were lighter moments though, even dances from time to time. Grace said that one of the doctors had told her she was a fine dancer. But he also commented on her figure, joking that she was all "bottom and bust". Then came the electric shock treatment, which she was given without an anaesthetic. Grace said it was awful and she never wanted it again.'

Eva reached over and squeezed my hand. It was time for me to leave, but she wasn't finished.

'I have a surprise for you,' she said. She picked up a large buff envelope, opened it, and took out two photographs and an airmail envelope.

'This is a picture Grace took and sent me,' Eva said, picking up the first photograph. Maurice and I, clad in loose woollen swimming trunks with shoulder straps, are standing on a ledge beside a fountain between two unknown young women. I am wearing a white sunhat and we are posing theatrically, our heads turned sideways and tilted upwards. The other photograph was of Grace, her hair tied back, holding me as a baby in a garden in Morden, the town where she had her first experience of life in a mental hospital.

'I was going through some old boxes in the attic before I left,' said Eva, 'and found the photographs. Unfortunately, I couldn't find the one I was really looking for. It was a lovely studio portrait of your mother, taken in the early 1930s before she was married. I think she had several made and sent them to family and friends as Christmas presents.'

She paused.

'But, while I was rooting around, I did find this.'

She held up the airmail envelope with several King George VI stamps on it and handed it to me.

'I received this from your mother in August 1940,' she said. 'I am sure it is the last news I had from her.'

I drove back to London in a strange state of exhilaration and exhaustion. I had been to a place where I had never been before, down a long, dimly lit tunnel to a pre-war city in which I was a small child living with my mother. It was a world that I could not remember but Eva had produced such a powerful narrative that it was not hard to visualise the period and its central character. The experience had been extraordinarily vivid but it was over. The last chapter lay beside me on the car's passenger seat: Grace's final letter to her beloved friend and, in all likelihood, her last word to me.

# 16

THE ADDRESS WAS 30 LONGRIDGE ROAD, EARLS COURT, London, SW5, and the date 27 August 1940. Her first letter had come from her mother's address in Finchley so it seemed clear that she had moved back to Earls Court, where she had spent her teens and met my father. The gap between the two letters was just under three months, during which Maurice had had his third birthday and a dramatic change had taken place in all our lives. The letter was, like the last one, typewritten on thin airmail paper that proved remarkably durable; apart from yellowing a little, the pages remain crisp and strong. It was four and a half pages long and, once again, I believe she had typed it at the office.

She wrote from a besieged city. The German air raids, leading up to the Blitz and the Battle of Britain in the following weeks, were on in earnest. People slept fitfully behind blacked-out windows, in improvised air-raid shelters, and deep under the surface of the earth on cots and wrapped in blankets on the platforms and along the connecting passages of London's Tube stations. The clamour of ambulance and fire engine bells filled the streets, and it only took a few seconds for people to recognise the difference between the anguished wail of the sirens indicating bombers were on their way from the heartening sound of the 'all clear'. At night, searchlights stitched ribbons of bright, clean light across the sky and, when a raid was on, the anti-aircraft guns broke into a frenzy of popping, the shells bursting high above the city like a gigantic Guy Fawkes display. Thirty thousand Londoners would die from the bombing over the next five years but no members of our family, sundered and scattered, would be among them.

Eva, my dear,

I was pleased to hear from you – yours of 12th July. I'm enclosing some snaps of the children, also one including Mother and Olive and a friend taken at the Finchley Open Air Pool one Sunday morning about two months ago.

I was very shocked to hear your hair had turned white. Don't worry so much Eva. I know you are very highly strung. I think I am even more so and, maybe because I've experienced such a lot of private 'blitzkrieg', I've now got this sickening nervous reaction well in hand. I seem to have acquired a new strength. I guess I have now grown up—and out!—although I'm under ten stone [140 pounds] and getting more graceful contours every day. The wear and tear of the daily rush is not conducive to heavy-weight proportions. I really think it's worse for you away from it all—the apprehension of anything is always harder to bear than the actual danger. The raids are certainly 'on'; last night was the longest that we've had in London, from 9.30 pm until 4 o'clock this morning!

Having set the scene, Grace launched into her life since she had last written to Eva, a period that had seen a 'lot of water flowing under my bridge'. The saga began when the brother of her mother's landlord killed himself in the flat above where Lucy, then sixty years old, Grace, and the two of us were living. Another calamity to add to the collapsed ceiling and the fire. The event shook the two women badly and seemed to have produced a cataclysm in Grace's life, or perhaps it was just the tipping point after other disasters. In any case, it led her to the heart of the matter and, for me, to a belief that I was finally closing in on the truth.

Acting under Doctor's orders, I had to make arrangements to get the children away, and also to alter my own life. Contrary to expectations, George was a great help and it has brought us closer together than ever before. I do not mean in a husband-and-wife relationship—nothing will ever do this because we are not of the same aura—but I think that from now and ever afterward we shall be the best of friends. My perspective of everything and everyone is so much broader these days and I have realised just how fundamentally sound George is. I'm not saying that because he has proved himself so good that he is now perfect. But I have realised these past few weeks how different events in people's lives bring out various traits in their characters.

Having complimented my father for something that was not yet clear, she focused on her mother, whom she described as a case. A major crisis had developed over Maurice and me being taken away from her home, a decision that Lucy Islip adamantly opposed.

She thought the children were going away for a holiday and that was fine. I was acting under terrific strain but managed to do all these things as quietly as possible. I beseeched Mother to take a holiday but she was thoroughly obstinate and wouldn't be advised. Therefore, I warned her that I would have to leave and, soon after the children had gone, the next day actually, I thought I could stick it out for the week. But the Doctor said he would have two cases on his hands if I didn't act as I thought I should. Therefore, I left a note for Mother the next morning, saying I was making a change since she wouldn't. I told her I'd be home at the weekend and would write to her.

Grace was adamant about never living with her mother again.

I go home twice a week and tell her all is well (Olive says I ought to be in Parliament!) but that I cannot trust her with any information. Yet if she has patience and faith in me, she will find herself and everyone else much happier in the long run. I am terribly sorry for her but I have found that I must be very firm to be kind. Also, when I saw the children in danger, that gave me the strength of ten and kept me resolved. There's no doubt, is there honey, that when the mother in us is roused, we can fight anything and win through!

What was the 'danger'? Unfortunately, she did not explain. She went on to say that Olive shared her view of their mother, essentially that she was an interfering and disruptive influence in their lives and, between the lines, a fearsome figure. The sisters achieved a catharsis of sorts. 'Olive and I agree that at last we are free from that fear we had of Mother,' Grace concluded.

She turned to her own family, saying that my father had taken a flat and installed a housekeeper, a Belgian widow, 'evidently a very good woman, and the children have taken well to her. This is a great weight off my mind as children do possess that gift of distinguishing the "right" from the "wrong" people.'

All this was happening at one remove. Grace, perhaps sharing a flat with Olive, was in Earls Court, and Maurice and I were with my father and the Belgian widow somewhere else. Grace talked of my father writing to her with news of the new ménage and presumably he put his new address on the letter. Or maybe not. His intentions became clearer as the letter went on. It was evident that Grace was not going to get an invitation to come over and see us any time soon.

At the time of the disturbance, I was all prepared to tell George that I would set up with him again, that we would manage on what little he was earning. When we met, however, he didn't even ask me but told me of his ideas and plans for the future!

Actually, my whole soul rejoiced that it was not to be that we should live together again. I do like and respect him but I was so anxious not to repeat past mistakes, especially after all the hell we went through as a result. My point is that as long as the children are happy, and George is too, I don't mind what I go without, or don't do. However, I am ready to go back and make a good job of it, if present arrangements fail. I will do anything to help. I think if love leads one's actions, no serious trouble will occur.

Poor Grace. She was whistling in the dark, hoping to patch things up and give the marriage another go, being rebuffed, and rationalising that it was for the best as long as everyone else was happy. Not surprisingly, she missed her babies.

'I haven't seen the children for over a month now,' she wrote, indicating our father had taken us away around the end of July.

I think George is a bit scared in case my arrival at the new household will upset the balance. I understand perfectly that he must feel a little—or a lot—apprehensive. After all, he has had enough of women's moods and reactions to last him the rest of his life! Therefore, I've suggested that I meet him with the infants out next Saturday and maybe in time the housekeeper and I will become friends. As George said, he doesn't think it wise for me to expect to enter the flat as a friend in the ordinary sense as people will talk and say what a strange situation.

I did suggest, you see, that I could go over there and help with bathing the children and washing their clothes. I assured him that I would not go in a critical frame of mind, but only with the desire to help and be a friend to all.

I wondered if my father was looking for an excuse to keep her away, or he was genuinely worried about the impression his household might be making. Both, probably. It struck me that 'people', presumably the neighbours, would be chatting away about him anyway. Picture the scene. A middle-aged man, with a foreign name, an accent, and two young children, turns up out of the blue. He is immediately joined by a woman, another foreigner, whom he calls his 'housekeeper'. What's going on here? Who are these foreigners? Where is the kids' mother? Shouldn't the authorities be informed?

Grace obviously believed that the ban on her seeing us was temporary because she confidently wrote:

> While I do intend to take the children out of Mother's life, I shall, in good time, take them to visit her, although I do not intend to divulge their address or my own. She must not be permitted to worry any of us.

This was depressing reading. Behind Grace's rationalisations and hopes, my father's plan was increasingly clear.

'Sometimes, I've just ached for the kids,' Grace wrote.

> But, to be perfectly honest, I do love my job and this sort of life better than being at home all day, especially as George and I are not in love with each other. If that were as it should be, I know I'd enjoy whatever I had to do. Therefore, as we both see it, if the children are happy this way, it is better all round. Also, my temperament, especially when I get depressed, is not the best tonic for the boys and George is far more suited to guide and bring them up.

There was one more paragraph, which I read with growing dread. It was heartfelt, optimistic and, as it transpired, tragic.

> I love the children so much that I will be guided by their happiness. Although I feel very lost at times. I feel I shall always do the best for them, even though to the world I may be pleasing myself. I don't feel as if I've lost them, which shows me, conclusively, that the best has happened. Eventually, George will take them to Seychelles and then I shall be really happy for them. Their education and a good social background will be assured. And somehow, sometime, I'll

go out to them. Anyway, I feel that God has been, and will be, very good to me if I try always to let my heart rule.

I put the letter down and poured myself a whisky. Even when I was most determined to find Grace, or at least to learn her story, I always felt that there was a danger I might discover too much. Wasn't it better to let a mysterious and unhappy past lie undisturbed? Maurice had come to that conclusion and I had heard accounts of others, who having lost a close relative or been adopted, wrestled with the same dilemma. There is no right or wrong answer; either choice, to seek or not to seek, is valid. In the end, I suppose it depends upon temperament, and something subterranean, perhaps genetic, that guides an individual to reconnect or to disengage. In my case, there also seemed to be a curious serendipitous force at play, which became increasingly powerful as the story unfolded.

Her faith in my father intact, Grace ended the letter with a short sentence.

I feel that the children won't be parted from me until they are of an age never to forget.

Poor Grace. She had come to this conclusion after facing adversity in myriad forms. She had to care for two young children while living with an interfering and tyrannical mother on whom she depended for a roof over her head and a baby-minder when she was at work. Her marriage had collapsed. Money was scarce. A man upstairs had committed suicide. She had been in and out of hospital with mental health problems. The war was on in earnest, and bombs were falling.

Yet she seemed to have handled the situation remarkably well. She finally cut the cord with her mother, who had exerted a powerful hold over her and her sister, and reached an amicable arrangement with my father to take us away from her mother's house where we had been in some kind of unspecified danger. (Something worse than the falling ceiling and the fire?) While Grace's first letter had been silent on her health, this one talked frankly of 'depression', a 'private *blitzkrieg*', 'acting under doctor's orders' and 'a sickening nervous reaction'. Yet, she was back at work and had found a new place to live.

Grace's maternal instincts remained strong despite all the upheavals. She loved us deeply and 'ached' for us after we had gone. She not only trusted my father but was colluding with him to keep our new home, wherever it was, secret from her mother. Finally, she took solace in her belief that she would see us regularly wherever we were.

She could not have been more wrong. My father had another plan. For him the break was final. There would be no visits, no correspondence, no photographs, and no contact with any member of the Islip family. He intended to wipe the slate clean. This part of his life—and ours—was over, consigned to oblivion.

Why had he been so brutal? He had got what he wanted, motivated by an understandable concern for our well-being. Did he fear that Grace and her hostile mother would try to kidnap us if he allowed them near us? Or was there something deeper, a personal vendetta about which I knew nothing? Had she been unfaithful, and was this his revenge? Did he have a vindictive, ruthless side to him like some of his Seychelles relatives?

Grace painted a vivid though poignant portrait of herself: an intelligent woman full of life, lucid and rational with strong motherly feelings, and at times jaunty and optimistic, even as she described events that ranged from the tragi-comic to the disastrous. However, reading between the lines, the inescapable impression was of a young mother struggling to keep her sanity against heavy odds while putting on the bravest face possible. Unfortunately, her suffering only foreshadowed a greater tragedy. Far worse lay ahead.

## 17

As I sat there, fiddling with my glass, I realised how miraculous Eva's preservation of these letters had been, just two out of probably many, perfectly bracketing the crisis that changed our lives. Significant gaps in the story remained, but the narrative, with its cast of characters, critical dates, and revealing details, was in place.

My *Observer* friend, now officially my alter ego and he mine, had left for Vietnam and I was free for six months. Where to start? Well, the beginning seemed to be the logical place. I wrote a formal letter to Princess Beatrice Hospital in Earls Court, where I had been born, and received a strange reply from the Medical Records Officer. 'I have had an unsuccessful search to find anything appertaining to your mother,' the official wrote. The tone was sympathetic though, and she asked me to come in with my birth certificate but to 'wring [sic] before coming'.

We set up an appointment and I took the Tube to Earls Court where my parents had lived and first met, and where I had once shared a flat with friends while working at a summer job. On leaving the station, I turned right and walked down Earls Court Road to the junction with the Old Brompton Road where the hospital was located. Known originally as the Queen's Jubilee Hospital, it opened in 1887 to celebrate Queen Victoria's Golden Jubilee. In the early 1930s, a much larger, six-story structure replaced the old building, and was renamed Princess Beatrice Hospital in honour of Queen Victoria's youngest daughter. Grace had been one of the new hospital's early patients. At the reception desk, I asked for the author of the letter and an elderly woman, with her hair tied in a bun and spectacles perched on the end of her nose, appeared. She took my birth certificate and disappeared for a good quarter of an hour. When she returned, she looked perplexed.

'It's most peculiar,' she said apologetically. 'There is no trace of your mother being here. I have looked everywhere but I can't find a single reference to her, and it is not the kind of name that might easily be confused with any other.' She shrugged a little helplessly. 'I really am sorry, but there is nothing else I can do.'

I thanked her, picked up my birth certificate, which stated unequivocally that I had been born to 'Grace Rose de St. Jorre formerly Islip' on 'February 9, 1936', here, in this very building, and left.

As I walked back along Earls Court Road to the Tube station, my thoughts began to follow a conspiratorial path. Had my father taken his campaign to obliterate the existence of his former wife to another level? The cover-up had begun with ensuring there was no trace of her at home, followed by her non-appearance on the family tree, then on to Friern Hospital where she had been officially admitted before vanishing, and now her disappearance from the records of the hospital where she had delivered me? How far had his pain, his hatred, his obsession—whatever it was—taken him?

I stopped for a moment and took a deep breath. Perhaps I was becoming paranoid. There could conceivably be something wrong with my birth certificate although it clearly stated that it was a 'Certified Copy of an Entry of Birth', the standard method of issuing birth certificates in Britain. It was issued by the Kensington Registry Office and it would make sense to check its authenticity. Registry offices, it is said, are where everyone is 'hatched, matched and dispatched', so it seemed to be the right place to go. The office was in Chelsea's Old Town Hall, an imposing structure with a palladium frontage and a large main hall with a vaulted and painted ceiling that was more like a Beaux Arts ballroom than a municipal office building. I went in and explained my quest to an official, showing him my birth certificate. He took it and disappeared down a labyrinth of corridors. When he returned, he said that the certificate was genuine and accurate. It had indeed been issued there, on 7 March 1936 to be precise, but there was no additional information about it or about my mother.

'Your best bet,' he said, 'is to check with the central archives at Somerset House in the Strand. They have everything.'

Before doing that and since I was in Kensington, I decided to pay a visit to the site of Our Lady of Victories Catholic Church, just off Kensington High Street, the church where my father and Grace were married and I was christened. I knew that it had been bombed and gutted during the war and I expected to see a hole in the ground or a new office building in its place. However, when I arrived, I found myself standing in front of a new, modernistic church bearing the same name as the old one.

I entered through the main door. The church appeared to be empty. Leaflets and postcards were laid out on a table near the entrance and I picked up a small brochure describing the church's history. The old church, built in 1869, acted as the temporary cathedral of Westminster until the great neo-Gothic cathedral in Victoria opened in 1903. Then came World War II. 'On a black September night, 13 September 1940, German bombers struck,' the brochure read. 'Four incendiary bombs landed on the roof of the church and, in a short space of two and half hours, it was burned to the ground.' There was no mention of casualties and it ended on a triumphal note. 'The Blessed Sacrament was saved and taken by the priests to the nearby Carmelite Church.'

I sat down in one of the pews and tried to imagine what my parents' wedding had been like back in 1934. Olive and Grace must have been striking in their long gowns and my father had probably looked smart in one of his three-piece, tailor-made suits, his hair neatly parted and brushed back. But what about Lucy Islip? I had forgotten to ask Fernande or Eva about her. She must have been there although she strongly disapproved of the groom and his religion. A stickler for protocol, she would have been formally dressed, probably in old-fashioned clothes, carefully pressed and smelling of mothballs.

I wonder what this stern matriarch, an English Protestant through and through, made of the scene before her? She surely would not have approved any more of the Popish ceremony, with its clanging hand bells, the worship of the host held on high, the incomprehensible Latin prayers, the constant movement of the congregation— standing, sitting, kneeling, and standing again—and the clouds of incense that enveloped her, than she did of her new son-in-law. Did she suspect that the celebration of vows and the elaborate ceremony unfolding in front of her would end badly? And did she do her best to make sure that it did?

I was startled out of my reverie by voices near the side door of the church. A tall, cadaverous, grey-haired man in a priest's clerical collar was talking to a ragged-looking individual who was pleading for some money to buy 'a cup of tea'. The priest remonstrated with him but, finally, put his hand in his pocket. Surprisingly, he had a raucous voice and a strong Cockney accent, similar to that of his supplicant. The man's fist closed on a handful of coins and he scuttled off.

The priest looked up, saw me, and walked over.

'What a character!' he said with a laugh. 'He comes in 'ere moanin' that he's lost his bloomin' parents. He's at least eighty years old! I'm pretty sure he's gone AWOL from the old people's 'ome dahn the road. He's on his way to the nearest pub, you can bet your life.'

The priest introduced himself as Father Cross and I told him that I had lost only one parent. Could he help?

'You're in luck, my friend,' he said. 'All the old registers survived the bombing. One of God's small miracles. Come with me.'

We went into the presbytery and he pulled some ledgers down from a shelf and began turning the pages. He had no difficulty tracing my parents' wedding, as well as my baptism. I couldn't help wondering if my father had slipped up here, wrongly assuming that the records had been destroyed with the original church. I was discovering that once you latch on to a conspiracy theory, for which there is at least some circumstantial evidence, it is hard to let it go.

The details in the ledgers were sparse. The register of marriages simply recorded that George Louis de St. Jorre, bachelor, and Grace Islip, spinster, were married in the church by the Reverend Austin M. Oates on 31 March 1934, in the presence of Jack Cook and Olive Eva Islip. The entry in the baptism register, dated 5 April 1936, as it was inscribed on my dented silver christening cup, was a little more expansive. It provided the names of my godparents: Raymond Deltel, (a Seychelles name), and Isabel C. McDermott. The name of the priest, who performed the ceremony, Father John F. Marriott, was also there.

Father Cross told me that Father Oates was dead but Canon Marriott was still alive and lived in Wembley. He wrote down the address and produced official extracts of the two documents. He made two errors with the witnesses' names in the marriage certificate, which was in English on one side and in Latin on the other. He wrote Jack Cook's last name as 'Coak' and eliminated 'Olive', christening her 'Mara' Eva Islip instead. When I pointed out the mistakes, he laughed loudly, corrected them, and carefully initialled the changes. He picked up a rubber stamp with the church's name on it, pressed it firmly on an inkpad, and stamped the marriage certificate with a flourish. But when he turned to the baptism certificate, his aim was less sure and he almost missed. Another belly laugh. Too much communion wine? A whisky priest in *Kensington*?

He peered at the document closely.

'Isabel McDermott, godmother, eh?' he said. 'Sounds as if she was picked aht o' the crowd and asked to take the job.' He guffawed again and I felt it was time to leave.

Outside, I took a deep breath. The Catholic Church had changed since my school days. Yet, given the randomness of the whole affair, what this curious priest said might not be so outrageous after all. It would not have surprised me if Grace had forgotten to organise a godmother for the ceremony, and someone was hurriedly called up from the congregation to stand beside the baptismal font.

Somerset House is an elegant eighteenth-century building set back from a large cobblestone courtyard. Dozens of people were waiting to use the registries in the main hall. The instructions on the wall had a colour code: red for birth certificates; green for marriage; black for death. I sat down at a table and filled out an application form for a copy of Grace's birth certificate. I handed it, along with my own birth certificate, to an official at the reception desk. After a long wait, an office boy came back with a copy of her certificate, recording her official entry into this world, and returned me my own.

While I knew Grace's date of birth and her parents' names from my reluctant father, having her actual birth certificate in my hands was a new experience. From it, I learned that the Islip family was living in Whitechapel at the time of Grace's birth in April 1907. Grace's father was listed as 'Sergeant, Metropolitan Police' so the family was probably living in police quarters. Whitechapel, in the heart of London's East End, Jack-the-Ripper territory and a rough place.

I remembered Eva said that my grandfather had died when Olive was fourteen and Grace eleven, which made it around 1918. Had he been killed in World War I, or on the mean streets of Cockney London, 'in the line of duty'? I was pretty sure that policemen were not called up so it was unlikely that he had been in the trenches. My paternal grandfather in the Seychelles had also died relatively young but of natural causes, in a peaceful setting. Whatever happened, Lucy was left in the lurch. With no skills or work experience beyond being a housemaid, and with two young daughters to look after, she must have had a hard life.

I looked again at the boards on the wall with its colour codes. The system provided no easy way of cross-referencing the hatching, matching and dispatching stages of life. In short, I could not find out if, or when, Grace had died by using her birth and marriage dates. And trying to check the death registers randomly would have been a hopeless task. When I asked what I should do next, I was told I could make a written application to see the Registrar, which I did and left.

A few days later, I had a call from Somerset House saying my appointment with the Registrar was the following afternoon. When I arrived, the crowd of seekers seemed larger than ever and I sat for a while gazing once more at the colour codes on the big board. Eventually, a clerk took me upstairs to an anteroom and asked me to wait. He picked up a worn brown file, tied with a blue ribbon, and took it into the Registrar's office. A few minutes later, I was summoned and entered a large room with a high, vaulted ceiling. The Registrar motioned to me to sit down opposite his tidy desk.

A man in his mid-fifties, he had sparse grey hair carefully brushed back, apple-red cheeks and thin lips, compressed in a knife-edged line. He was wearing the senior civil servants' unofficial uniform of the day: pink and white striped shirt with a white detachable collar, a striped school, club or military tie, and charcoal grey suit. He looked at me over a pair of gold-rimmed, half-frame glasses.

'What do you want to know?' he said, rustling through the brown file with an almost sensuous pleasure.

'I'm trying to find my mother who disappeared during the war. She is probably dead but I don't know for certain.'

'Why don't you ask your father?'

'He died seven years ago.'

Silence. The old paper crackled as the Registrar rustled it a bit more. I could see long passages of typewritten text.

'Why didn't you ask him before he died?'

I explained: the family silence; the new life with a caring step-mother; and my father's illness and frailty during his last years. But now, I said, I would like more information in order to establish, once and for all, the full story.

'The Official Solicitor represented your mother *ad libitum,*' he said, relishing the Latin phrase, which I did not understand. I failed Latin at school and had to take it again to enter Oxford where I struggled once more with that dead language.

'If your father did not tell you,' the Registrar continued, 'he must have had a very good reason for not doing so. That is quite proper and sufficient cause, in my view, for not giving you any more information.' He paused, lips compressed. 'Why do you want to know anyway?'

Patiently, but with growing anger, I told him that my mother's life had always been a mystery. I wanted to know what happened between her and my father and why she had been separated from my brother and myself when we were very young.

'Surely, as one of the children of this marriage I have the right to know?' I said. 'My brother and I are the only surviving members of the family. And she was, after all, my *mother.*'

The Registrar smoothed the pages. He didn't seem to be looking for anything in particular. Perhaps he was playing for time. Perhaps he was just playing. Or, maybe, he simply liked the feel and sound of the yellowing paper.

'I would like to see those documents,' I said firmly.

Silence.

'Do they belong to the government or my family?'

'I can tell you nothing more than the grounds for the divorce,' he replied at last. 'Your mother was found to be "incurably of unsound mind" and had been continuously under care and treatment for a period of at least five years.'

He raised his head and peered at me over his half-frames.

'You may bespeak a copy of the decree nisi, which contains this information. I suggest you check with the hospital in Barnet.' He closed the file. 'You can apply to the Official Solicitor for more information. But I doubt whether he will tell you anything more than I have.'

His lips tightened into an almost invisible line as he closed the file and tied it up with the blue ribbon. I stood up. The desire to smash my fist into his smug bureaucrat's face, and grab the file, almost overwhelmed me.

On the way out, a messenger accompanied me, carrying the file.

'I can drop it off for you,' I said casually. 'I'll be passing the records office on the way out.'

He hesitated. 'Thanks, mate,' he said, 'but it's against the rules.'

Before leaving the building, I filled in a form to 'bespeak' a copy of the divorce document and it arrived at my flat three days later.

My parents' divorce was filed in the High Court of Justice (Probate, Divorce, and Admiralty Division) before the Right Honourable Sir Henry Barnard, Knight, sitting at the Royal Courts of Justice, Strand, in the County of Middlesex, on 18 March 1947. The petitioner was my father and the respondent my mother, represented by her guardian, the Official Solicitor. The respondent filed on the question of maintenance and costs but otherwise did not defend the suit.

The judge found that the petitioner had 'sufficiently proved the contents of the said Petition' and ordered the marriage 'to be dissolved by reason that the said Respondent is incurably of unsound mind and has been continuously under care and treatment for a period of at least five years immediately preceding the presentation of the petition.'

That meant Grace had been in a mental hospital at least since March 1942 when Maurice and I were already with the Linder sisters. The decree became absolute on 31 December 1947, giving my father and Edith the long-awaited green light to get married, which they did three days later.

A lengthy, handwritten note at the end dealt with the custody of Maurice and me, costs, and maintenance. At my father's request, we were placed in his custody 'until further order of the Court' and it was 'directed that such children be not removed out of the jurisdiction of the Court without its sanction.' My father was ordered to make Grace an allowance for maintenance of nineteen pounds, seventeen shillings and sixpence per annum. Out of this princely sum, seven shillings and sixpence would go to the Official Solicitor 'as the cost of an official visit to the Respondent;' six pounds, ten shillings would go to the Medical Superintendent of Friern Hospital, New Southgate, London, N11, or to the superintendent of any hospital where Grace might be, for the 'provision of extra comforts for the Respondent'; and the balance would go to the 'Public Assistance Committee for the costs of the maintenance of the Respondent.'

I still wanted to get my hands on that file with the blue ribbon. It seemed incredible that in modern Britain, a citizen, almost forty years old, was not allowed to see the official record of his own parents' divorce. But if that was Kafkaesque, the legal reasoning, as explained to me by a lawyer friend, was pure *Catch 22*.

The law stated, he said, that access to such a file could only be granted if the parties to the divorce gave their permission. Fine. But my father was dead and Grace might be, too. If she were alive, she could, hypothetically, grant it. But since Grace was deemed to be 'mentally incapacitated', permission rested with her 'guardian', our old friend the Official Solicitor. He would only do so if he decided it was 'to her benefit'. Since he was the sole judge of what was beneficial for Grace and what was not, he had complete control over the situation. That meant, my friend concluded, the chances of reading the file were zero.

# 18

For the next couple of weeks, I was busy working with a friend on an idea for a political thriller set in Northern Ireland. The province was in turmoil with riots, bombings, and assassinations as the Protestants and the Catholics went at each other's throats. It was good to have a new project and not to think about where to go with Grace and her story. The blank wall I had encountered at Somerset House was disheartening and made the search more difficult because I was hoping to find the names of new people in the documents, especially relatives or friends, who might be able to help. The conspiracy theory whispered insidiously in my ear once more. Were my father's fingerprints on the documents in that brown file, with its blue ribbon, as they seem to have been elsewhere? Had he left specific instructions preventing his children from gaining access to the details of his divorce? Was that implicit in the Registrar's guarded comment that my father 'must have had a very good reason' for not revealing the truth. (Cousin Fernande, curiously, had used exactly the same words.) While I had learned a great deal, I was still a long way from knowing the whole story.

Brian, my co-writer, and I presented our proposal to a publisher and, to our surprise, received a commission and a modest advance to write the novel. We celebrated with a boozy lunch at Rules restaurant on the Strand, bought a couple of gorgeous velvet fedoras at Herbert Johnson, the hat shop in Bond Street—forest green for him, magenta for me—and booked our trip to Ireland. We agreed to split the research; he would go to the North, and I would head for the Republic. Before we parted, we did the easy part, coming up with a title for the unresearched, unwritten novel. There it lay, pristine and, to our giddy minds, immensely evocative, at the head of a blank page: *The Patriot Game*. It came from a song of that name we had heard on a collection of Irish nationalist ballads. Dominic Behan, brother of the playwright, Brendan, wrote it, and we both liked it.

Our publisher was eager to put the book out as soon as possible so, after returning from our research forays in Ireland, we decided to go to my house in Mallorca and hammer it out down there away from London's distractions. I called Edith and said I would come up to Scotland for a brief visit before going to Spain. She didn't sound at all happy at the prospect of me writing another book, and wondered aloud how working only half a year for the *Observer* would affect my pension. I did not know the answer, nor had even thought about it, so I let that one slide.

It was calming to be back in Scotland and we enjoyed our simple routine of day trips, meals with Edith's friends, and quiet evenings of television and Scrabble. I never stayed long but sometimes I would bring work with me and do it on the dining room table overlooking the garden, the meadow, and the bubbling burn. We had slipped into a comfortable, semi-intimate relationship. For me, it wasn't quite 'mother-and-son' as I imagined it, but it wasn't a cool, formal 'stepmother-stepson' affair either. I suppose it was somewhere in-between, which left room for Grace, whether I found her or not.

The day after I arrived, Edith said she would like to drive over to Alnwick in Northumberland where she had begun her teaching career at the Duchess School. We set off through the verdant border country, past Hadrian's Wall, still a recognisable barrier after eighteen centuries of battering from the weather and pillage, and started searching for the school. It derived its name from the Duchess of Northumberland who had established it in 1808 as a school for indigent girls. During its long life, it had had moved several times. It took some finding but when we finally arrived, Edith said she didn't recognise it at all. It was not surprising because it had changed from being the small exclusive girls' private school it had been in Edith's time to a large co-educational secondary establishment, retaining nothing of the school Edith knew, except the name. After lunch in a country inn, we drove around the town, and she pointed out the house that she had shared with two other young teachers in the 1920s.

Back home that evening, she prepared a simple supper and we settled down in the living room, she with a cup of tea and me with a glass of malt whisky, Angus's latest recommendation, and a cigar. Edith had become addicted to watching snooker competitions on television but, on this particular evening, she suggested a game of Scrabble and pulled out the old, worn board on which we had played countless games going back to our time in Singapore. When the game was over, instead of going straight to bed as she normally did, she lingered, her mind still on her youth.

'The world has changed so much,' she said. 'I didn't really want to be a teacher and nowadays there is so much more opportunity for young women.'

'Was it that bad?'

'Not really, I actually enjoyed the girls' company and I made some good friends among the staff, but I always wanted to get married and have a family.'

I sensed an opening. 'When did you first meet Dad?' I asked cautiously.

'During the war,' she said readily enough. 'We were both staying in Scotland House in Buckhurst Hill. It was a boarding house not far from the High Street. Do you remember it?'

I shook my head.

'You boys were with the Linders by then and Dad told me they were elderly and he would soon have to find someone else to look after you. He was still working as a salesman and was travelling a lot. He really didn't know what to do.'

'When was that?'

'I'm not sure but it was probably late 1942 or early 1943. Anyway, I suggested he ask the local priest for his advice and he did. The priest recommended St. Dominic's Priory. I don't know if it really was the right decision but Dad was desperate and the war complicated everything. I remember how relieved he was. He thought it was fine because it was out in the countryside and safer than London. He was also pleased that the school was run by a Catholic order, which is the way he had been brought up in the Seychelles.'

'I was always grateful that you rescued us from the nuns,' I said smiling. 'But I never knew how we got there in the first place.'

'I don't think there was much of an alternative at the time. And you and Maurice didn't come out of it too badly.'

Not on the surface, I thought, but underneath? Four years in a grim place like that with no mother, and virtually no father. Who knew what the psychological cost had been?

Edith said no more on that occasion and I had learned not to push her. Once again, I felt the well was dry and, once again, I was wrong.

How wrong I discovered a week later after I opened up the house in Mallorca and walked down to the post office-barber shop in the village. There, among the usual clutter, was a letter from Edith. Strange, I thought, she didn't normally write until she had heard from me and knew I had arrived. I went back to the house where Brian had set up his typewriter and was reading through his notes. It was time to work, so I left the letter until the evening.

As the sun was going down, the long dust-flecked rays turning the mountain red and gold, and the warmth of the day lingering in the stone walls, I took a glass of *pastis* out on to the terrace, and opened the letter. Edith began by saying how much she had enjoyed our recent time together and how our trip to Alnwick had triggered 'a lot of youthful memories, mostly happy ones.' Then came something entirely different.

The following, John, is what Dad told me, which I have kept to myself ever since, but I will tell you now.

When I met Dad he was very, very down. You and Maurice were with Miss Linder and Dad, as I mentioned, was in Scotland House, in order to be near you. His flat had been bombed and his job was just about folding up. Captain Will [an old seafaring friend of my father] advised him to apply to the War Office, which he did.

Eventually, he told me about Grace. He was in digs next door to her people in Earls Court and that's how they first met. Grace's father was in the police and her mother was a Tartar!

I think they were married in 1934 or 1935. On their wedding night, Grace told Dad that she had only married him for security, which was a bad start to any marriage. It was all over when Maurice was just a baby. Grace did not want children and it was Hilda Whiteley [the wife of another shipmate] who told me that Dad looked after you and Maurice.

You made me think. Dad had so few personal possessions. I may have told you that he burnt or destroyed all the photographs and papers he had concerning Grace, including his divorce certificate. He used to tear up and burn letters after he had answered them.

He loved his garden and his home, and although he went back to the Seychelles twice, he said that he would not want to settle there for their outlook was so narrow.

Hilda and Cecil Whiteley knew Grace. Cecil is dead but Hilda is probably still alive and might be able to tell you where they lived and even where and when they were married. She can tell you much more than Fernande Cook ever knew. I am sorry I cannot be of more help, John, but write to Hilda.

I put down the letter and stared out over the valley to the great mountain rim that encircled the village. The sun had disappeared behind the rocky wall and the air was full of the scent of jasmine from the vine that hung down from the pergola over my head. I had misjudged Edith and I wasn't sure why she was telling me all this now. While I already knew some of it, the story of Grace and my father on their wedding night came as a shock. Would Grace really have said something like that? Would any woman, whatever she felt, say it? But, if she hadn't, would my father have made it up?

Whatever the truth, the marriage appeared to have overcome this disastrous start. Before I left London, a package from the Seychelles arrived. It was from my cousin, Maryse, the daughter of my Uncle Henri and Aunt Alice, with whom I had had dinner during my visit to the islands. Maryse had been in Switzerland at the time but now she was back because her parents had recently died. Among their papers, she found a bundle of letters written by my father to her father in the 1930s. Some were in English, others in French, and they were mostly about the plantation, its management—or rather mismanagement—family feuds, and the price of copra, cinnamon oil, vanilla, and patchouli. But one paragraph, in plain English, jumped out.

'Married life is very nice,' my father wrote. 'But the great drawback is the mother-in-law. I have already had a few words and told her straight to mind her own business. These damned people cause more trouble in family affairs than ten thousand strangers put together. At the very outset, I put my foot down and told her that if she had nothing better to do than try to cause trouble, she better stop at her own home, and that I was big enough to look after mine; so we have peace and quietness now.'

There was no date on the letter but I guessed it was early in the marriage before I was born, which would make it 1934 or 1935.

The only other letter in the bundle that had any personal information in it was another one in English and dated December 1930. It shed light on something Fernande had told me.

'I had to break my engagement,' my father confided to his brother. 'The reason was obvious, and it was rather a hard blow for me. Still, I pat myself on the shoulder for having been able to find out things in time, otherwise my life would have been hell on earth.'

What had he found out? Was it the American or the English woman, or somebody else? Fernande thought the engagement was probably to the American but knew nothing more. The mystery remained but I liked the image of him patting himself on his shoulder, physically easier and perhaps more logical than the idiomatic 'patting myself on the back' and an infrequent example of him tripping up over the English language.

I wrote back to Edith, thanking her for her frankness and said I would love to talk more about it all when I next visited her in Scotland. Meanwhile, Brian and I worked steadily on our book, writing alternate chapters and swapping them for comments and rewriting.

We had developed a clear plot outline and the writing and critiquing system seemed to work well. We were fully aware that we were not producing anything of literary value. It was a formula thriller and its highest aspiration was to have readers turn the pages as rapidly as possible. The fact that Brian's last name happened to be 'Shakespeare' was a mixed blessing. But we felt that the combination of our unusual names on the cover, underneath the catchy title, would stop book browsers in their tracks. It was the 1970s, we were still young, and our optimism knew no bounds.

One morning, Brian received a message from London saying that he needed to return as soon as possible to attend to a family matter. We had enough copy to show our publisher to keep him off our backs, so we cut our Spanish stay short and drove back to England.

I had written to Hilda Whiteley from Mallorca and a letter from her was waiting for me at my London flat. Her response was gracious and down-to-earth. She said she wasn't sure how much she could help me but she remembered Maurice and me as small boys, and would do all she could. She invited me to come down to her home in Worthing, not far from Brighton, on the south coast.

I had known the Whiteleys during my childhood but lost track of them as I grew up. Cecil, I recalled, was a lively, gregarious man who had been my father's best friend at sea and died two years after he did. Hilda was eighty years old, a compact, silver-haired woman with a no-nonsense manner who greeted me at the door of a house remarkably similar to Joan Cooper's in Bournemouth.

Hilda lived alone, she said, but often saw her children and grand-children and had adapted to her widowhood. She took me into her living room and we sat down opposite each other.

'I remember first meeting Grace when she and George came to tea with us just after they were engaged,' she began. 'Grace was wearing a pretty frock. She was a lively and vivacious person with lovely golden hair. She also struck me as being very clever. But they were not compatible, George didn't understand her.'

The Whiteleys saw a lot of us after we moved to Morden in south London because they were living in Wimbledon, not far away. Their house was close to the public baths and we must have gone there because I could still remember the smell of chlorine, the damp heat, and the shouts of the children in the swimming pool.

'Grace was not well at that time,' Hilda continued. 'One evening, George called me and I went over. It must have been around six o'clock. Grace was in bed, very tired, and didn't seem to know what was going on around her. You and Maurice were asleep. I stayed with her for the next four hours while George went up to Finchley to get Granny Islip.'

After the marriage collapsed, the Whiteleys stayed in touch with my father and Edith but lost track of Grace and her family.

'When I knew you were coming, I began to look around and found an old address book from the late 1930s,' Hilda said, holding up a small brown book. 'There's only one Islip in it, someone called Edith, but for the life of me I can't think who it might be.'

The address was in Chiswick in west London. I made a note of it and the telephone number, thanked Hilda for her help, and drove back to London. Back in my flat, I checked to see if Edith Islip had been on my original list of London Islips, culled from the telephone directory, but she was not among them.

That evening I had a call from Edith in Scotland. She said she was having some legal difficulties with the construction company that had built her Scottish bungalow and asked if I would go up and help her sort it out. When I arrived, her lawyer set up a meeting with the builder and promised to find a resolution that would ease Edith's concerns. I didn't really do much but I think Edith needed reassurance and perhaps a male presence. I said I couldn't stay long because I had to get back to London. On my last evening, we had a quiet supper and settled down in front of the fire in the living room.

I thanked her once again for her letter to me in Spain and told her about my visit to Hilda Whiteley who sent her regards.

'They were closer to your father and Grace than anyone else I know,' Edith said. 'I am glad Hilda could help you.'

She fell silent, staring into the fire. When she began talking again, it was almost as if she were talking to herself.

'My first sight of George,' she said, 'was him walking down the road in the pouring rain to Scotland House. You and Maurice were on either side of him, tucked in under his raincoat like ducklings under their mother's wings. Maurice had on a pair of strange home-made flannel shorts, which came down to his knees.

'After George left the sea in 1929, he had a hard time. He went down several notches to become a salesman, the only job he could get. He was not very good at it, had little money, poor prospects, and then made a bad marriage.'

Grace's mother was against the marriage from the very beginning, Edith continued, but they went ahead anyway.

'They spent their honeymoon on the south coast but returned to London after only one night,' she continued. 'That was after

Grace had told George that she'd only married him for security, not love.'

'Surely a woman wouldn't tell her husband that on their wedding night, even if it were true?'

'I really don't know. That's what George told me. The marriage bumped along for a while but began to fall apart just before the war started. There was a rumour that Grace had a lover around that time...'

'Did Dad say that?'

'Yes, but he never went into any details. He also told me that Grace had treated you boys badly...'

'Badly? How?'

'He said that she was irresponsible and would leave you on your own. You were little children and he feared for your safety.'

'I've heard she had some form of mental illness. Did he say anything about that?'

'No, he just said he was away a lot and couldn't trust her. Anyway, by the time I met him, he had left her and taken you and Maurice with him. He got that job at the War Office, as a marine inspector, and kept it until he retired. During the war, he was travelling all the time. You were sent off to live with the Linders whom he had met when he was a salesman.'

Edith paused. 'Grace had a sister, Olive, who was a teacher and very bright. George told me she became a bit gaga after she retired and died in the early 1960s.'

'How did he know? I thought he cut all ties with the Islips.'

'He stayed friendly with Stanley Belcham, who knew the Islip family, and could have been a relative. I suppose Dad heard it from him.'

I told Edith I had looked for Stanley Belcham but without success. Olive's death was a setback but not a surprise. She was older than Grace, and it had always struck me that the chance of finding both sisters alive was highly unlikely.

'Your father tried to obliterate his past,' Edith continued. 'We got married in a registry office in Leyton [east London], and he felt guilty about having committed a sin by going through a divorce.'

'A *mortal* sin,' I said, 'the kind that sends you to hell.'

'It's not something I understood, but it affected him.'

Edith, as a Presbyterian Scot, viewed the Catholic Church with deep suspicion. She never talked about it but it was part of her upbringing and she revealed her wariness in oblique ways. She also had an ingrained distrust of Jews although, when I once confronted her about some derogatory remark she had made about a Jewish friend of mine at school, she strongly denied that she was anti-Semitic.

'Dad never told anybody that he and I were married in a registry office,' Edith continued. 'And he never talked about your births or your early lives. It was as if you did not exist until after he had left your mother. George never made it clear that I was his second wife and your stepmother. I know this was confusing for you, but it was also confusing for me.'

Maurice and I not 'existing' until the break with our mother, hit home. That was exactly how I had felt for most of my life but this was the first time anyone so close to my father had actually put it into words. It was, paradoxically, chilling and cleansing.

Edith was not finished.

'Your father seemed incapable of forgiving Grace for whatever wrongs, real or imagined, she had done to him,' she said. 'Then, after his first stroke, he used to sit in his armchair, endlessly saying his rosary. He was an unforgiving man.'

# 19

ON THE DRIVE BACK TO LONDON, IT STRUCK ME HOW REMARK-
able Edith's revelations had been. I had always felt that she did not
approve of my search for Grace but was too diplomatic to say so.
I am sure she understood the logic of a son wanting to trace his
biological mother, but it was natural for her to feel upset because
she had worked so hard to replace a woman who had gone missing
long ago, a disappearing act that she had nothing to do with. Like
most people, she wanted to be part of a family and have the comfort
it provided in old age. Something, however, must have changed
for her to open up and tell me what she knew, secrets that she had
kept to herself for so long. Had she hoped that I would change
my mind, and all she had to do was wait, but then realised I was
serious about the search? Or, did she simply need time to adjust to
the possibility of a rival? Whatever motivated her, she had given
me new insights to my father's character and provided important
leads to other sources and, for that, I was grateful.

None of this had happened easily or quickly. Edith, like my
other informants, still all women, had taken her time. I had yet to
find a man who knew anything about what had happened and, as it
transpired, I never did. The slow release of information was another
curious phenomenon, as if the truth, even from those people eager
to help, were too toxic to be released in large quantities. Everyone
who had known my father and mother seemed to feel the need to
ponder before disinterring their memories and passing them on to
me. The flow was neither rapid nor constant. It came out like liquid
from a bottle with a narrow neck, drop by drop. Perhaps I was not
the only one finding it difficult to deal with the past. It never quite

let you go, but you had to make a sustained effort to draw it out. The reward, if you persevered, was the lifting of another veil.

When I arrived at my flat, I called the Chiswick telephone number that Hilda Whiteley had given me for Edith Islip. As it rang, I wondered if it was a good omen that her names linked my stepmother and my mother. A woman picked up. I explained briefly who I was and why I was calling. Silence. I waited. Nothing. Had we been cut off?

'You're Grace's son?' she exclaimed at last. 'Oh my goodness! I can't believe it. I'm her cousin.'

It was my turn to remain silent. My throat felt constricted. A living relative at last.

'I am in Notting Hill Gate,' I said. 'Can I come over and see you?'

'Notting Hill Gate, that's strange… your mother used to live there. Of course you can. You can come now if you want.'

I put the phone down and drove over to Chiswick as fast as I could. Edith Islip's home was in a row of late-Victorian terraced houses of weathered red brick with narrow windows. It was one of those quiet, tree-lined streets with no building over two-stories in height, a reminder of a London originally composed of villages that became incorporated, and sometimes absorbed beyond recognition into the maw of the ever-expanding metropolis. This quiet corner of Chiswick had successfully resisted.

A small, thin, neatly dressed woman opened the door and looked at me curiously, as well she might. She put out her hand and introduced herself as 'Bill', a nickname from her childhood, she said. She went off to make some tea, leaving me sitting beside an old-fashioned coal fire watched by Kim, a suspicious pug, and by a large number of Islips, captured in a faded photograph on the mantelpiece. They were in Edwardian dress and having a picnic in a park. Edith Islip returned with the tea and settled down by the fire. Kim immediately jumped on to her lap, gave me a baleful stare, and fell asleep.

She explained that the house had belonged to the family from the time it was built in 1890. She worked for the Inland Revenue—'but don't let that put you off'—and was nearing retirement. Looking at the photograph on the mantelpiece, she said the Islips came from Lincolnshire in central England. Her paternal grandfather, Broome Islip, and his wife, Caroline, had a typically large Victorian family, six boys and three girls. Her father, Cuthbert, was one of the sons and moved to London where he married and had three children—Percy, Marjorie and herself. Charles Islip, my grandfather, was Cuthbert's older brother, 'Uncle Charlie' to Bill and her siblings. The brothers were close and the two families spent a lot of time with each other. Olive and Grace were older than their cousins, but they all got on well.

I told her about my own past and how I had obtained her name and address from the widow of one of my father's old seafaring friends. She listened intently and asked me how much I knew about my mother and her family. Very little, until recently, I told her.

'Grace was a lovely girl, so lively, full of fun, and mischievous,' Bill said. 'She had long golden hair, straight and often plaited, so long that it came down to her bottom. She and Olive had a reputation for unconventionality. At one time, they took to Greek dancing and I saw a photograph of them both in Greek costumes. It's an odd coincidence that you are now living in Notting Hill Gate because that's where I remember having our best times with the girls. Uncle Charlie, their father, was in charge of the police station and they lived in police quarters. One Sunday, we all went over there in a pony and trap. When we arrived, Grace's guinea pigs were running all over the basement. Olive was more aloof, more serious than her younger sister.'

'What was their father like?'

'He was a big, strong, good-looking man,' Bill continued. 'We saw him often, both in uniform and relaxing at home. He was full of fun and we children loved him. Aunty Lucy, on the other hand, was an unpredictable, possessive woman. She put the wind up me, and Olive and Grace were scared of her too. There may have been mischief in that family but no rebellion.'

World War I took its toll on both families. Percy, Bill's only brother, died of wounds on the Western Front. My grandfather, as a policeman, was never called up and survived the bombing of London and the dangers inherent in his job. But he had no defence against the great influenza epidemic that swept through Europe and beyond at the end of the war, killing millions of people. He was an early victim.

'Grace was about eleven years old when he died,' Bill said. 'She adored him and his death affected her terribly.

'We were all a bit surprised when Grace married George because he was considerably older,' she continued. 'Some members of the family weren't happy about Grace marrying a Catholic. Olive also went off with a Catholic, too, but that was later on.'

She paused, as if uncertain of the right words.

'I felt a lot of sympathy for your father,' she said slowly. 'There was mental instability on Lucy's side of the family—a sister, I think—and he was never told about it. When he heard later, he was very angry.

'When Grace became ill, Lucy wanted to look after you and Maurice but Grace refused. She was really at fault and George did the right thing taking you away. During the war, I lost track of Grace and Olive but, quite some time ago, someone in the family told me that Grace was in hospital in East Kent. She had become very violent—throwing things around and threatening suicide. But she was much calmer after the operation...'

'The operation?'

'The frontal lobotomy,' Bill said matter-of-factly, 'That's how they treated violent schizophrenics in the 1940s and 1950s. I don't suppose they do it now.'

She paused, looking at me intently. 'I'm sorry, I didn't realise you hadn't heard about it.'

'No, I hadn't,' I said. 'Do you know if she's still alive?'

She paused again, stroking the somnolent Kim.

'I heard nothing more after the operation. I have a feeling that she died some time ago. But Olive will know...'

'Olive! I thought she was dead.'

'No, no... Faith, another cousin who lives in Peterborough, is in touch with her. Olive lived with someone who was in the antique business, I think, but he died. They lived in Kent where she still is.'

'How can I contact her?'

'I'll write to Faith. She doesn't have a telephone but she will know Olive's address and, if you give me your number, I'll call you as soon as I hear from Faith.'

Bill lifted Kim gently off her lap and placed him on a rug in front of the fire. We said goodbye at the door.

'You know, it's strange,' she said, 'Faith told me that Olive has also been delving into the family's past.' She looked up at me. 'I wonder if she knows as much about you as you do about her.'

Back in my flat, I felt drained and depressed. I had been concentrating so much on gathering information and following leads that I had not really thought much about who, what, I might find at the end of the road. Like a news story, the pursuit had taken over, leaving the emotions becalmed, as the adrenalin flowed and the focus narrowed with each new discovery. I did not really fully understand what a lobotomy was but I knew that it was radical brain surgery, and that was enough.

I wasn't looking forward to moping around waiting for Edith Islip's call and it was hard to concentrate on work or anything else. However, providentially, the *Observer* intervened. I had a call from the foreign editor saying he knew that I was 'off', but would I be up for a quick story in Sweden?

'Count Carl Gustav von Rosen, of Biafra fame, is back home,' he said. 'We would like to do a profile on him and I can't imagine a better person than you to do it.' (Flattery, I thought, will get you everywhere.) 'He lives in Malmo. A couple of days over there should do it.'

The next day, I flew to Malmo in southern Sweden and contacted the count who invited me out to his country estate. I had written extensively about him and his exploits in the *Observer* and in my history of the Nigerian-Biafran war, but had never met him. He opened the door and greeted me cordially. He was older than I expected, over sixty and a grandfather, with greying hair and deep-sunken blue eyes, certainly not the swashbuckling, dashing fighter pilot I had in mind.

Yet his life was the stuff of legend. His ancestors included crusading Knights Templar, fighters for Greek freedom, and Africa explorers. He went to—and was expelled from—Sweden's equivalent of Eton College, taught himself to fly, and once broke the world record for the longest single flight in a small plane. He flew missions for guerrillas in western Ethiopia during the Italian invasion, fought for the Finns against the Russians in World War II, flew in relief supplies to the smouldering Warsaw ghetto, and, during the recent conflict in West Africa, knocked out half the jet-studded Nigerian air force with the aeronautical equivalent of an Austin Mini.

We sat down and he explained in detail how he had started flying in relief supplies to Biafra. But he soon realised that the embattled country had no effective way of combating the Nigerian air force, which was equipped with Russian MiG fighters and Ilyushin bombers, flown by Egyptian and other foreign pilots. He arranged for the purchase of five small civilian single-engine SAAB MFI-9B trainers. He collected a group of pilot friends, painted the planes in camouflage colours, and fitted them with French-made Matra rockets. Leading this tiny squadron, dubbed the 'Babes of Biafra', von Rosen struck at Nigerian airfields flying in low and fast with devastating effect.

While many Nigerian fighters and bombers were destroyed on the ground and Biafran morale soared, von Rosen's daring raids did not change the course of the war. A year later, Biafra collapsed and was reabsorbed into Nigeria. Von Rosen, along with other foreigners who fought on both sides, was criticised for inserting himself into an African conflict. But he remained unrepentant.

'In the end,' he said, 'if you are an honest man and went to fight for Finland because it was close to your own country and because they were white people, there is no excuse for backing out of a similar situation because it is farther away and because the people are black.'

I had what I needed and flew back to London on a dark, wet February morning. As I climbed the stairs to my flat, I heard the telephone ringing. I ran in and picked it up. The caller announced it was the 'Inland Revenue on the line'. I stiffened but another voice came on.

'John, it's Bill Islip. I've been trying to get hold of you.'

She was excited, so excited that her tongue slipped for a second.

'I've had a letter from Grace—I mean, Faith,' she stammered. 'Olive is in Chatham in Kent—I have her address—her married name is Anderson and she is living there with her husband.'

She paused for breath.

'Grace is *alive*! She's in a mental hospital near St. Albans in Hertfordshire. Faith saw her three years ago but Grace didn't recognise her. Faith says she isn't always in control of her faculties but comes out of hospital occasionally to stay with Olive. Faith says please contact Olive first before going to see your mother.'

I scribbled down Olive's address—81 Chestnut Avenue, Walderslade, Chatham, Kent; no telephone number—and mumbled my thanks. Grace dead one moment. Grace alive the next. But Grace half alive? Did I really want to meet this brain-damaged woman who 'was not always in control of her faculties', yet who was my mother?

BUT OLIVE WAS WAITING, SOMETHING HAD TO BE DONE. I immediately wrote to her and explained how I had found her, and hoped that my sudden appearance would not be too much of a shock. I added that I felt I already knew her quite well through photographs and talking to relatives and friends. Could I come down to Chatham to see her?

She wrote back immediately.

Oh John!

I can hardly keep my hand steady this morning. I've just had a letter from Faith enclosing Edith Islip's letter with masses of information about you. You were four and Maurice three when I last saw you both so naturally I am overwhelmed at this astonishing resurrection.

DO come soon. I've so much to say that it'll take me years to unburden! Bill and I would love to see you. Come for the day and then after that, come and stay whenever and for however long you please.

I've known about you since your first article for the *Observer* about Aden. I read your Biafran book—not for Biafra's sake, but yours, trying to find glimpses of your life in it. I've never said a word to Grace in case I upset her, or was the means of upsetting your life if she tried to get in contact with you.

One of the most interesting aspects is this family tree infatuation. I read a book called 'Tracing Your Ancestors' and was filled with enthusiasm. I still am! Hope I can fill in some gaps for you. I can tell you lots about Charles Victor Islip. I can tell you lots about you. Maurice too!

Hurry up, John, get here soon. We're not on the phone but if you're pushed for time a telegram will be O.K. If that's too expensive, I'll wait for a letter.

I've never ended a letter with the word aunt—but here goes.

Your devoted and long suffering Aunt Olive (Anderson).

On Sunday, February 9th, which happened to be my thirty-ninth birthday, I left my flat in Notting Hill early in the morning and drove across London. I rarely look at horoscopes but, by chance, I had seen one in the *Evening Standard* the day before. About Sunday's birthdays, it said: 'Security that much more assured... there's a happy reunion with someone you'd lost touch with.' It was the right idea although too simple a thought to describe what was happening. Thirty-five years of separation—virtually two generations in the passage of time—and my transition from a small child to a man on the cusp of middle-age, made it more like a first meeting than a reunion. With Olive, it sounded as if it was going to be a joyous affair. But what about Grace? How would she feel, in her impaired state, about being reunited with her oldest son? Would it really be a 'happy reunion'?

It was a smoky winter's day, the sun somewhere behind the mist, as I drove across a tranquil Hyde Park where the daffodils were beginning to bloom. Clear of the sprawl of south London, a resurgent sun that would have pleased William Turner was breathing colour into the brown fields and dark woods of the North Downs. Kent used to be called the 'garden of England' and, as I drove up the long chalky incline that takes you to the top of the Downs, the landscape recalled the county's rural past.

Olive's house, a small bungalow standing amid an untidy garden, was in Walderslade, a modern suburb of Chatham, once a great naval base and now a backwater.

As I parked, I saw two faces at the front window. Olive stepped out, followed by her husband, Bill Anderson. She was short, a little stout, with a head of fine white hair that framed a rather square, attractive face. She did not look her seventy years, and, as she came towards me, she suddenly stopped, spread her arms in a theatrical gesture, and danced a little jig.

We embraced and held each other for a long time. She stepped back and looked me up and down while I stood there, feeling slightly foolish, grinning. She wasn't tearful just very, very excited. She took a long breath and introduced me to her husband Bill, who had been bobbing around behind her.

Bill was an Irishman, a Catholic from Belfast, and had come over to England at the age of twenty. He worked with greyhounds and spent most of his life at the racetrack, a betting man until the day he died but, fortunately, not a drinking one. A simple story yet, like much else in this tale, not as simple as it seemed.

The house was small—three rooms, bathroom and kitchen—and a bit shabby. Olive, it transpired, had many interests but houses and gardens were not high on the list, although she liked cooking, especially the not-always-successful experimental kind, and she enjoyed her food. Money was tight but she and Bill got by on their state pensions, supplemented by Olive's small teacher's pension. The good news, she told me, was that she had just finished paying off the mortgage on the house, which she had bought in the early 1960s.

We had lunch in what doubled as a dining room and spare bedroom in the front of the house. As we sat down, I had a strange feeling. Was Olive really my aunt? Or had there been some terrible mistake? Was I acting out a sinister charade with a couple of elderly impostors from a Hitchcock film? True, this stranger's name was Olive, but Olive *Anderson*. She did vaguely look like the person I had seen in snapshots from the 1930s. But those photographs were taken forty years ago.

The floodgates opened and Olive began to talk. I picked up my knife and fork then stopped, staring down at them. They felt and looked familiar. They were silver-plated and had 'St. J.' embossed on the handles. I looked up at Olive.

'We had a set of six of these at home,' I said, 'knives, forks, spoons...'

'Eight, a set of eight,' said Olive crisply. 'It was my wedding present to Grace. She chose the design and I ordered them from Mappin and Webb in Sheffield. When George left her, he took them with him, but, for some reason, he left her two of everything. When she went into hospital, she gave them to me.'

I suppose if I were a Christian I would have felt like doubting Thomas putting his hand into the hole in Christ's side, gouged by a Roman spear, a gory but unforgettable way of making the point. I gripped the knife and fork and told Olive of my moment of doubt.

'Don't worry, duckie,' she said sympathetically, 'I've felt the same way for the last few days. But, believe me, I *am* your aunt and you *are* my nephew.'

Where to begin? Olive jumped from one story to the next and my notes, scribbled that evening, reflected the leaps and bounds. She had a pile of family photographs, letters and diaries on the table. Spreading them out, she picked up a picture of my grandfather, and there stood the archetypal Edwardian 'bobby': tall, burly, waxed moustache, a stern but reassuring presence. After Lucy met, or picked up, Charles in Hyde Park, they began courting in the approved manner of the day. Things went well but when he proposed marriage, he had a surprise.

'Yes,' Lucy responded, 'but only after you are promoted sergeant.'

Promotion came in 1903, duly followed by marriage. Olive showed me a yellowing photograph of Sergeant Islip at the time of the wedding. He was in civilian clothes, dressed in high Edwardian style featuring a stiff upturned shirt collar and a grey silk cravat with a pearl-headed pin stuck in it. A watch chain stretched across an ample stomach, constrained by a tight-fitting waistcoat. His hair was brushed back, and the points of his moustache were waxed and twirled.

Olive rummaged among the photographs and pulled out three of her mother. One was taken when Lucy was about sixteen years old, another a little later, and a larger portrait when she was in her early twenties.

'That last one could have been a wedding photograph,' Olive said. In all the photographs, Lucy had her hair up and was formally dressed. The pictures revealed a progression from a rather sweet-looking young girl, with slightly parted lips and a suggestion of a smile in her eyes, to a more determined, serious-looking person, to a mature woman with a prominent nose, a tightly compressed mouth, and no hint of joy in her trim, wasp-waisted figure.

The newlyweds moved into police housing in Whitechapel in the heart of the East End. Olive was born there on 24 May 1904 ('Queen Victoria's birthday,' she said with a smile) and Grace followed three years later.

'Grace's second name, Rose, came from an aunt, one of Lucy's sisters,' Olive continued. 'As a child, I remember hearing of mental instability in the family, that my Aunty Rose was a bit soft in the head. My father once told me that when he was about to marry Lucy, he had informed his superiors in the police about Aunty Rose, describing her as a person with "mental aberrations".'

While my father was adapting to life in Britain and learning his trade in the Glasgow shipyards, Sergeant Islip was doing well in the Metropolitan Police Force, and proud of his growing family. As time went on, there was even a little money for extras, such as piano lessons and the occasional party dress.

Charles was an easy-going man and a bit of a tease. He was fond of Latin aphorisms, such as *tempus fugit* and *nil desperandum* and, like Lucy, had no accent to betray his rural or working class origins, unusual in that era. He was a teetotaller but liked his food and a cigar after Sunday lunch. Then he would take the girls to Hyde Park and play games with them. He adored his daughters and they adored him.

Lucy was more sharp-edged, a worrier and a nag. 'She had no sense of humour although she thought she did,' said Olive. 'She was also a snob and once stopped me playing with a girl at my school because she was the daughter of a cleaning woman and was 'common'. That was rich coming from a woman who had been a housemaid.'

Not long after Armistice Day in November 1918, Olive was at school when a girl turned to her during the break and said, 'What's wrong with you, Olive, you look pale? Are you ill?' When she got home, she heard that an ambulance had arrived at her home to take her father to hospital at the time of her break.

'Later, Uncle Cuthbert came to the flat,' Olive said, 'and I knew immediately from his face that Father had gone.'

A big, powerful man in his prime, he died at 4:30 in the morning, less than twenty-four hours after arriving at the hospital. Olive paused, looking down at her plate, no longer buoyant but unutterably sad.

'Mother lay down on a settee in our living room,' she said slowly. 'She didn't speak for four days.'

Their father's death was a disaster for the family. Both children were devastated, particularly Grace who was the more emotional and vulnerable of the two. Suddenly they had no income, apart from a minute police pension, and no roof over their heads. Lucy finally pulled herself together, and the family moved to the basement flat in Earls Court.

'Luckily, Grace and I won scholarships, otherwise we wouldn't have been able to stay at school after the age of fourteen,' Olive said. 'Grace left at sixteen because she was restless and wanted to work. She did a secretarial course and got a job, which she loved. I stayed at school until I was eighteen and then went to a teacher training college in south London. I didn't want to be a teacher but there wasn't much else that a woman could do in those days.'

I thought of Edith facing the same dilemma about that time— she and Olive were virtually the same age—and ending up with the same result. Olive qualified in 1924 and went to teach in an elementary school in a Yorkshire coal-mining village called Jump where she could barely understand the children's accent, and they could barely understand hers. Four years later, she got a job in London and moved back in with Lucy and Grace in Earls Court.

'Grace met George in the spring of 1933 when they used to walk to Earls Court Tube station to go to work. Grace was going out with a man from her office called Leslie at the time, and I remember they went off to the Lake District together for two weeks that summer. He wanted to marry her but he said they would have to live with Lucy for a bit because he didn't have a place of his own. "No thanks," said Grace.'

Olive searched through the pile of papers and photographs on the table and extracted a tiny pocket diary.

'This is for 1933,' she said, turning the pages. 'Here we are, Friday, November 10th: Grace and her new chap going strong. November 14th: George St. Jorre calling again—proposed to Grace. November 17th: Mother worried over the St. Jorre affair—called on various people to find out more about him. November 26th: Grace definitely parted with Leslie and is marrying St. Jorre. December 7th: Grace engaged today. Diamonds.'

When Grace first brought him home, Lucy was immediately hostile.

'It was hate at first sight,' Olive said. 'Right from the start, she disliked him. I don't know why. "Who is this man?" she would say, "What do we know about him?" I suppose she was suspicious because, to her mind, he was a foreigner, and a Catholic to boot. Also, he wasn't doing well as a travelling salesman. Lucy tried to dissuade Grace, pointing out that this was not his first engagement. But if Mother was stubborn, so was Grace. She was the rebellious one who stood up to her. She had a violent temper, too. I was different. Munich. Appeasement. That's me!'

I asked about my father's former fiancée.

Olive shook her head. 'We didn't know any details. It all happened some time before he met Grace and I am not sure how we knew about it. For her part, Grace had had quite a few boyfriends whereas I stayed close to Mother. George once said to me, "Are you going to be tied to your mother's apron strings for the rest of your life?"'

'Didn't you have boyfriends, too?'

'Not with a face like mine, not a chance,' she said. 'I had terrible acne until I was about forty. I remember I was in a train once, and the man sitting opposite me got up and moved into the next compartment. A doctor at London Hospital said that my acne was the worst case he had ever seen. I was very insecure until quite late in my life.'

I looked down at Olive's hands. They were small, plump and remarkably smooth for a seventy-year-old woman. I reached out and squeezed her hand. She looked up at me. 'Oooh, duckie,' she said with a radiant smile.

At the wedding and the reception, the Islips and the de St. Jorres kept well apart.

'During the honeymoon, I telephoned Grace to see how things were going,' said Olive. 'The first thing she said was that she had told George on their wedding night that she didn't love him.'

I was stunned. George telling Edith the story was one thing. But hearing it independently from Olive, who had heard it from Grace herself, put it on another level.

'That's incredible! Did she say why she'd married him?'

Olive shook her head. 'She didn't explain. I didn't know what was going on between them, and it wasn't any of my business.'

'This is for 1936 when I had recently returned from Canada,' she said, picking up another diary. 'Sunday, February 9th: Grace's baby boy born at 4.15 today. Monday, February 10th: Saw the babe about six o'clock. Just like a little old Jew. I longed to rush out and buy him a suit and bowler hat. Grace looked wonderfully well. Sat up knitting and seemed A.1.'

Olive laughed. 'Sounds silly now, doesn't it?' She flicked the minute pages. 'Sunday, March 1st: Mother went to see Grace. Came home very distressed. Both of us cried.' She looked up. 'Grace was not well then but she recovered later. Monday, March 2nd: Popped over to see Grace tonight for half an hour. She doesn't look too bad but no spring in her. Esau—that's you—red in the face.'

Maurice was born on 11 June 1937 when we were living in Morden in south London. Olive was still with Lucy in Finchley, north London.

'You were quiet and withdrawn as a child,' she said, 'but you were your father's favourite. Grace used to put olive oil on your hair and massage it into your scalp. She told me she didn't want another child. They had money problems and she said she couldn't cope. But when Maurice came along, he was a sunny little fellow, very outgoing and cheerful.'

I told her that a reversal of character seemed to have taken place. I had become the extrovert and Maurice the introvert. Also, I remember Maurice being the favourite while I, as the older child, always got blamed if anything went wrong. He probably remembered it the other way round.

Olive confirmed that Grace had her first breakdown in Morden after Maurice was born, probably in the summer or autumn of 1937. George was away and a neighbour saw us wandering around alone in the garden. Grace was found in the house, lying down and completely disoriented. She was taken to Cane Hill Hospital in Coulsdon, treated, and released after a week.

Shortly afterwards, she had a relapse and returned to hospital.

'Your father took you away and put you in a children's home,' Olive said. 'But you were not treated well, so George asked Lucy if you could stay with her for a while and she agreed.' Olive paused. 'It was the middle of winter, January or February 1938, and you were both in an unhappy state. You slept in Lucy's room and Maurice, who was only about six months old, slept in mine. He would wake up in the middle of the night, moaning and crying inconsolably. I really didn't know what to do to comfort him, poor mite. Maurice's first words were, "there, there," in a soothing tone, which he must have copied from me.'

'You were withdrawn, silent, and watchful,' she continued. 'Your favourite game was loading up a wooden box with stones, pushing it to one end of the garden, unloading it, pushing it back, and then starting all over again, loading and unloading. You'd do that for *hours*. During the day, Lucy, who was then in her early sixties, used to take you and Maurice out in a pram and sing "Onward Christian Soldiers" slightly out of tune and in a quavering voice. You couldn't pronounce "Maurice" properly so you called him "Moy". He would follow you everywhere.'

Olive got up, went into the living room, and came back with a small round stone. 'You found this somewhere,' she said, 'and brought it to me. You held it up to show me and kissed it passionately.

'On another occasion, I took you over to Joan Cooper's house and left you there for about an hour while I did some shopping. When I came back you were sitting on a step, between the kitchen and the dining room, exactly where I had left you,' said Olive. 'You were about three years old and not a happy child.'

'Did the house in Finchley have a big room with a tiled floor?'

'It did. That was the kitchen and it looked out on to the back garden.'

I told her of my memory of Grace and she nodded. 'That was the house.'

In 1939, Olive moved to Ramsgate in Kent. Things were not going well between Grace and George, or between the two of them and Lucy.

'You and Maurice had a terrible time, with constant rows going on around you,' Olive said. 'At times you were neglected. Maurice became really thin and both of you were very unhappy. I once took the two of you away from London, down to Ramsgate, to recuperate. Maurice had bad diarrhoea and had to be starved for twenty-four hours to get rid of it. Times were also so hard financially.

'My last memory of you was after George took you down to Exmouth in Devon during the summer of 1940,' Olive continued. 'You returned a little man, very sophisticated. You pronounced 'Ex-mouth' very precisely. I remember everyone standing around looking at you as you washed your hands. I can see you now. Later, you were sitting beside me in bed in Mother's Finchley house. You turned to me and said: "You cannot look back. We must go forward."'

She paused, searching for the right phrase. 'We loved you,' she said. 'But we didn't enjoy you.'

The domestic turmoil reached a crescendo in the summer of 1940, and George decided to act. 'Mother wanted to keep you but Grace agreed with George,' Olive said. 'He found a place in Blackheath and a Belgian woman, a widow, to look after you. Grace visited you there once, but that was it. She never saw you again.'

Grace passed through a succession of mental hospitals: Coulsdon in Morden, south London; Friern in Barnet, north London; Shenley in Hertfordshire; and finally Napsbury, also in Hertfordshire, where she was now. She had been violent at times and was treated with electric shocks. In the early 1950s, she had the frontal lobotomy operation. None of this had much effect on her illness, Olive said, but she calmed down and was able to leave the hospital for short periods.

Grace was on a mixture of drugs. After so many years in mental institutions, the hospital had become her home. Recently, she moved from a ward of sixty patients to one containing forty and seemed happy there. From time to time, she would come out and spend a weekend with Olive, but a month ago, she had blotted her copybook by walking out of the hospital grounds during the night. She was eventually found wandering in the woods with her legs and arms badly scratched. Olive went to the hospital and Grace told her that, when she returned to the ward, the nurses kissed her, and she was happy again.

Granny Islip, suffering from dementia, joined Grace in Napsbury Hospital in 1961 and died there two years later. At her deathbed, Grace turned to Olive, who was weeping, and said: 'I can't cry, Olive, I can't cry.'

After her debts were settled, Lucy left two hundred and fifty pounds. Bill, who had been listening and nodding, said, 'Ulav gave Grace half of the money for clothes and cigarettes. She's a terrific girl this Ulav, you know. She's the only Islip who's ever cared for Grace.'

Olive reached across and put her smooth hand over mine. 'I used to dream of you and Maurice for years, right into the mid-1950s. I heard nothing of you until 1947 when Beryl, an old college friend who was living in Ilford in Essex, wrote to me. She said that her daughter was at Woodford County High School and had told her that her domestic science teacher, Edith Ross, was getting married to a Frenchman who had two boys. "Could they be Grace's boys?" she wondered. I was sure it was George and you two but I did not tell Mother. She would have tried to find you, probably in a cock-eyed way, and embarrass everybody concerned. I didn't tell Grace either.'

When I mentioned my father's fear of returning to Woodford after he and Edith came back from Singapore, Olive said it was because Beryl had actually met him and Grace in her Ilford home, not far from Woodford, just before they were married. He knew Beryl would be in touch with the Islip family and did not want to take the risk of her knowing where he was, so it was safer to stay in Ealing, on the other side of London. Another loose end tidied up.

'I lost track of you for another ten years or so,' Olive continued. 'Then I received a letter from Stanley Belcham, our cousin, saying that you were going to Oxford and Maurice to Durham. He had probably promised George not to say anything more. Another decade went by before the next piece of news came. The daughter of an old friend of Mother's sent me a story about Aden that you had written for the *Observer Magazine*. There was a photograph of you in it. "Do you think this could be Grace's boy?" she wrote. "It seems likely by the dates."

'I wanted to contact you at the *Observer* but thought it best to lie low and not burst, unwelcome, into your life. I never said anything to Grace but simply told her that I was sure you and Maurice were all right.'

'How did the final break happen?'

'"He'll come when Mother is out," Grace told me. "It's better that way."'

Olive paused and looked at me, cocking her head. 'It's amazing that you and Maurice ever did anything, that you didn't become hippies with flowers in your hair,' she said. 'George did the right thing, you know, I can see that now. But the whole thing was disastrous, catastrophic, a tragedy.'

I DROVE SLOWLY BACK TO LONDON, A PACKET OF FAMILY photographs beside me, a head churning with impressions, and a heart full of sadness. Yet Olive had been marvellous, an irrepressible survivor of turmoil and tragedy. I realised how much I needed her, not only to complete the story of the missing years, which she was doing, but also as an indispensable intermediary for the reunion, which was about to happen.

When I reached Blackheath, where my father had placed us under the care of the Belgian widow, and where my mother had seen us for the last time, I stopped at a pub and ordered a pint of beer. I drank it quickly and ordered another.

*'He'll come when Mother is out,'* Grace had said. *'It's better that way.'*

I leaned back and closed my eyes. I tried to imagine her sitting alone at a table in that tiled room, smoking a cigarette, and staring into space. My father had been and gone. Night had fallen and perhaps an air raid was under way—the rumble of bombers, sirens howling, the pop-pop-pop of anti-aircraft guns, and searchlight beams sweeping the blue-black sky. In the bedroom, two small empty beds. And later, the slow realisation that she would never see her babies again. A mother's grief compounded by mental demons. A young life trapped in locked and violent wards. Draconian remedies. As I left the pub, I was close to tears.

Two days after visiting Olive, a giant birthday card with a French nineteenth-century still life on the cover arrived. Inside it read: 'With best wishes, lots of love, Grace, Bill and Olive' and below: '9th Feb '75. What A DAY!'

That afternoon, Olive called me from her neighbour's telephone to say we could see Grace at Napsbury Hospital the following day.

We arranged to meet at Victoria station the next morning. Accompanying Olive was an old school friend, Anne Skibulits, a slender, elegant woman of Hungarian and Swiss origin. Anne had worked as a secretary most of her life, never married, and lived near Brighton, on the south coast. Unlike Joan and Eva, she had managed to remain in contact with Olive through war and peace.

She looked at me curiously.

'This is amazing,' she said. 'I am sorry but I still can't quite get over you turning up like this after all these years. The last time I saw your mother was when she was very ill in hospital in Coulsdon. It must have been 1939 or perhaps 1940. She didn't recognise anyone and just played with a bit of wool. It was the saddest thing.'

She reached into her bag and took out a large envelope.

'I won't hold you up but I wanted to give you something I've had for a long time, and I think you should have it now.' She handed me the envelope. She did not say what was in it, and I didn't ask. I simply assumed it was another piece of my past, once again from a feminine hand.

I thanked her and we said goodbye. We were in a hurry so I put the envelope, unopened, on the back seat. I asked Olive if she had recovered from the excitement of the last few days. 'Recovered, duckie?' she said with a laugh, 'I'm revelling in it. When you came down to see us the other day, I felt that I had to tell you everything because you might never come back. And when Bill first saw you through the curtains, getting out of this old French car in a long leather coat with a Spanish basket over your shoulder, he turned to me and said, "He's a *hippy*."'

During the journey, Olive told me Bill Anderson's story. He grew up in a poor Catholic section of Belfast, left school at the age of fourteen and got a job in a handkerchief factory. Two years later, his mother who was heavily pregnant, fell ill. He ran into the street and found a priest who went up to his mother's bedroom and told him that she was dead. The baby was born alive, only to die eighteen months later.

'Bill was shattered,' Olive said. 'He told me he slept beside his mother's corpse for two nights and wanted to commit suicide.'

When he was twenty, he married a young Catholic girl. He was not in love with her and did not want to get married. But she was eager and both families were behind the marriage so Bill gave in and agreed. Directly after the wedding, however, he changed his mind. That same afternoon, with the marriage unconsummated, he went down to the Belfast docks, bought a one-way ticket, and took the ferry to England. He never went back.

Olive met Bill, five years her junior, in London during the war and they started an affair. In 1946, Olive took the plunge and left her mother to live with Bill in Brighton where he worked at the local greyhound track. Three years later they moved to Chatham where Olive got a teaching job at an elementary school.

'Bill never saw or spoke to the girl he married since the day of the wedding,' continued Olive. 'But he's still legally married to her so I'm not really "Mrs Anderson", though that's how everyone knows me. I've kept very quiet about it for thirty years.'

Their marital situation caused financial problems and heartbreak. When Olive was due for promotion in 1951, she stopped teaching altogether because she was worried that her 'marriage lines' would be investigated and the awful truth that she was 'living in sin' revealed. The result was near penury for the next five years. Bill's earnings from the greyhounds as 'head lad' (more than a kennel boy, less than a trainer) were erratic. They had to live in a caravan with no running water, electricity or sanitation. 'That's where I spent my fiftieth birthday,' Olive said.

Olive's position carried a serious stigma in those days. The simple phrase 'living with a man' outside wedlock implied a shaky morality at best but usually meant a woman of demonstrably loose

morals, a bad role model for the young. (Not unlike the irrepressible, free-living Miss Fenton whose morals, at least according to
Edith, were so loose as to be unmoored.) While Olive broke with
tradition by living with a married man whom she loved, she said
she always felt guilty, and a social pariah. She never spoke about
Bill's marital status to her mother although the old lady was probably aware of it.

Olive found part-time work in a shop that sold postcards and, in
1955, the house in Walderslade came up for sale. She managed to
borrow the money for the deposit (one hundred and ninety pounds)
and obtain a mortgage although Bill had to sign the papers because
a woman wasn't trusted to hold the note. In 1956, she decided to
risk exposure and return to teaching. To her great relief, the school
did not pry into her private life beyond asking her for the date of
her marriage. She gave the day she had first gone off with Bill ten
years earlier.

As we approached the hospital, Olive said that she had written
twice to Grace since our reunion. The first letter was to tell her that
she would be coming to see her and had a 'surprise' for her. The
second, initiated by the need to soften the shock, explained that
the surprise was 'someone you haven't seen for a long, long time'.

Napsbury Hospital, built in Victorian times, is surrounded by
lawns, flowerbeds and tall trees. The birds are singing, there is a
damp wind, and the sun breaks through as we drive in. Spring has
arrived early with bulbs bursting with fresh, green shoots and leaves
appearing on the shrubs, unaware that it is only early February. I
wait outside in the driveway as Olive goes to fetch Grace. This part
of the hospital is open. It is visiting day and several patients are
walking in the grounds. There is no mistaking them. They have
sunken faces, stiff, unwieldy limbs, half-mast trousers, scarecrow
raincoats, and expressions of painful introspection.

I wait. A bunch of yellow tulips in the car. A packet of Benson
and Hedges cigarettes in my pocket. ('She loves cigarettes,' Olive

said. The ash between the breasts.) A loaded camera, but will I use it? Thirty-five years.

Olive appears at the entrance with a plump grey-haired old woman, a vacant look on her face. Another surreal moment. Can this stranger really be my mother? Am I being dragged into a macabre piece of theatre, plotted and directed by a phony and sinister aunt? Ridiculous. I have run out of sanctuaries for ambivalence and denial. There is no turning back.

I approach this woman, my mother, towering over her. She looks much older than Olive although she is actually three years younger. Her hair is straight, short, the grey mixed with white. Her skin sags a little and has a yellowish pallor. Her eyebrows are virtually colourless. She has a round face and the distinctive long nose, slightly bulbous at the end, familiar from the old photographs. I have her nose, no doubt about it.

Over her right eye, there is a small scar. (The lobotomy?) Her mouth is wide without much shape. Olive told me she is always losing her dentures but does quite well without them. A long furry tongue moves restlessly around her gums and between her lips, a habit shared by many of the patients. Her eyes are pale, grey-blue, and large. She is wearing a plain, faded blue dress with some stains on the upper part, and a brown cardigan. Underneath her rumpled stockings, I can see pieces of sticking plaster on her legs where she cut herself during her recent escapade. She has on bright blue velvet slippers, sweet and childish, sad and unforgettable.

Grace looks up at me, a clear, direct gaze.

'Who are you?' she says. 'I don't know you. What is your name?'

I look down at this little old woman with the clear, direct gaze and say: 'John de St. Jorre.' It sounds silly in retrospect but it is less melodramatic, and less traumatic for her perhaps, than something like, 'your long lost son, John.'

My mother stares at me, her firstborn, blankly. I smile. What else can I do? No point in saying anything. There is nothing to say.

She has no more reason to recognise me than I do her. Has she understood who I am? I have no idea. We are strangers yet we are as biologically close as two humans can be. This dishevelled old woman carried me in her womb for nine months and gave me life.

Standing and staring at each other is unbearable. I abruptly turn aside, murmuring about something I have in the car—any excuse to escape. Olive is chatting volubly, diverting Grace's attention. The big sister, who remained at her side, is something she can grasp. Never has Olive's garrulousness been more useful or appreciated.

I return with the flowers. Olive and I link arms with Grace, one on either side, and we walk slowly towards the hospital. This is better, physical contact, side-by-side, no need to look at each other, and no attempt to talk. The earth smells of fresh rain and the birds are celebrating something or other. Olive chats away but I can see that she is as nervous as I am. We go to the cafeteria and while Olive orders some tea and cakes, I offer Grace a cigarette, which she takes with a half-smile. It's like wooing a woman, the old-fashioned way ('Would you care for a cigarette?'). Grace says she likes smoking and the middle finger of her left hand is stained with nicotine. I have found a conversational vein.

A tall woman, another patient, comes over to our table and looks down at me.

'Where were you born?' she asks abruptly.

'Kensington.'

'Can you give me two bob?'

I give the woman two shillings and she drifts off without another word.

Olive arrives with the tea and, as we drink, Grace tells us about her 'walk'. She fell into a grating in the dark and was lucky to get out with nothing worse than cuts and bruises on her shins. She apparently left the hospital grounds and the police picked her up four or five miles away the following morning. It was a shock, she says, and she hasn't been out of the hospital since. She says she has got her appetite back but she looks tired with heavy wrinkles around her eyes. She talks lucidly and clearly and, like Olive, with no discernible accent. She asks for another cigarette and I give her the packet. She puts it and the matches into a tatty, red imitation leather handbag. She begins to drift off, slipping into polite but vague responses, 'Yes, yes, very nice, I see, oh yes…' Sometimes she stops and hums to herself.

All around us are other patients, most of them sitting in a kind of catatonic silence. One thin man, with a bald pate like a monk's tonsure, prowls around the tea room. He sits down for a few seconds, then he is up again, pacing backwards and forwards, on patrol. A young woman, pale and forlorn, sits on a couch. She pulls her feet up and hugs them like a child who is cold and tired. Another Grace, struck down in her prime?

A woman with ginger hair piled up on her head and fanned out at the back like a peacock's tail comes up to us. She is carefully but heavily made-up with a crimson gash of a mouth.

'What did I tell you?' she says belligerently to Grace.

Grace looks at her but says nothing.

'I told you someone was coming to see you today. So there!' She spins on her heel and walks away.

I feel as if I am in the middle of a piece of modern theatre with distraught characters coming on stage, uttering a few nonsensical lines, and stalking off.

Olive tells Grace we came by car and she is impressed. I mention that I walked past Negretti and Zembra in Bond Street the other day. Didn't she work there?

'Yes,' she says, 'for Paul Negretti. I also remember two other men who worked there, Mr Burns and Mr Sayers.'

Olive and I talk about Joan and Eva, and Grace says, 'Joan was your friend, wasn't she Olive?'

She appears to have no recollection of Eva and the letters she wrote during the war. We leave the cafeteria and go to Laurel Ward, her home. It is a set of bright, clean rooms that includes a lounge, dining room and small kitchen. There are electric fires, a colour television, magazines, even books.

A nurse is clearing the dining room table. Grace takes the tulips into the kitchen and bustles around putting them in two separate vases and placing them on tables in the lounge. We sit down and she lights a cigarette.

I tell her about Maurice and Dorothy and their family.

'Oh yes, good,' she says looking at me and then around the room. She sucks on her cigarette, cheeks deflating.

We talk about the time of day or night when Maurice and I were born. She can't remember.

'It was all confused, wasn't it?' she says.

'How old do you think John is?' asks Olive.

'Forty,' she says quickly, giving me that direct look.

We laugh, almost right. She can't remember my birthday but thinks Maurice was born in June. He was. Then, without any prompting, she says:

'He was ten pounds and you were eight. Yes.'

We are delighted. She seems to be connecting with me, and with the past. Olive mentions my curly hair, and I say it's strange because both she and my father had dead straight hair, and so does Maurice.

'Do you remember what you used to do to John's hair, Grace?' Olive says.

'No,' she says blankly.

'You used to rub olive oil into it and perhaps that's what made it curly.'

'Yes.' She has left us again.

'Do you want us to go now?' Olive asks.

'Yes, I do,' she says emphatically but so direct and honest that it is appealing.

'I'll see you to the door,' she says formally. When we reach the lobby, I instinctively kiss her on the lips and she responds. Something deep down inside me makes me do this although I am still not sure she knows who I am. It had been like that with Olive, hugs and kisses from the outset, a physical spontaneity and warmth on both sides, something I never felt with Edith and couldn't fake, although it would have been the kindest thing to do.

I wait at the entrance while Olive accompanies her back to the ward. I watch them walking down the corridor, hand-in-hand. Olive stops and presses some money into Grace's hand. They turn a corner and disappear. My last sight of her is of a small girl with her big sister. The girl is wearing bright blue velvet slippers.

## 22

ON THE WAY BACK TO LONDON, OLIVE SAID THAT WHILE SHE was walking with Grace to meet me, she tried to build on the letters she had sent and prepare her for our visit by asking her to guess who the 'surprise' was. Grace first said 'Bill', then 'Faith', the Peterborough cousin. When Olive said it was a man she hadn't seen for a long time, she offered 'Harold', another cousin who gave her away at her wedding. Olive also told her that George died ten years ago. Her only response was a sympathetic 'Oooh'.

I dropped Olive off at Victoria and went home. I slumped into a chair feeling as if a vacuum pump had been attached to my emotions and left running. On the table was the envelope that Anne Skibulits had given me. I got up, went out on to the balcony, watered the fuchsia, and took a few deep breaths of damp London air.

I went back in and opened the envelope. Inside were three photographs. Two were small snapshots of Olive in her teens. In one, there was a touch of Maurice and, in the other, oddly, a suggestion of his wife, Dorothy. The third picture was much larger, a studio portrait of Grace in slightly soft focus but well preserved and mounted on thick-weave cloth paper. The photographer's name and 'Kensington' were written at the bottom right hand corner, as an artist would sign a painting.

Grace was wearing a black chiffon blouse with a large bow at the throat, and pendant earrings. Her hair was parted at the side and brushed straight across her forehead. She looked youthful, attractive, poised but pensive, a little sad. On the back she had written: 'With best wishes for Christmas 1933—Grace.' The photograph was taken, I now knew, around the time she became engaged to my father.

That it had finished up in my hands was another small miracle of preservation. It was, I felt certain, the same studio photograph Eva Lebel had thrown out three months before she spotted my name in the *Observer*.

I looked at the picture more closely. This was how my mother looked a few months before her wedding. I could see nothing in common between this pretty, rather wistful young woman in front of me and the ageing, scruffy, disconnected woman at the hospital. Was it possible that these two people could be one and the same? The sadness returned. I put my head in my hands and this time the tears came.

Depression is often described as a black cloud that envelops the sufferer. I had never been truly depressed before, spared, I thought, because of a simple defence mechanism that I had developed at an early age. When things got bad, I imagined something even worse and, as a result, felt a little better because, well, things weren't as bad as they could be. This time, however, Grace's story hit me hard. Try as I might, I could not glimpse the hint of sunlight behind that dark cloud.

Meanwhile, a letter arrived from Olive, written the day after our trip to Napsbury.

'I felt like a piece of unleavened bread this morning,' she wrote. 'Really it was a stupendous day yesterday, an enormous strain on the nervous system. I am beyond speech, a record as far as I am concerned. I know it amuses you that I talk so much, but there's a solid reason for so doing. I may die at any time and I'd simply have to come back if I thought I hadn't told you all I could remember!

'I can't imagine how you felt about it all,' she continued. 'But whatever else happens, John, I'll always be grateful and happy that you found us. It's a fairy tale to beat all fairy tales.'

I wrote back echoing the power of the experience and thanking her for being such a good intermediary. I also mentioned how down

I felt after seeing the studio portrait of Grace because the contrast with what she had become was so brutal.

A few days later, I called the hospital and spoke to Sister Meehan who was in charge of Laurel Ward. She said Dr Birmingham, Grace's doctor, could see me during my next visit.

'Grace is a lovely person,' she said in a soft Irish accent. 'She often told me about her husband and her two boys. She was delighted with the reunion and hasn't stopped talking about it. Grace is very intelligent, you know, but I don't think she could live outside.'

The weather was kind the day Olive and I drove back to Napsbury, a warm sun, a soft breeze, and spring exploding around us. Grace was sitting in the hallway that led into Laurel Ward. She was alert, happy, excited, and much better dressed than last time. She was wearing a pale blue dress, maroon cardigan (a present from Olive), and smart blue leather shoes. Her jewellery consisted of a red bead necklace and a silver bangle on her wrist. She had washed her hair and it was held in place with an old-fashioned slide, the way she had probably done it as a young woman in the 1920s. Her hair was almost entirely grey and white but, when the sunlight caught it, I could see a flaxen glint, a reminder of the long golden tresses she'd had as a child.

She stood up and we embraced. She bent down and lifted her skirt, unhooked a stocking, pulled it down, and showed us, with pride, how well her calf had mended. Her legs were fish-belly white, short and withered. A spasm of sadness. I turned away.

She looked in much better health, however, and was clearly delighted to see us. She had asked for my photograph and I gave her two, one in colour and the other black and white. Olive had brought her some chocolate and sweets, and I gave her a packet of cigarettes. Grace reached for the cigarettes and lit one, sucking in her cheeks and puffing vigorously. She said she bought her own from her wages for work in the needle room, sewing pillowcases, curtains, sheets and buttonholes.

She took a great delight in introducing us to a couple of her friends, including the Anglican padre who visited the hospital regularly.

'This is my sister, Olive, and here is my son, John,' Grace said without hesitation.

Such a simple, commonplace phrase yet never had it seemed so memorable.

The patient with the peacock's tail hairdo came over and said she was sure someone was coming to see her today, someone from the past, just like me. She moved away and Grace politely asked what I did for a living. I told her about journalism and writing books and she nodded sympathetically.

'Do you do shorthand and typing?'

'I taught myself to touch-type with a Pitman book, but I never learnt shorthand.'

'I used to earn my living by shorthand and typing,' she said proudly. 'I spent ten years doing it and I liked it. I didn't like home, except to live in.'

Sister Meehan arrived. Dr Birmingham was in the ward office. I excused myself, leaving my mother and my aunt chatting and laughing with Sister Meehan. I could have been the parent leaving two children while I went off to talk to the management. When I looked back a cloud of blue cigarette smoke hung over the trio.

Dr Birmingham was a small, dark-haired, slow-speaking Irishman around my age. His manner was serious, sympathetic, and direct. He didn't mince words, indulge in medical jargon, or resort to euphemisms. In his lexicon, 'mad' was 'mad'.

He had only been at Napsbury for four months, he said, and had talked to Grace on three occasions. But he had secured the full record, such as it was, and wanted to share it with me, a refreshing change from the thin-lipped, odious registrar at Somerset House. I immediately felt at ease with this young doctor.

'The reports on your mother in her early days in hospital are very sketchy and totally inadequate,' he said, opening a large file.

'The treatment of mentally ill patients in the 1930s, 1940s, even the 1950s, was appalling. Things only changed in the last fifteen years. Until 1959, a person could be confined to a mental institution on the simple recommendation of a doctor—it didn't have to be a specialist, a general practitioner would do—and with the approval of a single relative.

'Your mother originally suffered from post-natal depression after the birth of your brother and was admitted to the Cane Hill Hospital in Coulsdon Hospital, Morden,' he continued. 'The record here states it was in 1936 but that is a clerical error. She is recorded as having three children, also an error.'

He explained that post-natal depressions are common in young mothers and are routinely treated with drugs in hospital. Patients are rarely kept in for more than a week and social workers visit them regularly when they return home. 'The idea is to place the woman in a normal environment as quickly as possible,' he said.

'The reverse of what happened to Grace?'

'Exactly. Thirty or forty years ago, women in her condition were allowed to deteriorate and then locked up with genuinely mad and often violent people.'

He paged through the file.

'Your mother was clearly an intelligent and sensitive woman but she was under a lot of pressure. Her marriage, according to these records, was not a successful one. There is no record of her husband visiting her at any time. Her mother was also a problem. She is described in a social worker's report as "a fearsome, tyrannical woman".

'The loss of Grace's father when she was eleven years old may have had a damaging effect. Also, her sister Olive may have been jealous of her as the more sparkling of the two, and as the younger sister who got married and produced children.'

'But Olive was the only member of the family who took care of her,' I protested.

Dr Birmingham shrugged. 'The records do not show that she paid much interest in her medical condition—no appeals, inquiries, requests for tests and so on.'

Was it jealousy or Olive's fear of dealing with officialdom because of her phony marriage? Why hadn't my father visited Grace in those crucial early days when they were still a couple? Had he already turned against her? Or perhaps the records were at fault? Each revelation seemed to bring with it a new line of inquiry, and new doubts.

'The final blow,' Dr Birmingham said, 'was the removal of her children and the knowledge that she would probably never see them again.'

He paused, leafing through the file. 'After Coulsdon, Grace was moved to Friern Hospital in north London,' he continued. 'The 1940s seemed to have been a particularly bad time for her. It appears she had ECT—electronic convulsive treatment—but she remained deeply disturbed, sometimes violent and... well, mad. Here are a doctor's comments at that time. "She is obese, childish."' He read the extract with withering contempt. 'Later, he refers to Grace as "it".' Dr Birmingham paused. 'In those days it was almost as if the authorities wanted to certify people, to make them mad.

'In 1950, your mother was moved to Shenley, four miles from here,' he said, reading from the file. 'She went out from time to time but it was not a success. On one occasion, she was working in a hotel as a cleaner but had to return to hospital because she started throwing the guests' things around. She was moved here in 1953 and was operated on in the same year. The operation was a leucotomy, a bilateral leucotomy.'

'What's that?'

'It's less radical than a frontal lobotomy, which is a punitive operation for violent patients and usually reduces them to vegetables. Grace's operation was for...' he read from the report... '"extreme anxiety and anguish".'

'What does it do?'

'The effect is to calm the patient. It impairs the memory but not the intelligence and distances the patient from daily life. It makes patients more biddable—ready to do what is bidden, more docile. Leucotomies and lobotomies are rarely performed these days. They are generally regarded as primitive and savage medicine. Drugs, psychotherapy and ECT have taken their place.

'Grace was discharged after the operation and returned to live with her mother in Finchley,' he continued. 'But she was soon back here again. In February 1960, she was discharged once more but returned in June of the same year. In 1961, she went out again only to be sent back on a compulsory order, signed by her mother who would soon follow her here as a patient herself.

'In the 1960s, it was the policy to discharge as many patients as possible,' he said. 'Your mother spent six months working as a chambermaid in a hotel in St. Albans. But the management complained that she would stand and stare at the customers, and was rude when reprimanded. She couldn't explain what was happening and was returned to the hospital.'

'What's the diagnosis?'

'She is classified as a chronic schizophrenic,' he paused. 'Whatever that means.'

I realised that I knew so little about the disease or, indeed, about mental illness in general. When I thought about schizophrenia at all, I imagined that it implied a person was schizoid, suffering from some form of split personality. But, as Dr Birmingham explained, schizophrenics' symptoms are quite different.

'Schizophrenia is sometimes called the "cancer of the mind",' he said. 'It's a chronic, severe, degenerative bio-chemical brain disorder that can be treated but rarely cured. For the afflicted, an early stage of dislocation is usually followed by apathy or agitation, the hearing of voices, a sense of alienation, delusions, and a loss of contact with reality. Many of these symptoms are present in other mental illnesses, such as manic depression, and people with split or multiple personalities. The combination of symptoms, however, makes schizophrenia peculiarly distinctive and destructive.'

In the 1960s I had skimmed, rather than read, a book called *The Divided Self: An Existential Study in Sanity and Madness* by R. D. Laing, a popular and controversial Scottish psychiatrist, who was twenty-eight years old when he wrote it. Laing was a Freudian and based his theories on his own case-work. One of his central arguments was that what we call 'madness' is merely another state of consciousness, which is as valid as the 'normal' kind. Other Freudians went further, viewing schizophrenia as not a serious psychiatric disorder at all but as 'another reality', a mental state that had creative and even spiritual merits. Some even argued that it was a rational reaction to an unbearable situation.

I mentioned this to Dr Birmingham. He responded with a brief summary of how the debate in the medical world over the origins of schizophrenia had developed since *The Divided Self* first appeared. In simple terms, he said, there were two schools of thought. The 'hereditary' advocates believed the illness was transmitted through the genes, while the Freudian 'environmentalists', like Laing, felt that pressures in the family and in society were largely responsible for the disease. In between, there was a great fuzziness where both elements were thought to play a part.

'Grace had an aunt with mental problems,' I said, 'but it's not clear what they were.'

'Genes may play some part. The doctors here, myself included, tend to favour the environmental thesis. But we still know very little. Nothing is proven.'

'What happens now?'

'Your mother is a pleasant, intelligent, rather eccentric person,' he said. 'It's almost certainly too late to find out what really happened in the late thirties. She herself will probably have forgotten. She has spent almost forty years inside mental hospitals, much of it under crowded conditions with people who were mad, violent, beyond all hope. She has had a severe operation on the brain. She has been on drugs continuously and still takes two powerful ones daily, plus a periodic injection to tranquilise her and help her sleep.'

He closed the file and looked up. 'How did she react to your reappearance?'

'After the initial surprise, she seems to have accepted me as her son and she appears happy about it.'

'That's good. A family reunion like this has been known to have extreme effects, either a miraculous recovery or a retrograde movement into deep depression. In the 1940s, she probably blocked off memories of you and your brother as a self-defence mechanism against going completely mad. But, in her case, I don't think either of these eventualities is likely. The most common pattern with people in her condition, and at her age, is for them to become burnt-out schizophrenics. All that means is that they descend slowly and calmly into a normal old age, no crazier or crankier than other old people, and are often transferred to an old people's home.'

'And Grace?'

'Well, theoretically, she could leave here if there was someone to look after her all the time. But she would find it hard to cope and could possibly feel more isolated in those conditions. And since she behaves eccentrically from time to time, like taking that night walk, we expect her to remain in hospital for the rest of her life.'

I returned to the ward where Olive and Grace were sitting over a cup of tea. Grace was talking and seemed to be enjoying herself.

I suggested a drive to St. Albans, the nearest large town. Grace was reluctant at first but Olive quickly persuaded her. As we left, Grace turned to Sister Meehan.

'They have invited me out to tea in St. Albans,' she said, 'and I have acquiesced.'

She was impressed with my car, although it was the ageing Peugeot, dented and dusty. She would like to drive, she said, and wondered how much it would cost to take lessons. Olive mentioned a figure and she fell silent. But soon she was chatting away again. We drove into the town and had an old-fashioned English tea, with finger-sandwiches and cakes, in a restaurant near the cathedral. Grace chuckled to herself from time to time but otherwise behaved quite normally. She had forgotten Maurice's profession and I reminded her. She responded with one of her favourite expressions: 'That's right... yes.'

Some of her questions were those of a curious, intelligent teenager. 'What is the difference between *assurance* and *insurance*,' she suddenly asked. 'How much would a portable typewriter cost? Three guineas?' Her mind was still in the world of the old British currency. It was as if she had woken up from a long sleep and only remembered the era before mental illness closed her eyes. Other comments verged on the childish. When Sister Meehan had asked her what she liked best, she said without hesitation: 'Cigarettes, sweets, and money.'

After leaving the restaurant, we linked arms and wandered along the main street. She was fascinated by the shops, especially the jewellers and the women's clothing stores. I suddenly caught sight of the pair of us in a shop window. Thirty-five years ago, we had probably walked by many similar shop windows, hand-in-hand, mother and child.

She said she would like to go out on her own to the shops but was worried that she might lose her way. 'Sometimes I forget to turn corners,' she said.

As she was getting into the car, she squeezed Olive's hand and laughed her strange laugh.

'Are you tired, Grace?' I asked as we were driving back to the hospital.

'No,' she said, 'I'm happy.'

Back in the ward, I noticed a piano in the corner of the living room.

'Do you play the piano?' I said, looking down at her long slim fingers.

'I spent two years learning as a young girl, but I haven't been able to play since my breakdown.'

This time, Grace didn't want us to leave. She said she was getting better, 'much better'. Did she really want to leave the hospital, I wondered? Did she believe she could cope with the outside world after almost forty years 'inside'? Who would look after her? Olive? Me?

Her eyes closed occasionally but she was aware of it. 'It's the pills they give me after lunch,' she said in a clear voice.

She had a sense of humour, impossible to describe. At times she struggled for words to express herself, eyes rolling a little, hands weaving. She laughed a lot, often at herself, but the laugh, like everything else, faded quickly as she relapsed into her own sound-proofed world. She did not complain, nor display self-pity. On the contrary, she seemed to have a calm awareness of her condition and her prospects. It was only when I looked down that I felt a stab of sadness. Her legs, her poor legs. She sat with them tightly wrapped round each other, frail and bony, her stockings irremediably rumpled. But this time the bright blue velvet slippers, which I will always associate with her, were nowhere in sight.

I told her that I was going to see Eva and Joan, her old friends from the thirties.

'I didn't like Eva,' she said abruptly.

I mentioned the letters she wrote to Eva in 1940.

'Perhaps they were forged,' she said.

She wanted us to stay longer but Olive had to get back to Chatham to attend to Bill and Sugar Plum, her cat. This time Grace insisted on walking us to the main entrance, not just to the ward door. I told her I would visit her again the following week and we'd go for a drive in my car. I felt like a parent promising a young child a special treat. Grace mentioned that one of her friends in the hospital was going to see *Aladdin-on-Ice* in London, but she would not be going because she did not like long bus journeys. She would watch television instead. Our individual lives, plotted to follow different routes, had to continue. The reunion so far was life-enhancing but not life-changing.

Having balked at using the camera during my first visit, I persuade Grace to have her picture taken. We go out to the hospital's driveway. The light is failing; so is my resolve. Grace stands in front of me, staring blankly at the camera. It's too sad, I can't do it. It was a bad idea. Through the viewfinder, I see Olive bend down and whisper something in Grace's ear. She lifts her head, looks straight at me, and laughs. Click, it's done.

## 23

BACK IN MY FLAT, I FELT EXHAUSTED BUT RELIEVED. GRACE had been a different person this time and, notwithstanding Dr Birmingham's cautious diagnosis, a transformation of some kind seemed to be taking place. What was particularly encouraging was her accepting me as her son after the initial 'Who are you?' greeting, and evidence that her memory was functioning. How she really felt about suddenly meeting me whom she had last seen as a four-year-old child was a mystery, impossible to filter through the long years of separation and the damage suffered in a succession of mental hospitals. However, through the fog, I sensed a maternal dynamic at work. The black cloud was beginning to move on.

My immediate task was to let Edith and Maurice and Dorothy know what had happened. I dallied with the idea of calling them but settled for letters. It would be easier to explain the situation and allow for a more nuanced way of breaking the news, especially in Edith's case. After all, she had chosen that method to reveal what she knew about my father and Grace, even though we'd had plenty of opportunities to talk about it earlier. Meanwhile, there was virtually no chance of them hearing about the reunion from anyone else at this stage, so I had time on my side.

I wrote to Maurice and Dorothy first and gave them a short version of Olive's story of our early life and the visits to Grace in hospital, without any of the graphic and painful detail. I said that sadness was mingled with happiness but ended on an upbeat note about how well it had all gone considering the huge time gap and Grace's mental history, and what a wonderful find Olive turned out to be. I ended by acknowledging Maurice's different view of the whole idea of reconnecting with our past, and said I would probably have felt just like him if I had been the younger brother with no memory of our mother. I left it up to him if he wanted to get in touch with Olive and Grace.

Turning to Edith was more difficult. The simple solution was not to tell her anything and let her assume that I had given up the search. But what if she found out from Maurice or Dorothy, or some other way? I didn't want to tell Maurice and Dorothy to keep the reunion a secret because it sounded too conspiratorial and unnecessary in the new, open world we lived in. It would also be highly hypocritical. After all, I was the one who had opposed the burying of family secrets in the past. Moreover, Edith had come clean with me, albeit over a lengthy period, and I should be straight with her although I knew it would hurt. The trick would be to soften the impact as best I could.

I wrote her a short letter, mainly about my work in London, the flat, which I was repainting, and the likelihood that I would be going to the Middle East when I returned to the *Observer*. Near the end, I said that I'd had a breakthrough and found Olive. She had taken me to visit Grace who was in a mental hospital and not well. I finished by saying that, although I was happy to have found them both alive, she, Edith, would always be my 'Mum'.

After I mailed it, I wondered about her reaction. For years she had worked to make my father, my brother and me happy, and build a family life that we never had. Would she feel betrayed? Edith was a sensible, practical woman and, at one level, I was sure she would understand why I wanted to find Grace. Yet, with my father gone and Maurice in distant Canada, I was the only member of the family around, the person who visited her quite often, chatted with her on the telephone, and wrote to her frequently. I had also become friendly with some of her Scottish friends who, with the exception of Angus, regarded me as her attentive and loving firstborn son. She was bound to be upset. How could she not be? Perhaps I shouldn't have told her? It was too late, the letter had gone, and all I could do was to wait.

During the following days, I went down to Chatham and Olive came up to London. She was used to hopping on to buses and into trains, and I met her at Victoria Station and dropped her off there at the end of the outing. She and Bill did not travel together because someone had to stay behind and look after Sugar Plum.

About a week after I had written to Edith, her reply arrived. I opened it with some trepidation. She began, like me, with the safe stuff, comments on my work and the flat, and her social activities in Scotland. Finally, a new paragraph with a single sentence.

'You must be happy now that you have found your mother.'

That was it, nothing more. I put the letter down and stared out of the window. The sentence was plain enough, a statement without ambiguity. Yet, it contained an emotional undercurrent. With Edith, I had always been careful to say, and write, 'Grace' when referring to my mother from the moment I first raised the subject the day my father died. Edith had done the same. 'Mother' and 'Mum' were, by mutual consent, her preserve, titles that she had earned, and become entrenched by use over the years.

But here, contrary to our practice, she referred to Grace as my 'mother', making a point and giving her comment a slightly bitter flavour. Edith was clearly upset, but what could I do? There was no point trying to explain further what I felt by letter, telephone, or face-to-face. That would almost certainly make things worse. The only way was to adopt the old family tactic of silence and, with luck, end the matter. Henceforth, I would never mention Grace, Olive, or any of the Islips again. I would treat Edith exactly the same way as I had done before the reunion. I did not think she would bring the subject up but, if she did, I would respond as briefly as possible, and steer the conversation into safer waters. There had always been compartments in my mind, separating the two mothers, although there were times when they connected. From now on, they would be sealed shut.

Not long after Edith's letter arrived, a reply came from Maurice and Dorothy. Each of them wrote a short note, essentially welcoming the developments. While there was nothing negative in Maurice's response, I sensed that he was less excited than Dorothy because he showed no sign of wanting to get in contact with either Grace or Olive. But he did say he fully understood why I had spent so much time on the search and congratulated me on the result. He added that his interest in the family had always been in our French ancestors during the seventeenth and eighteenth centuries before they left France, the 'thoroughly dead de St. Jorres', as he put it. (When he retired, he dug deep into the genealogical records in France and the Indian Ocean islands and wrote a scholarly and fascinating family history, tracing our male line back to seventeenth-century Normandy.) Dorothy, for her part, seemed happy and intrigued about what would happen next. However, I am sure she realised that this was a personal matter for Maurice alone to handle.

One morning, I had a call from Olive, using her neighbour's telephone. She said she had received my letter reporting the latest news and understood Edith's attitude and thought it wise to behave with her as if nothing had happened. As for Maurice's reaction, she simply said with a laugh: 'He may not be anxious to take on a mother, as well as a talkative aunt.'

I knew that she would love to meet Maurice and his wife but her innate sense of discretion prevented her from saying so, and I felt I could do nothing to help at this stage. The real reason she had called me was to say that Dr Birmingham had given his permission for Grace to come out and stay with her for a few days. I drove down to Chatham and Grace recognised me immediately.

'Hello, darling,' she said.

Olive had prepared lunch and we all sat around the table in the front room, just like a normal family. In the place settings, Grace and I had the 'St. J.' silverware, sharing what was left of Olive's wedding present. I gave Grace some eau-de-cologne and perfumed soap, packaged together in a gift box. She thanked me and wrote on the box: 'Grace de St. Jorre from my baby-man John de St. Jorre.'

There it was, the baby and the man, compressing the lost decades. Later, when I turned the box around, I saw that she had added some disconnected words, suggesting the other side of the story. 'Control'. 'Lonely'. 'Lose'.

During the meal, which Grace managed perfectly well without her teeth, she became quite animated. For the first time, she talked about my father.

'He always dressed very smartly,' she said. 'He liked to wear a bowler hat and he took size six and seven-eighths, a big head. He was in love with me and I was with him. We married in love.'

I glanced at Olive who looked startled, a new twist to the story. I was dying to question Grace about the other version, which had two material witnesses to back it up, one of them sitting beside her. But she was in full flow and I didn't want to interrupt her. Also, given her present condition and that small scar at the side of her forehead, I wasn't sure how far I should go when it came to probing, or challenging, her memories.

After lunch, we moved to the living room, and Grace lit a cigarette. She picked up an atlas and said she recalled going to Tangier and Kitzbuhel in the 1920s. I helped her find them in the atlas, and then she turned to a dictionary and started to page through it.

She looked up at Olive. 'What's a lesbian?'

Olive told her.

'John's got a lesbian girlfriend,' Bill said.

'A *Lebanese* girlfriend!' exclaimed Olive, hooting with laughter.

Grace turned to me. 'Have you been married?'

'No.'

'You've had lovers?'

'Yes, but no marriages.'

'If you remain a bachelor, I will give you money.'

She asked about Maurice. I described him and reminded her that he was a successful mining engineer. She listened attentively.

'Has he got his own teeth?'

I assured her that Maurice was naturally fanged.

'Do you remember me?' she said suddenly.

I told her of my single, abiding childhood memory, about the large, tiled room, the snow, and her laughing. But I didn't mention the breasts or the cigarette ash. It was my turn to control the family narrative.

'Do you like your names?' Grace asked me.

'I do.'

'I chose them, English names, John Anthony. I never called you Johnny or Jack, you know, just John or Baby. And it was always Anthony to me, not Tony. That's Italian, isn't it? Just John Anthony because I'm English.'

'George chose Maurice's names,' she continued. 'They were French names—Maurice, George, Felix.'

I noticed her poor, wasted legs again. The rumpled stockings were still rumpled, held up just above the knee by suspenders that had become twisted so that they ran down the front of her thighs instead of along the side.

Occasionally, she could be quite droll, and not, I felt, by acci-dent. Bill was clowning around and talking about his 'seventeen rich widows in Canada'. Grace took some plates out of the room and, as she passed him, she turned to him and said crisply. 'You are some man, aren't you?' She was gone before he could think of a reply.

In the afternoon, Grace and I went for a walk along the main road and into a series of meadows connected by a public footpath. It was a bright spring day with a light breeze carrying the scent of elderberry flowers and warm earth. We walked slowly, hand-in-hand, sometimes chatting, and other times in silence. I had become used to her silences but this time it was different. The pauses were mutual and didn't spoil the flow of our thoughts and the rhythm of the conversation.

We talked of animals. 'I have always been frightened of horses,' she said. 'But cows are... grand.'

I said I had ridden horses but never trusted them, especially after one I had been on in Hyde Park in London sat down on a sandy track, with my legs still wrapped around its belly, and refused to get up. The discomfort was bad enough, but worse were the disdainful looks of the more skilled riders as they passed by.

She smiled and stopped.

'You're of me, born of woman,' she said, looking at me intently. 'I can remember the nurse giving you to me after you were born. I didn't have much milk though. I remember feeding and bathing you. I knitted you a pretty blue cardigan. Maurice had a bad time when he was a baby. He was frightened and cried a lot.'

I asked Grace about her father. She looked down at her feet.

'The night after he died,' she said quietly, 'I dreamt he was standing in my bedroom doorway. I missed him so much. They say dreams come true. But he didn't come back. Some dreams don't come true, do they?'

'This one did,' I said.

She looked up at me enquiringly but did not say anything.

'That one day I should find you.'

She smiled. 'Yes... Yes.'

She was suddenly interested in my career and wanted to know how many books I had written. I told her, not entirely truthfully, 'only two.' (*The Patriot Game* was not quite finished.) She had looked at Olive's copy of my Nigerian Civil War book and, amazingly, remembered that Hodder & Stoughton had published it.

As we were walking back to the house, I asked her about eating without teeth. Wasn't it difficult?

'Oh,' she said with her funny laugh, 'I have teeth in my head but none in my smile.'

When I returned to London, I called Dr Birmingham and asked him if I could come and see him. He agreed and we arranged to meet at the hospital the following week. Things seemed to be going well with Grace and I began to wonder if more could be done for her. Meanwhile, Olive came up to London and I took her to tea at the Dorchester Hotel overlooking Hyde Park where her parents had first met in another age. When we had settled down, I asked what she thought about Grace.

'It's an amazing transformation,' she said. 'I haven't seen her so interested and so involved for years. She seems to remember new things every time you see her. And she also seems much happier than she's been for a very long time.'

'Do you think she could come out of hospital?'

'Permanently?'

'Yes.'

'I've thought about it many times, duckie,' Olive said slowly, 'many times. She's certainly making progress but she would still need constant care. We tried it in the past, for a week or two, but something always went wrong. She couldn't sleep, or she'd go out without us knowing, and we'd have to scour the neighbourhood looking for her. After a time, she gets nervous and restless and wants to go back to the hospital. She feels safer there. Also, I have to think of Bill. He is fond of Grace but I don't think he could have her living with us in our little house.'

'I suppose, in theory, I could look after her,' I said. 'I'm not married. I have a flat. I am free…'

'But you have to work and travel, John. You have a life to lead. She needs full-time care.'

'What about hiring a nurse?'

'Very expensive and not always reliable.' She paused. 'I know you want to help but see what Dr Birmingham says. Poor Grace, she used to be such an independent person.'

It was true that we all had our lives to lead and nothing was likely to change at this point. However, there was always hope and, for me, a kind of change had already taken place. Grace, my mother, was real and present even if I did not see her often and she remained physically remote in the hospital. I noticed this psychic shift when I had to fill in a form for a foreign visa and provide my date and place of birth, a routine exercise I had performed many times before. But this time it felt different, more significant. I thought of Grace and the hospital where I was born, a real person, a real place.

Before I went to see Dr Birmingham, I did some research on the treatment of schizophrenia. *Pears Medical Encyclopaedia* described leucotomy in some detail.

'The division of some of the prefrontal fibres, which connect the front part of the cerebral cortex to the rest of the brain, are severed to a greater or lesser degree,' it read. It went on to warn that the operation was a measure of last resort. 'The possibility of permanent damage to the mental function makes it advisable to reserve leucotomy for cases where all other methods have been tried and failed and there is no reasonable hope of spontaneous recovery. A leucotomised patient, whose emotions are shallow and behaviour unreliable, may be better than a demented one as far as relatives and attendants are concerned. But the patient has lost something which cannot be recovered. Recent tremendous progress in drug therapy of mental conditions has made surgeons even more cautious about taking irrevocable measures. The operation, once quite commonly performed, is now rarely used.'

Intrigued, I did some more research. Leucotomy, I discovered, was the brainchild, if that is the right expression, of Egas Moniz, a Portuguese neurologist, who first tried it on humans in 1935 after an American experiment with two chimpanzees. An accomplished self-publicist, Moniz spread the word that his leucotomy operation was safe and effective.

Leucotomy, deriving from the Greek words 'cut' and 'white', involved the use of a pencil-sized device called a leucotome, which worked by pressing a plunger at one end that extruded a wire loop at the other. Moniz drilled holes over the frontal lobes in the patient's skull, inserted the instrument, released the loop and, with a rotating movement, snipped off some of the white neural fibres.

While that sounded pretty haphazard and barbaric, it got worse. Three versions of the surgery came into use. The prefrontal leucotomy, which Grace underwent, was followed by the prefrontal lobotomy, a more radical procedure involving a knife instead of a leucotome to cut away the brain tissue. The third method was transorbital lobotomy conducted with two simple instruments: an ice pick and a small hammer. The pick was inserted through the eye socket between the upper lid and the eye and tapped further in with the hammer. The pick was then swirled around, rather like an egg-beater, severing the fibres.

The controversial inventor and practitioner of transorbital lobotomies was Dr Walter Freeman, a flamboyant American neurologist who became Moniz's leading disciple in his home country and coined the term 'lobotomy'. He travelled far and wide across America in his self-styled 'lobotomobile' and performed nearly 3,500 operations, many on children, over two decades. He operated in hospitals, clinics, his office, motel rooms, and patients' homes. His most notorious operation was on John F. Kennedy's mildly retarded and emotionally erratic sister, Rosemary, reducing her to a semi-vegetative state at the age of twenty-three. He was eventually disbarred for a botched operation that killed a patient.

Moniz's career as a lobotomist was cut short in 1939 when he was shot by a former patient. The attack left Moniz semi-paralysed and with a useless right hand. But he was awarded the Nobel Prize in 1949 for 'the discovery of the therapeutic value of leucotomy in certain psychoses'. The award helped legitimise the operation and the practice spread far and wide. Grace was one of the people caught up in a veritable tsunami of lobotomies. Poor Grace, she had little good luck in her life but this was probably the worst break of all.

At the hospital, I told Dr Birmingham about the progress we had made and wondered about the possibility of Grace coming out.

'All that's good,' he said. 'However, one upheaval in Grace's life is enough for the moment. I would not recommend changing her treatment as a permanently hospitalised patient for the time being.'

'She seems to enjoy her time out with her sister,' I said, 'and I understand that there have been no more walks in the night.'

He looked at me gravely. 'I think it is important not to rush things. She has spent most of the last forty years in hospitals. Let's take another look at how she is progressing in a few months' time.'

## 24

IN LATE SPRING, I DECIDED TO RETURN TO SPAIN TO FINISH my part of the Irish thriller. I visited Olive on my journey south, and she promised to keep me up-to-date with Grace's progress. Typically, her first letter arrived before I did, lying amid the same barber's clutter and uncollected mail that had cushioned the revelatory letters from Joan Cooper and Edith. Strangely, two more letters, with a similar impact and rounding out the story that the first had started, would soon nestle there.

Olive's first offering was not in the same category but it was full of news. If ever the written word could be said to bubble, it would be in Olive's letters. This one was bursting with activities of her family and her daily life. She had spread the word about our reunion to her relatives, who were also mine, and I felt myself being drawn into the maternal side of my family that had been missing for so long.

I had put Olive in touch with Joan Cooper and the two old friends started corresponding after a gap of thirty-five years, culminating in Joan inviting Olive to come and stay with her in Bournemouth. She quoted a comment she had made about me in one of her letters to Joan because she thought it would amuse me. 'John came here on his way to Spain,' she wrote. 'I pumped him with as much information as I could about the family but, as he says, "She can *talk!*" Haven't heard a word since but I can't blame him. It must have been a lot of family to swallow at one gulp.'

She was right. It had been overwhelming. However, the depression I had experienced after first meeting Grace, and seeing how she had looked before she was married, had lifted. The subsequent visits to the hospital and the time spent with Grace in Chatham had been so different, and Olive reported further improvement.

She also threw out memories from the past like pebbles into a frothing stream.

'I've just remembered how George grew the most wonderful tomatoes while you were all living in Morden,' she wrote. 'He just planted them anywhere, in circles, no system of any kind. Mother was furious! They were so marvellous and shouldn't have been!'

Furthermore, she sprinkled her letters with things that had caught her attention. 'I heard a comment on the radio the other day,' she wrote in one letter. 'It was someone talking about British journalists. "They are socially ambiguous," he said, "but they are certainly not gentlemen."' I told Olive later I took it as a compliment.

One day, I was surprised to find a letter from Maurice among my mail on the marble counter. We didn't normally write to each other but spoke on the telephone from time to time, and exchanged birthday and Christmas cards. There were two letters inside the envelope: a cover-note to me, and a copy of a letter he had written recently to someone with whom we had both been in contact.

Not long before I found Grace, an unknown woman had written to me asking for help. Like the Cooper sisters, she had seen my name in the *Observer*. Her name was Rosemary and she explained that she was adopted at birth, had grown up harmoniously with her adoptive parents, whom she loved, and was happily married with three young children. However, at the age of forty, she felt the time had come to find out more about her biological mother.

Rosemary managed to find a copy of her birth certificate that revealed her mother's maiden name was de St. Jorre. She was born in the Seychelles and was one of my many cousins. With help from family members, I obtained her mother's address, passed it on, and copied the correspondence to Maurice. Rosemary wrote her mother a carefully worded letter expressing the hope of establishing a connection but promising not to intrude in her life, stressing that she had a settled and happy life of her own. She received a short, brutal response. Her mother wanted nothing to do with her and told her never to contact her again. Rosemary was mortified and bitterly angry, but she could do nothing about it.

I told Maurice and he wrote to her. His letter made fascinating reading because he chose to use our family story as a way of expressing his sympathy for her, and to show 'how traumatic events can determine the way one reacts for the rest of one's life.'

'I am not sure what John told you about our parental history,' he wrote, 'but in a way it is as tangled and sad as yours.'

Our parents divorced after the war and my mother wound up in a mental institution and was lobotomised, probably for something not much more than post-partum depression after my birth. I never knew her. John has some brief memories of a happy, smiling person; I have no memories at all. As children we were told that she had died and were discouraged from asking any questions about her. I never saw a photograph of her until I was close to fifty.

My reaction to all of this was twofold. First, I used my father as a counter example; anything he did I would at least consider the opposite as the first possibility for any action. Second, I oriented my life around that of my friends or my work; existing family ranked a very distant third at least until I married and had a family of my own. As soon as John had both independence and time, he set off in pursuit of the truth about our mother. He recently found her alive in a London mental institution but severely impaired because of the lobotomy.

I haven't seen her, but that is my choice. Even though I live in North America, I could go but I choose not to. I have always considered her dead. All this is sad because I am sure that my father and my mother were not bad or mad people, but they were caught up in their own problems and those foisted upon them by the Depression and the Second World War.

I guess my point is that there are certain inexact parallels between your mother's reaction to your approach, and John's and my attitudes towards our missing mother. I hope your mother will reconsider her attitude but I suspect that she will have to come to this on her own. Any pressure on her will probably be counterproductive.

I had always thought that this was how Maurice felt. For him, the story about our mother dying at an early age was literally and emotionally true. I thought we made it up, but perhaps Maurice was right, and someone told us that she had died although I cannot think who it might have been. Maurice had never expressed his feelings in writing before, or in such detail, and I thought the way he did it here was honest, moving and, ultimately, sad. It was honest because he did not seek to blame one side or the other in the failure of our parents' marriage, and he recognised that the difficult times they lived through must have deepened their troubles. It was moving because, although his own position was clear, he had great sympathy for Rosemary, who had taken a different path, and for her suffering when her mother spurned her. Finally, it was sad because our parents' tragedy had alienated him from our father, in particular, and the family in general.

That he had chosen to tell the story via a third party was not surprising. It reflected our upbringing. Our father and Edith established the rules, sometimes explicitly, as with the shunning of our upstairs neighbour, or elliptically, like their silence about our mother. As children, we understood and obeyed. We buttoned up our emotions and kept our mouths shut. This meant we did not ask them about topics they did not voluntarily discuss with us. It also became second nature never to talk between ourselves about those things, even though we were close in other ways.

When we left home, things began to change. Maurice distanced himself from our family. He and I remained friendly but I was in the

Far East, Africa or the Middle East much of the time while he took off for Canada and rarely came back to England. His attitude towards our father was a surprise. He did not mention Edith, to whom he had always been respectful and loyal, but when he relegated our family in his priorities, Edith was part of it. In the end, the elaborate cover-up of our family history seemed to have stirred both of us to rebellion, and this was Maurice's way of doing it.

My way was to look for Grace. I knew that if I did not try, the mystery would have haunted me to the grave. Yet, had it not been for considerable help and some extraordinary luck, the quest could have easily ended in failure. I was erratic, hesitant, and distracted at times, and lacked a consistent plan. But when knowledgeable people emerged and pointed the way, I followed.

The succession of coincidences and breaks that I experienced during the search were so powerful that, at times, I felt some kind of external force was at work or, more fancifully, it was my mother's way of reminding me not to forget her. I also was fortunate, at the end of the road, to find a willing and enthusiastic enabler and go-between, the irrepressible Olive. Finally, and most important of all, Grace, after initial bewilderment, accepted me as her son and seemed proud of it. The rejection Rosemary encountered from her mother showed how radically different the outcome could have been.

In her next letter, Olive told me that she had asked Dr Birmingham if Grace could spend a few days with her in Chatham to celebrate Grace's sixty-eighth birthday. He agreed and Olive reported that she had never known Grace maintain such 'a concentrated attention to what she was doing or to talk so normally about all sorts of things.' One day, after an outing to Chatham, Grace turned to Olive and said, 'I am adapting to a natural environment.'

'Wasn't that a lovely phrase?' enthused Olive, 'and so exactly right to explain her progress in just one weekend at home. Her face this week has gradually changed to a proper shape—more like Grace, not a person in an institution.'

Olive said that Grace did not like the photographs I had taken of her during our second visit. 'I've shown them to her once or twice,' Olive wrote, 'just to give her a gentle reminder that teeth would be a definite improvement!'

Grace was also in the habit of writing long lists of disconnected words. Olive enclosed one with the words scrawled over an old Christmas card and scraps of paper. Grace seemed drawn to colours, which she wrote in columns: 'vermillion, cerise, scarlet, red, purple, mauve, heliotrope, magenta,' and so on. Scattered among the collection were a few references to me: 'John!' 'John comes.' 'Green French car.' 'John life reporter.' 'John returns.'

On a page torn out from a magazine, she wrote what was, in essence, the story of her life: 'Grace Rose Islip (I was)—Mr George Louis de St. Jorre—a Frenchman—married him—bore two babies, boys, John and Maurice—pretty—divorce—breakdown.'

Olive said that she had suggested to Grace that she should write a note to me. Grace agreed somewhat reluctantly but just stared at the notepaper. 'I don't know what to say,' she said. However, with Olive's help, she eventually got going.

The letter was in an airmail envelope. As I turned it over, I caught sight of a phrase, just visible through the thin paper. My heart missed a beat. I tore open the envelope and read my mother's first letter to me. It was written on flowered notepaper in a firm, clear hand.

Dear John,

I have washed up three times today.

Thank you for my birthday card.

Thank you for your letter. Do you like typewriting letters? I think that looks rather nice.

I return to Napsbury Hospital tomorrow (Wednesday). I am going to see Gladys Peagram, a cousin, as Olive sees me back on the Green Line bus.

I have enjoyed my week's stay with Bill and Olive and I am much happier now—recovering from my breakdown.

Thank you for the chocolate egg. It was delicious, a nice big one. Darling baby mine.

I don't think I can write any more. We will meet again soon. Lots of love,

Grace.

Three words, five syllables, hiding in plain sight, forging the final link that I had been only dimly aware was missing until that moment. I had found my mother, and now she had found me.

# 25

I FLEW TO NEW YORK IN LATE 1975 ON ICELANDIC AIR—THE steerage class of transatlantic travel at the time—clad for the rigours of a North American winter in a long, sheepskin-lined suede over-coat. When I stepped out into the pandemonium of JFK airport, the temperature was eighty-five degrees with matching humidity. Off with the coat and into a yellow cab driven by an Egyptian who, true to form, drove with a death wish, as if he were in Cairo.

In Manhattan, he dropped me off at the apartment building where a friend had invited me to stay until I found a place of my own. I rang the bell, he opened the door and we greeted each other. Sitting on the couch behind him, was a beautiful young woman. Her name was Helen and she greeted me with a dazzling smile. It seemed as if we had been waiting for the right time and right place to meet, and here we were.

I was in New York because I had been offered a year-long job by the Carnegie Endowment for International Peace to write a short book on South Africa aimed at the United States foreign policy establishment. Over lunch with another journalist, who had just finished a similar project on Ethiopia, he gave me the subtext of working for an American non-profit institution.

'Every morning when you wake up,' he said, 'the foundation's endowment has grown in the night. This is a serious problem for your masters. They have to spend the money otherwise they are in deep trouble with the Internal Revenue Service. It's your job to help them out.'

A few months later, Helen and Seth, her seven-year-old son from a former marriage, and I moved into a brownstone apartment in

Greenwich Village. Olive continued to write regularly and the occasional note came from Grace. Olive had finally acquired a telephone and when Grace next spent a weekend with her, I called them. They had been watching a 'riveting' England-France rugby match on Olive's small black-and-white television. Grace was reading a lot, Olive reported, 'which is very unusual and very heartening, and my neighbour has also noticed a great improvement.' Not long after, I received a postcard from Grace.

'To dear John from his Mum with lots of love and kisses,' she wrote. 'I am very pleased you phoned me and that I was resilient, whatever that means.'

I wrote back to her and enclosed a photograph of Helen and Seth who, with a little encouragement, wrote a short note. Grace responded quickly: 'They look most attractive,' she wrote. She thought Seth was 'very energetic' and 'sweet and strong'. She went on to say she felt better than when she had last stayed with Olive. 'I am on a diet and have lost a little weight, and am much happier.' She ended with: 'I am looking forward to seeing you all when you turn up next time. Much love to you, Helen and Seth. Always, Grace.'

In one of her letters, Olive recounted a recent conversation she had had with Grace about separation and divorce.

'I told her that although the adults suffered, it was the children who were shattered. "Imagine," I said, "if Father had left us. Imagine how we would have felt? Or suppose Mother had gone off with another man?"

'At that, both of us collapsed into gales of laughter and Grace said: "I can't imagine her doing anything so *frivolous!*" Wasn't that a lovely word?'

Grace's memory continued to surprise Olive. 'She rattled off your address in Morden, where you were living when she was first taken ill—something I've never been able to remember. Then she said she felt much better but added: "I'm not quite normal yet." Once upon a time, she couldn't put that into words.'

Olive's most exciting report came after Grace had spent a whole week with her. 'I've never had such a marvellous time with her,' Olive wrote rapturously. 'She was so stable, so interested in every-thing, it was unbelievable. She was able to hold *long* conversations, never lost the point of the discussion, watched T.V., and laughed in all the right places. After a couple of days, she was reading for two or three hours at a time. We went for walks around Rochester where she commented on various ancient buildings. Oh! I can't begin to tell you how miraculous this normality was.

'What thrilled me was that she didn't have any sign or symptom of relapse. She slept every night—therefore so did I! Not since she became ill, have we had such a joyful week together. She asked me about how you and I met, and sat enthralled by the story. I give the credit of this tremendous improvement all to you. I wish you could have seen her at the end of the week.'

I wish I could have seen her, too, but I simply could not leave New York. Was a miracle about to occur in Laurel Ward? Probably not, but miracles, even Dr Birmingham conceded, could happen. Olive reported the changes to him, and she sent me his response.

'I am pleased to hear that you found Grace to be so much better when she visited you this time,' the doctor wrote. 'On the whole, I think she has been generally better lately and, certainly, she very much appreciates her holidays with you and the contact she has with her son.'

It was evident that he did not think anything dramatic was occurring. But, like all the doctors in the hospital, he had dozens of patients to look after and might not be fully aware of Grace's current condition. I was eager to see for myself.

In the summer, Helen and I went to England, drove down to Chatham, and spent a day with Olive, Bill and Grace who was out of hospital for a few days. Grace's hair had been washed and set, her nails painted, and she looked bright and cheerful. Only her stockings had missed the make-over. They were as wrinkled as ever and held up precariously just above the knee by garters.

After we embraced, she looked at me. 'You have a steady face,' she said reflectively. 'You are older, but not old.'

I introduced Helen who, seeing a book open on the side table next to where Grace was sitting, asked her if she enjoyed reading.

'I do but I can't concentrate for very long.'

'What do you like doing best?' I asked.

'Smoking,' she said quickly.

Olive and Bill had banned cigarettes for the time being so Grace asked for one of my small cigars. She smoked half of it, coughed a lot, and gave up.

'How did you and Maurice get along with Edith and your father?' she suddenly asked.

'Very well,' I said, unsure of how much I should say.

Olive went off to make some tea and came back with a large fruitcake. After we all had some, Grace eyed a slice still on Helen's plate. 'Are you going to have that piece?' she asked. 'No, I'm full,' said Helen. Grace reached out and ate it with pleasure.

After the cups and plates had been cleared away, Bill sang a popular song from the 1930s and the sisters joined in. Grace remembered some of the words and sang in a sweet, gentle voice. I can't remember the song but it created a bittersweet moment, back in time, when they were all young, hopeful and happy before the world they lived in changed forever, and their lives with it.

Grace said that she felt she was recovering from her breakdown but was 'not quite herself yet'. She seemed to be aware that it was necessary to return to the hospital. I wondered what she thought of the institutional life there where all she did was work, eat, take her pills, watch television, and smoke away her weekly wages. I also wondered how she would feel if she were given a chance of leaving and living in a world that she no longer knew. It was impossible to tell.

During the afternoon, I noticed something that had escaped me earlier: sibling rivalry. Olive clearly loved being at the centre of things and treated Grace more of a child than she really was. Perhaps it had been the other way around in their youth when Grace was the lively, sexy one, with boyfriends, while Olive stayed in the shadows, loyal to her strait-laced mother and a prisoner of her acne.

Near the end of our stay, Grace suddenly said, 'When did George die?'

I told her.

'Were you with him?'

'Yes, I was.'

'Did he ever talk about me?'

I leaned forward and took hold of her hands. 'Never. Maurice and I grew up knowing nothing about you, or Olive, or your mother, or indeed anybody in your family. Nobody talked about the Islips, and we were not encouraged to ask. It was very confusing, and very sad.'

She looked down and did not comment. She still seemed able to cut herself off from the world yet, paradoxically, I felt we were closer than ever.

On the way down to Chatham, I had thought of what to say if Grace asked me when Maurice would be coming to see her. *I am not sure*, I planned to say. *He lives in western Canada and is working hard. I have told him all about you and Olive and I am waiting to hear from him.* But she never asked me, yet she had spontaneously brought up my father and Edith in our conversations. Did she suspect the truth?

She looked up at me, her face unclouded, back with us once more. 'Are you and Helen going to get married?'

I glanced at Helen who smiled. 'Very likely,' I said.

Shortly after returning to New York, we received a letter from Olive with a brief 'thank-you' note from Grace inside. Olive reported that Grace was well and had said that she liked Helen whom she thought 'a sensible and very nice girl'. The conversation ended as follows.

Grace: 'Is Helen black?'

Olive: 'Yes, she is. What did you think she was?'

Grace: 'I thought she was well-tanned.'

'As you drove away,' Olive wrote, 'Grace said, "I am going to cry," and she shed a few tears.'

A week later, a letter from Grace arrived.


Dear John,

Darling, how busy you are & clever, I think. Olive showed me your work and I am very proud. I have been knitting a sock and reading a lot. But I have also been restless and wish I were well again although Olive says I look better physically.

Olive is visiting me this afternoon & keeps me in touch with you.

Are you happy? Please write to me quickly and take me out in your car, John.

Olive showed me two pictures of her and Bill with a little monkey. I'd like the monkey.

I am well and nearly normal. You enjoy good health, don't you?

August was very long ago & that was the last time I saw you (& Helen).

All my love, Grace, xxxx

P.S. I shall have no excuse for not writing as Olive has given me this pen.

Au revoir and a happy New Year. It's quite warm. I dream a lot. Olive has been getting at me to arrange for new dentures (I liked Helen's dentures) but they hurt me & don't suit me well.


In February 1978, Helen, with her beautiful natural teeth, and I were married in New York by a gay Methodist minister in his stylish living room, just off Washington Square in Greenwich Village. He offered us the choice of the normal Methodist marriage service and a secular version, the identical liturgy but with all references to the deity removed for the comfort of non-believers. We chose the expurgated version and Seth, then eight years old, gave away the bride. I wondered what Grace's reaction would be since she had once offered me money to stay single.

I called her and told her the news. She sounded cheerful, her voice clear on the transatlantic line.

'That's wonderful, darling,' she said.

'I'll be coming over soon and will see you then.'

'That will be fine. I look forward to seeing you and Helen.'

'Look after yourself,' I said.

'I always do,' she replied.

## 26

WHEN I HAD FINISHED MY SOUTH AFRICAN BOOK, I REJOINED the *Observer* covering the United Nations but also making forays to the American hinterland, Canada, El Salvador, and Egypt. From time to time, we went over to England to see Olive and Grace who was still in hospital but spending more time with Olive than in the past. In January 1979, the paper sent me to Iran to cover the Islamic revolution. I broke the journey in London and called Olive. Grace was in a hospital in London, she said, having an ulcer from her tongue removed, and I could visit her there.

I found Grace sitting up in bed in a ward with five other patients. She appeared happy to see me and stuck out her tongue to show me the hole where the ulcer had been.

'It doesn't hurt much,' she said, 'but my tongue feels like sandpaper.'

I gave her some French perfume and a packet of cigarettes. She said she was not allowed to smoke in the ward but could do so in the patients' common room. She seemed disoriented, probably due to the unfamiliar surroundings, and began to drift off. I chatted about Helen and Seth, life in New York, and the Tehran assignment.

She listened but did not say much, except for the almost dreamy 'Yes... Yes... Yes' that I knew well. When I did not keep the flow of conversation going, she started reciting her word patterns, another sign that she was not at her best.

'Suicide, sea, scaffold, remain, quit... which is it?'

Taken aback, I hesitated. 'Remain,' I finally said.

'I am in a university here,' she said, suddenly alert.

'What are you studying?'

She paused and gave me one of her direct, clear-eyed looks.
'Courage,' she said.

The next day I flew to Tehran. The Shah had gone and Ayatollah Khomeini had arrived but not yet taken over. An uneasy interregnum was under way, with noisy, sometimes violent, street demonstrations, and a final showdown seemed imminent. I had been there for three days when I received a cable from the *Observer* at the hotel. My mother had died of a stroke.

I could have flown back to London. Tehran airport was often closed but, if you were patient, it was possible to get in and out. The *Observer* would have understood although not been happy because I would have left a major story uncovered. However, it didn't take me long to decide to stay. I felt that I could do nothing to help. I knew Olive would be able to handle the funeral arrangements and although my presence would boost her morale, it was not essential. Maurice, far from England and preoccupied with his professional life, probably felt the same way about not returning for our father's funeral fourteen years earlier.

I was in Iran for six weeks. On my way home, I stopped off in London and went to see Olive in Chatham. She said she had recovered from Grace's sudden death, but she was more subdued than usual.

'It was awful, I didn't even know she was ill,' she said. 'I had a call from the hospital, and a nurse, whom I had never heard of, said Grace had been dead for three days. I was shattered. I couldn't believe our little Grace was gone. You were on your way to Tehran. I called Helen but she didn't know where you were and when I spoke to someone at the *Observer* he said he wasn't sure which hotel you were staying in.'

'Someone knew and reached me,' I said. 'Why didn't the hospital call you earlier?'

'When Bill and I went up to Napsbury the next day, they told me it was a mistake. Grace hadn't been dead for three days before they called but they should have called me earlier anyway. She took ill on the Friday and died early Sunday morning. That eased my despair and bewilderment but it was still painful because I wanted to see her when she was first taken ill. Now, I'll never see her again.'

Olive began to cry and I put my arms around her and held her close. I told her why I had not returned to England for the funeral.

'Don't worry, duckie,' she said, brushing away her tears. 'I understand.'

She admitted that having to handle all the bureaucratic and funeral formalities kept her busy and her mind off her grief. She decided that Grace should be cremated, mainly because it was less costly than digging a grave. She asked for the resident Anglican minister at Napsbury Hospital, whom she knew, to conduct the funeral service and it was held at the local crematorium. Apart from the minister and a crematorium official, Olive and Bill were the only people who attended.

'I economised on the cremation,' said Olive, 'but I wanted her ashes to be with Father and Mother in London, even though it was double the cost of interring them locally. I was told that they would put the casket in a kind of pocket at the foot of the grave, so no digging was necessary. That was just as well,' she said, brightening a little, 'because the gravediggers were on strike!'

Grace's estate, when the tallying was complete, totalled sixty-two pounds ninety pence, split between Maurice and me. Grace was seventy-one when she died on 4 February 1979. She had spent forty of those years in mental institutions.

I told Olive that I would like to visit Grace's grave but had a flight booked to New York the next day, so we agreed to go when I returned to London in three months' time. We met in Notting Hill and took a bus to Kensal Green Cemetery in north London. It was a gloomy, overcast day with thunder in the air as we entered the cemetery through the main gate. Headstones had fallen down, weeds covered the grave sites, and even the paths were overgrown. There seemed to be no one in charge.

The confusion started with the piece of paper in Olive's hand. On it were written two different section numbers, both with a question mark. Another problem was that although the grave had originally been registered under the name 'Islip', Olive had changed it into her name, 'Anderson', after her mother died. Then, recently, a 'de St. Jorre' had been added. But Olive was confident we would find it because she had been there only weeks earlier when Grace's ashes were interred. We set off down one of the long avenues.

We searched and searched but in vain. Finally, we found someone who worked there. He did his best to help us but still nothing. No sign of Grace, no trace of Charles and Lucy. We persevered for another half hour and it began to rain. We looked at each other and decided there was no point in continuing. I reached for Olive's firm, smooth hand and felt its reassuring warmth. The Islips, apart from the one at my side, had vanished once more.

## 27

I WROTE TO MAURICE AND DOROTHY ON MY RETURN TO THE UK telling them about Grace's death and they replied with their condolences. Olive, I knew, would like to see them both but she never mentioned it to me, and I never said anything to Maurice. I debated whether to tell Edith the news and, in the end, decided not to. Neither of us had talked about Grace since Edith's ambiguous one-line comment when I first told her of the reunion. Knowing Grace was finally gone might have reassured Edith, but I thought it better to stick to the original plan of total silence, taking refuge in our traditional family *omertà*.

Eighteen months previously, I had taken Helen to Scotland to meet Edith after Helen had met Olive and Grace in Kent, concluding the grand tour of my divided family. Edith was gracious and hospitable, and if she was disappointed in me for my choice of partner, she did not show it. Since we were not yet married, Edith put Helen in my bedroom and I made do with a sleeping bag on the living room floor, reminding me of how Edith and my father had separate bedrooms in the Woodford flat before they were married.

One night we all played Scrabble and, near the end of the game, only two tiles, face down, remained on the table. It was Edith's turn. She looked at them and then, touching them alternately with her forefinger, she said:

> Eenie meenie miney moe,
> Catch a nigger by his toe,
> If he hollers, let him go,
> Eeenie meenie miney moe.

She picked up the tile she had last touched, placed it on the rack with her other letters, and studied them carefully. I looked at Helen who shrugged and smiled.

After we were married, Helen suggested a name for her new mother-in-law, 'Mother Edith', following an American custom. This pleased everybody, especially Edith, since it underlined her position as the family matriarch.

In early October 1981, I received a call in New York from one of Edith's neighbours. She had fallen on the step outside her back door and broken her hip. She was in hospital and, when I called her there, she said she'd had an operation and was making good progress. She wrote to us a few days later, we replied and, from time to time, I talked to her on the telephone. Then I had another call, this time from a nurse at the hospital. Edith had died of pneumonia. It was November 6th, her father's birthday.

Maurice, who was working for a mining company in northwest Canada, joined me at J. F. Kennedy airport in New York and we flew to Scotland together. I hadn't seen him for three years and he was, as ever, a tall, thin, loping figure with thick straight hair, flecked with grey, and a face wrinkled from long exposure on high mountains and ski slopes. The scars from the cycling accident on Dartmoor had softened with age but were still visible. It was curious that Maurice had spent much of his adult life either in the depths of the earth, as a mining engineer, or at its highest reaches as a passionate rock climber and mountaineer. Both were lonely, dangerous places where he found achievement and solace.

We arrived in Edinburgh in the afternoon, rented a car, and drove through the Scottish Borders to the hospital in Galashiels. The sky, which seems closer to the ground in Scotland than elsewhere, was the colour of pewter and a gusting wind chased the clouds over the hills. The doctor told us that Edith had recovered from her broken hip but pneumonia set in afterwards, as it often does with elderly patients lying prone for long periods.

'At this stage, old people tend to react in two different ways,' he said. 'They either decide to fight or to give up. What happens next is largely a matter of willpower. Your mother decided not to fight.'

At the time of her death, Edith was seventy-eight years old. She had chronic bronchitis, severe arthritis, and a deep-seated feeling that she should not, under any circumstances, become a burden to her relatives and friends. She had made elaborate preparations in advance for an accident or a medical emergency. The neighbour who found her discovered a bag already packed with a list of instructions about extra things she might need, how to contact family members, and the way her affairs should be handled. In the end, I think Edith decided that she would rather die than bother anybody. Her final words in her last letter to me were: 'Sorry to be such a worry to you.'

The undertaker arrived at Edith's house almost before we did. He was a businesslike fellow with a small moustache and a tendency to laugh at the wrong moments. He referred to the body using a number of euphemisms but slipped up once, calling it the 'remains'. He said he would make all the arrangements and then startled us by asking if we had 'any other interments in mind'.

We spent the next five days organising the funeral, and disposing of Edith's house and possessions. It was the longest period we had been together since our teens. Maurice was as quiet as ever but not uncommunicative. On two occasions, he called me 'Dorothy', a sign perhaps that, despite all the time apart, we were still close. He was both practical and astute in winding down Edith's affairs. While I began to wilt, sadder than I thought I would be, he set about clearing the house and instructed the solicitor not to advertise the funeral because it might draw attention to the unoccupied property. If he was upset, he kept it to himself.

In the evenings, we had dinner in the hotel in Hawick where we were staying, and usually had a beer or two afterwards. The death of Edith had not only brought us together in this quiet corner of the world but also took us back into the past.

'I sometimes wondered why she ever hooked up with Dad,' Maurice said one evening. 'He was no catch in any sense of the word. But he did provide an instant family, and after a lifetime of spinsterhood, perhaps that was enough.'

'It was unlikely that she would ever have children of her own,' I said. 'She and her three sisters had been spinsters all their lives and, when her chance came, she took it. That aside, I think she was genuinely in love with Dad, and he with her, and it worked out pretty well for both of them. And for us.'

Somehow or other, the biking accident came up, and Maurice surprised me by taking full blame for it, saying it was his decision to fiddle with the front brakes, not mine. It was a relief to hear it but I continued to feel guilty because, as the older brother, I should have made sure the brakes were working properly before we crossed the moor.

Our four, motherless years at St. Dominic's still lay heavily on his mind and this time he linked the ordeal to his attitude towards Grace.

'I never had any inclination to go and look for her, and I am still not sure why,' he said. 'Perhaps the experience of St. Dominic's convinced me that the past was something best forgotten as quickly as possible.'

'That's understandable.'

'I wonder if your motivation to search for Grace might have been weaker, perhaps non-existent, if you hadn't been there,' he continued. 'Just imagine if you had lived a humdrum lower middle-class life for those years, you may have felt differently about her.'

I was not sure he was right because I had a vivid and intimate memory of Grace before I went to St. Dominic's and it kept me focused on her. Also, I was older and possibly less traumatised by the school. Sixteen months of seniority doesn't sound like much but, in childhood, it is a significant difference, which diminishes and eventually becomes meaningless as you grow older. When we arrived, Maurice was a tender five-year-old, one of the youngest in the school, whereas I was a relatively mature seven-year-old. However, if he was right, it meant that our time at the school influenced us in diametrically opposite ways. He buried the past, and I dug it up.

Among Edith's papers, I found her marriage certificate. It showed that she and my father's registry-office wedding in 1948 had been witnessed by Jenny, Edith's elderly spinster sister, a gentle soul, and our fascist landlord, an odd pair. My father's divorce from Grace was recorded, as was his current residence, the house in south London where we had lived in the early part of the war but long since left. Edith's address was our flat in Woodford where he was actually living. I suppose the proprieties of the day precluded them from admitting they shared the same roof, not to mention cohabiting with the fascist landlord. The assumption would be that they were 'living in sin', which they weren't. Nevertheless, that anomalous situation had lasted for six months and I often wondered how Edith explained it to colleagues at school or friends in the neighbourhood. For long known as a single woman, the virtuous Miss Ross, it could not have been easy. That she was prepared to share the flat with us, regardless of what people thought, showed an independent streak, and commendable courage in that morally corseted age.

The funeral took place in the small stone Presbyterian church on the hillside at the end of Edith's property, clearly visible from her living room window. Her neighbours, including my veterinarian friend Angus, and other friends turned up in force and gave her the send-off she deserved.

When I told Olive about Edith's death, she said she would have liked to have met her but realised it was 'a feeble wish'. Olive quickly became an integral part of our lives and those of our young children, Jenna and Shane. Whenever we were in England, we spent time with her and Irish Billy, and they visited us in Spain. After Bill's death in 1982, Olive came to see us in Washington DC, aged eighty, notwithstanding an arm broken in a recent fall, and got to know teenage

Seth. Olive kept up a lively and voluminous correspondence, writing in a clear, confident hand. She loved reading. At the back of her diary for 1933, she had a list of eighty-two books, which she had read, skimmed, or started but not finished, with brief critical comments on most of them. When I called her on her eighty-ninth birthday, she said: 'I'm reading Charles Dickens' *Little Dorit*... oooh, duckie!'

Her letters and conversation were brimming—frothing, at times—with her latest discoveries, impressions and memories. When she was living in London during the 1920s and 1930s, she had gone to the theatre and ballet as often as she could afford it. She had seen Charles Laughton and Flora Robson in *Henry VIII*, Richard Tauber in concert, and once went to the Ritz Hotel where Mary Pickford was staying. Somehow she and a friend got in, made contact with the star, who invited the two excited young women to tea, and Olive walked out with her idol's autograph. At the age of eighty-five, Olive read a book that she liked by the British writer Katherine Moore, then almost ninety, and wrote to her. Katherine Moore replied graciously and thus began an enthusiastic, wide-ranging correspondence—they never met—which lasted until both were too old to continue.

Olive's relationship with Bill seemed stable. She was rather maternal in her dealings with him and he played the role of the naughty little boy. All that was fine but it went beyond a joke when, one day, Olive told me agitatedly that Bill was 'having an affair' with a woman down the street. Neither Helen nor I took it seriously, nor did Olive's friends, but she was convinced. She was deeply upset, at times anguished, and talked about 'divorcing' him.

The drama ended with Bill's death in 1982. Olive was in Florence, on one of her art excursions. When she returned she found Bill had stopped eating and looked 'like a Belsen victim'. The doctor did not seem to know what was wrong and gave him something to improve his appetite. A month later he was dead. The autopsy revealed that he died from liver cancer.

I saw Olive shortly afterwards on a trip to London to write an article on Savile Row tailors for *Town & Country*. The magazine booked Helen and me into a suite at the Dorchester Hotel, my only experience of showbusiness journalism. As we sat in the hotel's grand tearoom, Olive told us she had been distraught but it wasn't clear what upset her most, Bill's alleged infidelity or his death. After the funeral, she calmed down only to discover that Bill, whose name was on the title deed, had left the house to his sister. Under the threat of becoming homeless, Olive had to hire a lawyer and eventually sorted it out.

My family was not the only one to embrace her. Not long after Bill's death, Maurice and Dorothy and Danielle, their youngest daughter, flew over from Canada and drove down to Chatham to spend the day with her. She was delighted and wrote us a long letter about the visit. The Canadian side of the family kept in touch with her until the end. Thus, Olive was finally reunited with both her nephews whom she had cared for with love, though not enjoyment, long ago.

Olive lived in her modest bungalow in Kent until she was ninety-one when she started having blackouts and becoming disoriented. One day a neighbour found her on the bedroom floor and when I arrived, she was in hospital, a place she had never been before except to visit others. On the advice of her doctor, I moved her to a residential home.

'I'm being crucified,' she told me when I visited her. 'I'm a lost soul and it's my own fault. The only thing I want to do is to die.'

On another occasion, her spirits revived.

'It's priceless, duckie,' she said, sitting up in bed. 'Two old creatures from Rochester came to see me. I had never seen them before and had no idea who they were!'

Yet she was bent on escaping, on 'doing a bunk', just as Maurice had from St. Dominic's during the war. Perhaps it was in our genes.

'I go absolutely pink trying to think of some way to get out,' she said. 'But I'm so stupid!'

During one visit, she brought something up that we had never discussed.

'I always wanted to be cherished,' she said, 'but I never was.'

'What about your mother when you were young?'

'Mother? Never!'

'Well, your father then?'

'Father? He cherished Grace. She used to sit on his knee. But somehow I was never invited.'

'Bill?'

'Good heavens, no. He was too busy looking to see if other women were paying attention to him.'

Poor Olive, she spent much of life looking after people—Lucy, Grace, and Bill—and she buried them all. The great survivor died on 21 August 1996 at the age of ninety-two, four months after she had moved into the residential home. Up to the end, she remained vivacious, talkative, and funny, although rather deaf. The move from her home, which she loved, was the turning point, as it is with many old people. We were in Canada with Maurice and Dorothy when the news came. Helen and I, with our children, flew back for the funeral and, Dorothy, who had come over to visit her mother, joined us in the quiet country church on the North Downs where Olive and I had sat many times during our outings together. She was cremated and her ashes buried in the ancient churchyard with her name and the bare details of her life inscribed on a slab of granite. I haven't been back but at least I know where that Islip lies.

The years pass, gathering speed, and increasing the distance from my father, Grace, Edith, and Olive. But when I see an old black and white photograph, catch a wartime melody, smell mothballs or dried lavender, walk along a familiar street, or hear a story connected with their lives, they return as if it were yesterday.

The past affected Maurice too, although in a different way. In early 1998, I went to London to research a book just as Maurice and Dorothy were finishing a visit to England. We did not manage to see each other but spoke on the telephone before they returned to Canada.

At the end of my trip, on a whim, I decided to go back to St. Dominic's Priory for the first time since leaving the school over fifty years earlier. When I asked for directions in Cuffley, the nearest town, people were puzzled. Nobody seemed to know anything about the convent school but when I mentioned the name of the property, a light dawned. 'Oh, Ponsbourne Park,' a man in an estate agent's office said, 'You mean Tesco's management training centre!'

I drove to the crest of the hill and stopped. The undulating meadows and parkland below me, as well as the house itself, were virtually unchanged from the time I had turned and looked back on that summer's day in 1947 when my father took us away for the last time. The only difference was a swimming pool in front of the house and a nine-hole golf course on the grounds where Maurice and I had grazed hungrily on 'sourgogs' and where I, along with a couple of friends, were initiated into the rites of masturbation by a precocious twelve-year-old with thick-lensed glasses and a large penis.

The manager let me wander around. The refectory was still a dining room but the chapel had become a lecture room. Aspiring supermarket managers were studying barcodes, shelf-stocking and marketing techniques where the mysteries of the Catholic faith were drilled into us. The elegant rotunda, with its classical portico, which served as the antechapel, was still there with its tiled floor and domed ceiling of blue mosaic and gold stars. The pictures of Jesus and his bleeding heart, the crucifixes, the statues of the Virgin, and the smell of incense had vanished though not from my memory where they remained fresh and vivid.

Some of the nuns were buried on the grounds in a far corner of the property. I crossed the lawn at the side of the house and struggled through the undergrowth. Crows were squawking overhead; two wild ducks took off from a small stream, shedding water from their wings; and a rabbit scampered off into the woods. I climbed over a fence and found half a dozen neglected tombstones with names on them. The lettering was blurred by mildew and grime but just legible. A headstone bore a large cross and the words: 'Pray for the Dominican Sisters Buried Here.' The dates ran from 1937 to 1970, and among the names were Joseph McDonnell, Rosemary Grogan, Baptist McGrath, Michael O'Brien, Magdalen Brennan and Agnes McVeigh—the flower of Irish womanhood.

There was no trace of Mother Bernadette, the Mother Superior, or Father Cottrell, the priest, but the last name stirred a memory: Sister Agnes bearing down on a seven-year-old boy, carefully penning his Sunday letter home to his 'Mammy and Daddy'. In that dank wood, amid the rotting vegetation and neglected grave stones, I could see her narrow, mean face and her flash of contempt as she tore up the letter and stalked away muttering, 'Your poor father.'

The manager said that the school had closed in the early 1970s and became, in turn, a hotel, a private club and finally a supermarket training centre. Before leaving, I bought a postcard of the house and grounds.

The nearest Dominican convent was in St. Albans. I called and was put through to the nun in charge of the archives. I asked about Mother Bernadette and the others. 'Oh dear me,' an Irish voice answered, 'they've all gone to their eternal reward. Did you have happy memories of the school?' I paused for a moment and then gently put the phone down.

Back in Spain, I went to the village post office to send the postcard to Maurice. I was about to mail it when I noticed something on the counter top. I picked it up and stared at it. It was a postcard, identical to the one in my other hand. I turned it over. A Canadian stamp. My name and address. A familiar signature.

Maurice had done what he and I vowed we would never do. He had gone back to the school, a few days before I did, his first visit, like mine, in more than half a century. On the postcard, he described his impressions, unaware that I was about to follow him. He noted that the chapel had a dual use. In the evenings, it was a discotheque. '*Sic transit ecclesiastica*,' he ended.

# EPILOGUE

When I returned to Kensal Green cemetery in 2009, I spent a good hour searching for the graves of my mother and her parents before giving up. I stepped back on to the path, took a final look at the weed-covered mounds, folded my map, and walked away. On my way to the main gate, I saw my guide and told him I had found nothing.

'Sorry, mate,' he said, lighting a cigarette. 'You were in the right place, all right. But, you know what? I believe some people don't want to be found. Strange, in'it?'

A family was ahead of me. Two small girls, their parents close behind, ran, skipped, and hopped their way through the gates. The grey autumn day was coming to a close, the wind was picking up, and London's damp was creeping into my bones. It had been a frustrating afternoon. Where was that grave? But, as I walked out into the living world, the dark mood lifted. I didn't need to see my mother's name written on some cold, weather-stained stone amid tangled undergrowth. I had my memories, and that was enough.

# ACKNOWLEDGEMENTS

OVER THE YEARS OF WRITING THIS BOOK, I HAVE HAD THE indispensable help of a number of people. I would like to thank old friends Paul Spike, Larry Malkin, Robert Cowley, and Louis Atlas for their advice, ideas and unshakeable belief in the story, and Gillon Aitken for his wise counsel and for passing the manuscript to Matthew Hamilton, a talented editor, who worked hard and skilfully on it. Jessie Keyt, with her screenwriting expertise, helped me improve the structure and narrative, as well as coming up with the title. At a critical stage, Don Fehr, my agent, brought to bear his long experience as an editor, and boosted my flagging morale with his faith in the story.

I would also like to express my deep gratitude to those who took the time to review the book before publication, namely, Paul Theroux, John Cornwell, Simon Winchester, Donald Trelford, Charles Glass, Judy Bachrach, Anne Casement and Paddy Hayes.

Throughout, my wife Helen, who not only knew the story but is in it, proved to be as good a critic as she was a sympathetic reader. My brother, Maurice, with his memory, his honesty about his feelings, and his fine editing skills, immeasurably improved the story. *Darling Baby Mine* is, in a sense, part of a family continuum that he started with his own book, *Ten Generations of the Jorre Family*, which traced the history of our paternal ancestors back to seventeenth-century France. Special thanks to Dorothy, Maurice's wife, for her unswerving support then and since, and to Maryse and Irène, my dear cousins, for critiquing the chapter on the Seychelles where they grew up on the family plantation.

Finally, I owe a huge debt to more old friends, Jeff and Anne Price and Charlie Glass, who all liked the book and led me to Naim Attallah and Quartet Books. Naim saw merit in the story and immediately agreed to publish it. If the book attracts and entertains readers, it will be to his everlasting credit, along with Grace Pilkington, publicity manager, and James Pulford, editorial manager. If it doesn't, the fault will lie with me and no one else.

JOHN DE ST. JORRE
*Newport, Rhode Island, March 2017*

*Right*: Studio portrait of my mother inscribed 'With best wishes for Christmas 1933, Grace'

*Below*: 'Darling Baby Mine'. Grace and me in London, 1936

My father and me, Exmouth,
Devon, 15 August 1939

*Left*: John aged four, and
Maurice aged three, 1940

*Bottom*: Maurice and me at
Finchley Public Baths, with
unknown women, 1939

George and Grace on their
wedding day, 31 March 1934

Olive and Grace as
teenagers—carefree
and happy

*Top Left*: Grace and George in a London park, 1934
*Top Right*: Grace on holiday before she met George
*Below*: George, Grace and Fernande, a Seychelles cousin, in Devon, 1934

Grace, shortly after the reunion, February 1975

Joan Cooper and her sister, Eva Lebel, Olive and Grace's best friends in London in the 1930s

*Top*: George and Edith
on their wedding day,
3 January 1948

*Right*: With my family
(Helen, Jenna and Shane) and
Olive in London, late 1980s

*Below*: Bill Anderson and
Olive, Chatham, Kent, 1975

*Above*: Reunited after thirty-five years with aunt
(Olive) and mother (Grace), February 1975

*Below*: Helen with Seth, around the time of our
wedding. He gave away the bride

*Above*: Shane, Jenna, Olive (with broken arm) and Helen, Islington, London

*Right*: Mother and son, February 1975